Lecture Notes in Business Information Processing 380

Series Editors

Wil van der Aalst ⓘ
RWTH Aachen University, Aachen, Germany
John Mylopoulos ⓘ
University of Trento, Trento, Italy
Michael Rosemann ⓘ
Queensland University of Technology, Brisbane, QLD, Australia
Michael J. Shaw
University of Illinois, Urbana-Champaign, IL, USA
Clemens Szyperski
Microsoft Research, Redmond, WA, USA

Ewa Ziemba (Ed.)

Information Technology for Management

Current Research and Future Directions

17th Conference, AITM 2019
and 14th Conference, ISM 2019, Held as Part of FedCSIS
Leipzig, Germany, September 1–4, 2019
Extended and Revised Selected Papers

 Springer

Editor
Ewa Ziemba (iD)
University of Economics in Katowice
Katowice, Poland

ISSN 1865-1348   ISSN 1865-1356   (electronic)
Lecture Notes in Business Information Processing
ISBN 978-3-030-43352-9   ISBN 978-3-030-43353-6   (eBook)
https://doi.org/10.1007/978-3-030-43353-6

This Springer imprint is published by the registered company Springer Nature Switzerland AG
The registered company address is: Gewerbestrasse 11, 6330 Cham, Switzerland

Preface

Four editions of this book appeared in last four years:

- *Information Technology for Management* in 2016 (LNBIP 243)
- *Information Technology for Management: New Ideas or Real Solutions* in 2017 (LNBIP 277)
- *Information Technology for Management: Ongoing Research and Development* in 2018 (LNBIP 311)
- *Information Technology for Management: Emerging Research and Applications* in 2019 (LNBIP 346)

Given the rapid developments in information technology and its applications for improving management in business and public organizations, there was a clear need for an updated version.

The present book includes extended and revised versions of a set of selected papers submitted to the 17th Conference on Advanced Information Technologies for Management (AITM 2019) and the 14th Conference on Information Systems Management (ISM 2019) held in Leipzig, Germany, during September 1–4, 2019. These conferences were organized within the Federated Conference on Computer Science and Information Systems (FedCSIS 2019).

FedCSIS provides a forum for bringing together researchers, practitioners, and academics to present and discuss ideas, challenges, and potential solutions on established or emerging topics related to research and practice in computer science and information systems. Since 2012, proceedings of the FedCSIS are indexed in the Thomson Reuters Web of Science, Scopus, IEEE Xplore Digital Library, and other indexing services.

AITM is a forum for all in the field of business informatics to present and discuss the current issues of IT in business applications. It is mainly focused on business process management, enterprise information systems, Business Intelligence methods and tools, decision support systems and data mining, intelligence and mobile IT, cloud computing, SOA, agent-based systems, and business-oriented ontologies.

ISM is a forum for computer scientists, IT specialist, and businesspeople to exchange ideas on management of information systems in organizations, and the usage of information systems for enhancing the decision-making process and empowering managers. It concentrates on various issues of planning, organizing, resourcing, coordinating, controlling, and leading the management functions to ensure a smooth operation of information systems in organizations.

For AITM 2019 and ISM 2019, we received 45 papers from 24 countries across all continents. The quality of the papers was evaluated by the members of Program Committees by taking into account the criteria for papers relevance to conferences topics, originality, and novelty. After extensive reviews, only 10 papers were accepted as full papers and 12 as short papers. Finally, 13 papers of the highest quality were carefully reviewed and chosen by the chairs of the two conferences, and the authors were invited to extend their research and submit the new extended papers for consideration to the LNBIP publication. Our guiding criterion for including papers in the book was the excellence of publications indicated by the reviewers, the relevance of subject matter for improving management by adopting information technology, as well as promising scientific contributions and implications for practitioners. The selected papers reflect state-of-the-art research work that is often oriented toward real-world applications and highlight the benefits of information systems and technology for business and public administration, thus forming a bridge between theory and practice.

The papers selected to be included in this book contribute to the understanding of relevant trends of current research on and future directions of information technology for management. The first part of the book focuses on information technology assessment for future development, the second part presents methods and models for designing information technology, and the third part explores various aspects of information technology implementation.

Finally, I and the authors hope readers will find the content of this book useful and interesting for their own research activities. It is in this spirit and conviction we offer our monograph, which is the result of intellectual effort of the authors, for the final judgment of readers. We are open to discussion on the issues raised in this book, as well as look forward to the polemical voices, or even critical, as to the content and form.

January 2020   Ewa Ziemba

Acknowledgment

I would like to express my gratitude to all those people who helped in making AITM 2019 and ISM 2019 research events a success. First of all, I want to thank the authors for extending their very interesting research and submitting the new findings to publish in LNBIP. I express my appreciation to the members of Program Committees for taking the time and effort necessary to provide valuable insights for the authors. The high standards followed by them enabled the authors to ensure the high quality of papers. I am deeply grateful to chairs of AITM 2019 and ISM 2019, namely Witold Chmielarz, Helena Dudycz, and Jerzy Korczak for their substantive involvement in the conferences and efforts put into the evaluation of papers. Their work enabled us to ensure the high quality of the conferences sessions, excellent presentations of authors research, and valuable scientific discussion. I acknowledge the chairs of the FedCSIS 2019, Maria Ganzha, Leszek A. Maciaszek, and Marcin Paprzycki, for building an active international community around the FedCSIS conference. Last but not least, I am indebted to the Springer-Verlag team, especially to the heads Ralf Gerstner and Alfred Hofmann, without whom this book would not have been possible. Many thanks also to Christine Reiss and Raghuram Balasubramanian for handling the production of this book.

Organizations

AITM 2019

Chairs

Frederic Andres — National Institute of Informatics in Tokyo, Japan
Helena Dudycz — Wrocław University of Economics, Poland
Mirosław Dyczkowski — Wrocław University of Economics, Poland
Frantisek Hunka — University of Ostrava, Czech Republic
Jerzy Korczak — Wrocław University of Economics, Poland

Program Committee

Witold Abramowicz — Poznań University of Economics, Poland
Frederik Ahlemann — University of Duisburg-Essen, Germany
Ghislain Atemezing — Mondeca – Paris, France
Agostino Cortesi — Università Ca' Foscari Venezia, Italy
Beata Czarnacka-Chrobot — Warsaw School of Economics, Poland
Suparna De — University of Surrey, UK
Jean-François Dufourd — University of Strasbourg, France
Bogdan Franczyk — University of Leipzig, Germany
Arkadiusz Januszewski — University of Science and Technology in Bydgoszcz, Poland
Rajkumar Kannan — Bishop Heber College, India
Grzegorz Kersten — Concordia University, Canada
Ryszard Kowalczyk — Swinburne University of Technology, Australia
Karol Kozak — TU Dresden, Germany
Marek Krótkiewicz — Wrocław University of Science and Technology, Poland
Christian Leyh — TU Dresden, Germany
Antoni Ligęza — AGH University of Science and Technology, Poland
André Ludwig — Kühne Logistics University, Germany
Damien Magoni — University of Bordeaux, LaBRI, France
Krzysztof Michalak — Wrocław University of Economics, Poland
Mieczyslaw Owoc — Wrocław University of Economics, Poland
Malgorzata Pankowska — University of Economics in Katowice, Poland
Jose Miguel Pinto dos Santos — AESE Business School Lisboa, Portugal
Maurizio Proietti — IASI-CNR, Italy
Artur Rot — Wrocław University of Economics, Poland
Stanislaw Stanek — General Tadeusz Kosciuszko Military Academy of Land Forces in Wroclaw, Poland

Jerzy Surma	Warsaw School of Economics, Poland, and University of Massachusetts Lowell, USA
El Bachir Tazi	Moulay Ismail University, Morocco
Stephanie Teufel	University of Fribourg, Switzerland
Edward Tsang	University of Essex, UK
Jarosław Wątróbski	University of Szczecin, Poland
Pawel Weichbroth	WSB University of Gdańsk, Poland
Tilo Wendler	Hochschule für Technik und Wirtschaft Berlin, Germany
Waldemar Wolski	University of Szczecin, Poland
Cecilia Zanni-Merk	INSA de Rouen, France
Ewa Ziemba	University of Economics in Katowice, Poland

ISM 2019

Chairs

Bernard Arogyaswami	Le Moyne University, USA
Witold Chmielarz	University of Warsaw, Poland
Jarosława Jankowski	West Pomeranian University of Technology in Szczecin, Poland
Dimitris Karagiannis	University of Vienna, Austria
Jerzy Kisielnicki	University of Warsaw, Poland
Ewa Ziemba	University of Economics in Katowice, Poland

Program Committee

Daniel Aguillar	Instituto de Pesquisas Tecnológicas de São Paulo, Brazil
Boyan Bontchev	Sofia University, Bulgaria
Alberto Cano	Virginia Commonwealth University, USA
Domagoj Cingula	Economic and Social Development Conference, Croatia
Beata Czarnacka-Chrobot	Warsaw School of Economics, Poland
Robertas Damasevicius	Kaunas University of Technology, Lithuania
Pankaj Deshwal	Netaji Subash University of Technology, India
Yanqing Duan	University of Bedfordshire, UK
Monika Eisenbardt	University of Economics in Katowice, Poland
Ibrahim El Emary	King Abdulaziz University, Saudi Arabia
Susana de Juana Espinosa	University of Alicante, Spain
Marcelo Fantinato	University of São Paulo, Brazil
Renata Gabryelczyk	University of Warsaw, Poland
Aleksandra Gaweł	Poznań University of Economics and Business, Poland
Nitza Geri	The Open University of Israel, Israel
Leila Halawi	Embry-Riddle Aeronautical University, USA
Krzysztof Kania	University of Economics in Katowice, Poland
Andrzej Kobyliński	Warsaw School of Economics, Poland

Christian Leyh	TU Dresden, Germany
Krzysztof Michalik	University of Economics in Katowice, Poland
Roisin Mullins	University of Wales Trinity Saint David, UK
Karolina Muszyńska	University of Szczecin, Poland
Walter Nuninger	Polytech'Lille, Université de Lille, France
Nina Rizun	Gdańsk University of Technology, Poland
Uldis Rozevskis	University of Latvia, Latvia
Marcin Jan Schroeder	Akita International University, Japan
Andrzej Sobczak	Warsaw School of Economics, Poland
Jakub Swacha	University of Szczecin, Poland
Symeon Symeonidis	Democritus University of Thrace, Greece
Edward Szczerbicki	University of Newcastle, Australia
Oskar Szumski	University of Warsaw, Poland
Bob Travica	University of Manitoba, Canada
Jarosław Wątróbski	University of Szczecin, Poland
Janusz Wielki	Opole University of Technology, Poland
Dmitry Zaitsev	Vistula University, Poland

Contents

Information Technology Assessment for Future Development

Perceptions Towards the Adoption and Utilization of M-Government Services: A Study from the Citizens' Perspective in Saudi Arabia

Mohammed Alonazi[1,2(✉)], Natalia Beloff[1], and Martin White[1]

[1] Informatics Department, University of Sussex, Brighton, UK
{M.Alonazi,N.Beloff,M.White}@sussex.ac.uk
[2] Prince Sattam Bin Abdulaziz University, Al-Kharj, Saudi Arabia

Abstract. The government of Saudi Arabia has adopted M-Government for the effective delivery of services. One advantage of adding the M-Government channel to government services is that it offers unique opportunities for real-time and personalized access to government information and services through the advantage of wireless technology. However, a low adoption rate of M-Government services by citizens is a common problem in Arabian countries, including Saudi Arabia, despite the best efforts of the Saudi government. Therefore, this paper explores the determinants of citizens' intention to adopt and use M-Government services, in order to increase the adoption rate. This study was based on the Mobile Government Adoption and Utilization Model (MGAUM) that was developed to improve adoption. Data was collected from 1,882 Saudi citizens, and the final sample consisted of 1,286 valid responses. The result of the descriptive analysis presented in this paper indicates that all the proposed factors in our MGAUM model were statistically significant factors in influencing citizens' intention to adopt and use M-Government services, and thus help to increase the adoption rate. Perceived Usefulness, Perceived Ease of Use, Perceived Mobility, Social Influence and Perceived Compatibility were particularly influential on citizens' intention, whereas, Perceived Trust, Culture, Awareness, Citizens Service Quality and System Quality were also influential to some degree.

Keywords: E-Government · M-Government · Saudi Arabia · Mobile technology

1 Introduction

Governments from across the world have digitized their services to citizens through mobile technologies and the Internet, which has arguably improved communication between citizens and their governments, to provide better access to services and information as well as improving government accountability, transparency and public governance [1–3]. Mobile government (M-Government) has also been widely implemented by developing service delivery channels that use wireless and mobile technologies [4, 5]. In this study, M-Government is thus defined as the use of mobile technology to deliver and

© Springer Nature Switzerland AG 2020
E. Ziemba (Ed.): AITM 2019/ISM 2019, LNBIP 380, pp. 3–26, 2020.
https://doi.org/10.1007/978-3-030-43353-6_1

improve E-Government services and information to citizens, commercial organisations and all government agencies. Previous studies have either regarded M-Government as separate to E-Government or as an extension or replacement of it [5, 6]. Kushchu and Kuscu [4] note that as it offers the public a valuable extra means to access services and information, it can be considered an advance in government service delivery. Although E-Government and M-Government work on the same principle, the latter is distinguished by features that are particular to it:

- Mobility is the main advantage for citizens utilizing M-Government services, as citizens can access the network from anywhere and at any time [7].
- Citizens can instantly receive messages from government service providers on their mobiles [8].
- The mobile phone has recently become the primary way people communicate over distance in many countries; and has thus arguably become a part of everyday life for many people [9, 10]. Therefore, being able to access government services via mobile devices might be the best route for citizens.
- Accessing government services and information on their phones means citizens neither have to visit the service provider in person nor go home to use their computer in order to do this [8, 10].
- Access to the Internet may depend on economic factors, i.e. the extent of Internet access in a particular country, and how many citizens have access to computers providing mobile services can overcome these limitations [4, 6].

An M-Government system provided by wireless technology, will give citizens opportunities for personalized access to government services and information in real time [7, 11]. This is especially beneficial for users in remote areas as M-Government services have the advantages of being affordable and easily and immediately accessible. Further, a relatively low level of digital literacy is required to operate them successfully [7, 12]. Given these features, the adoption of an M-Government system benefits both citizens and governments.

The Mobile Government Adoption and Utilization Model (MGAUM) has been developed as a framework from which to analyse factors affecting adoption and use of M-Government services [13]. This study aims to investigate and understand Saudi citizens' perceptions towards the adoption and utilization of M-Government services in developing countries, particularly Saudi Arabia, in order to increase the adoption rate of M-Government services. The remainder of this paper consists of the following sections: Sect. 2 outlines background and context, Sect. 3 covers the research methodology; Sect. 4 contains a descriptive and statistical analysis of the findings, Sect. 5 contains the research discussion and Sect. 6 is the conclusion.

2   Background and Context

Despite M-Government systems being available for several years, citizens' adoption of e-government services in general and M-Government services in particular still falls below expectations [1, 2, 14, 15]. Furthermore, in Saudi Arabia, like in most developing countries, M-Government implementation is still in its infancy and there are many challenges related to implementation, adoption and use [1, 16, 17]. Factors such as the rate of mobile device and Internet penetration and their security, reliability and effectiveness, affect how successful a government will be at implementing M-Government and user adoption and accounts for global variation [11]. However, there is a lack of research that allows a clear understanding of how factors such as these might impact the adoption and use of M-Government services. This study rectifies this problem by providing a theoretical model purposely developed to carry out empirical research in this area. The results of this research will yield new insights about the key factors influencing the adoption of Saudi M-Government, which will be invaluable to policy makers who require strategies that will result in faster and more efficient adoption of M-Government services; as well as providing new information for researchers in the field and the ICT industry.

Research carried out in a number of different areas such as Malaysia and rural China [12, 18, 19] have made use of adaptations of the Technology Acceptance Model (TAM) and provided examples of how a number of social, cultural and technical factors can usefully be included in the TAM to provide insights into the influences on citizens' intention to utilize M-Government systems to access services and information. Cultural and technological factors like culture, trust and lack of necessary infrastructure have been demonstrated to be significant by comparative studies of M-Government adoption in developing and developed countries [20, 21].

The adoption of M-Government in Arab countries, however, still requires further research. Studies conducted in these areas [21–25] have revealed that factors such as trust, citizens' perceptions of the compatibility of M-Government with their lifestyles, culture, awareness and the quality of the system are significant. Further, these studies show that there have been no empirical studies of M-Government adoption in Saudi Arabia that includes factors like compatibility or culture. Similarly, there are no studies that take the quality of both technical and human factors into account or that investigate the issues from the viewpoint of the providers in addition to the intended users. There is clearly a need to carry out further research into Saudi M-Government adoption. In order to analyse factors that affect users' adoption and use of M-Government, the researcher has developed a model called the Mobile Government Adoption and Utilization Model (MGAUM). The Mobile Government Adoption and Utilization Model (MGAUM) has been developed as a framework from which to analyse factors affecting adoption and use of M-Government services [13].

3 The Research Methodology

The study was conducted in Saudi Arabia; and the questionnaire was distributed to Saudi citizens (public users) who were at least 18 years old, irrespective of whether they had used mobile government services or not.

3.1 The Research Instrument

The research instrument (questionnaire) was distributed electronically (via Email, Twitter and WhatsApp) and manually in different cities in Saudi Arabia. This method is opportunistic, and the questionnaire was distributed to public users in government agencies, some universities and public areas such as parks, coffee shops, and shopping centres. The main reason behind the questionnaire being distributed electronically and manually was to get broader and more comprehensive results. Questionnaires given to participants manually were to be collected by the researcher who would also be on hand if the participant has any questions. Once incomplete questionnaires had been eliminated from the survey, the total valid responses constituted a sample of 1,286 Saudi citizens. SPSS was used to analyse the survey study data.

The survey questionnaire contains 76 items (Appendix), details and justifications for all questionnaire items and associated hypotheses can also be found in the first author's PhD thesis [70]. All questionnaire items are developed and modified from items used in previous research into both E-Government and M-Government [26–35]. All items were measured with a 5-point Likert scale ("Strongly agree", "Agree", "Neutral or do not know", "Disagree" and "Strongly disagree"). To ensure enough data had been collected to conduct a thorough analysis, the questionnaire had to be relatively lengthy. Questionnaires were distributed manually which contributed to achieving a higher response rate and meant that the researchers could clarify points for the participants if necessary.

3.2 Reliability and Validity of the Study

To be considered reliable, a research instrument needs to produce similar results if used in comparable conditions and be relatively free of errors [38, 39]. As part of the pilot study for this research, Cronbach's Alpha was chosen to assess the reliability of the questionnaire, as the internal consistency of the constructs used in the questionnaire had to be established; in other words, the extent to which items measured the same things when referring to a specific independent or dependent construct, and how these related to each other. Cronbach's Alpha is the test that is most commonly used to calculate and evaluate internal consistency, and thus reliability [40]. Cronbach's Alpha operates with a scale of 0 to 1, with 1 being the highest reliability, a value for independent and dependent variables of 0.6 is considered to be adequate [41]. Table 1 indicates the Cronbach's Alpha study results for the complete research instrument, and demonstrates that the reliability of each of the constructs (independent and dependent variables) lies within the range of what is thought of as acceptable in academic research.

If a research instrument measures what the researcher intended, it can be said to be valid [42], and its validity is thus the extent to which it does this and provides the information required [43]. Face and content validity were chosen to be investigated rather than construct or criterion validity. Face validity is designed to establish the extent to which the purpose of the instrument is clear even to a lay person with only basic education [44]. There is a high level of face validity if the questionnaire items are unambiguous and clear; if the items are seen as difficult to understand or confusing, then the face validity is low [44]. The face validity of each item was ascertained in the pilot study to ensure that the model's factors measured what they were intended to measure; and items deemed to lack sufficient clarity, unambiguity or relevance were deleted or revised accordingly. Six academics, with expertise in this field, were requested to review the items in the research instrument; and their reviews of the content of the study demonstrated that all the items had a high degree of face and content validity.

Table 1. Internal consistency of the study survey instrument (Appendix)

Measured variable	Number of items	Cronbach's Alpha
Perceived Usefulness (PU)	7	.898
Perceived Ease of Use (PEOU)	4	.862
Social Influence (SI)	3	.779
Perceived Compatibility (PCOM)	2	.868
Perceived Trust (PT)	7	.715
Culture (CULT)	5	.616
Awareness (AW)	4	.842
Perceived Mobility (PM)	3	.776
Citizens Service Quality (CSQ)	8	.920
System Quality (SQ)	7	.745
Intention to use M-Government (ITU)	4	.894

4   Research Findings

This section provides an overview of respondents' demographic characteristics: age, education level, occupation, use of mobile and the Internet, knowledge of M-Government before participating, experience and how they rate using M-Government.

4.1   Respondents' Demographic Data

Table 2 illustrates that of the final sample 813 participants were male (63.2%) and 473 were female (36.8%). The highest percentage of participants was in the 18–30 age group, the largest number held a bachelor's degree and over half the participants (46.7%) were government employees. All participants had Smartphone devices, with a large majority using mobiles and the Internet in daily life (96.4% and 93.3% respectively). Approximately three-quarters of the respondents (76.7%) have some knowledge about M-Government services in Saudi Arabia, whereas 22.9% had no knowledge. Moreover, the majority of participants (90.5%) already used M-Government services, but 9.5% had never used it. Also, the survey asked the participants who had already used M-Government services to rate their general experience. The result showed that 40.3% were very satisfied, 44.3% were satisfied to some extent, with only 5.9% not satisfied with M-Government services. Furthermore, 22.6% of participants reported that the requirements of the intended M-Government services were not clear and 26.6% of them reported that the system quality of M-Government services was not good.

Table 2. Demographic data, adopted from [35]

Variables	#	%
Gender		
Male	813	63.2
Female	473	36.8
Participants' age in years		
18–30	692	53.8
31–54	512	39.8
46–60	76	5.9
Over 60	6	.5
Participants' education level		
Secondary school or less	222	17.3
Diploma	330	25.7
Bachelor's degree	484	37.6
Master's degree	183	14.2
Doctorate degree	67	5.2
What is your occupation?		
Unemployed	110	8.6
Student	462	35.9
Governmental employee	600	46.7
Private sector employee	88	6.8
Self employed	26	2.0
What kind of mobile device do you have?		
Smartphone	58	100
Non – Smartphone (Traditional phone)	6	.5
What brand of mobile device do you have?		
iPhone – IOS	974	75.7
Samsung – Android	237	18.4
Windows phone	6	0.5
Nokia	3	0.2
Others brand of mobile, mention it please	60	4.7
How often do you use the mobile?		
Daily	1234	96.0
Two or three times a week	34	2.6
Two or three times a month	12	.9

(*continued*)

Table 2. (*continued*)

Variables	#	%
How usually do you use the internet		
Everyday	1209	94
Several days a week	54	4.2
Several days a month	17	1.3
Did you know what is the meaning of M-Government before participating in this Questionnaire?		
Yes	986	76.7
No	294	22.9
Have you ever used any Saudi mobile government service (Application/Website) such as Absher services for ministry of Interior, Ministries of education and universities?		
Yes	1164	90.5
No	116	9.0
How do you rate your experience of using M-Government in general		
Very Satisfactory	518	40.3
Satisfactory to some extent	570	44.3
Not satisfactory	76	5.9
What are the reasons that made your M-Government experience unsatisfactory (You can choose more than one answer?		
The requirements of the intended m-Services were not clear	290	22.6
System quality not good	342	26.6
I did not get the expected results	153	11.9
The difficulty of using M-Government services	268	20.8

4.2 The Measures of Central Tendency

A single value that describes a set of data is a measure of central tendency and can be expressed as a mean, median or mode. As central tendency sums up an entire set of differing values, the researcher needs to use the mean, median or mode according to what is most appropriate for the specific conditions being described; although the mean, which is the sum of all the values divided by the total number of values, is the most common measure of central tendency [21, 22]. In the current study, the mean was considered the most appropriate way to calculate central tendency, Eq. 1.

Equation 1:

$$\bar{x} = \frac{X1 + X2 + X3 + \ldots + Xn}{n} \tag{1}$$

4.3 Likert Scale

Indeed, the mean, along with standard deviation to describe variability are the descriptive statistics recommended for use with a five-point Likert scale, which was chosen as the main instrument in this study's questionnaire [47]. The reason behind the choice of a Likert scale is that it is recommended as being the simplest and most practical way to measure strength of opinion; and a review of the literature shows that is most commonly and successfully employed in Information System (IS) research [48–51].

In the course of data analysis, the individual items in the Likert scale are combined into a single composite score/variable which measures the intended aspect either as a sum or the mean of the combined items [52]. Thus, the Likert scale is an interval measurement scale.

Weighted averages were calculated for the Likert scales, from Strongly Agree = 1 to Strongly Disagree = 5, so that the tendency of the composite scores could be ascertained. The numbers entered into SPSS are thus said to represent 'weight' and the weighted averages for the scale needs to be calculated to understand means. This is accomplished by dividing the distances between the scale values (4 in a 5-point Likert scale) by the number of values (5). Thus, the period length is $4/5 = 0.80$, which is used to calculate the weighted averages [53, 54].

The weighted average categories for each result are shown in Table 3; and each result is interpreted with the degree of influence for each factor calculated accordingly.

Table 3. Weighted averages for 5-point Likert scales

Weighted average	Result	Result interpretation
1–1.79	Strongly agree	Very influential
1.80–2.59	Agree	Influential
2.60–3.39	Don't know or neutral	Neutral or do not know
3.40–4.19	Disagree	Uninfluential
4.20–5	Strongly disagree	Very uninfluential

4.4 Descriptive Analysis of Data

The data collected was analysed with reference to each of the constructs in the MGAUM [13]. Participants' attitudes, intentions and behaviour towards adopting and using Saudi M-Government services were explored by means of responses to statements for which Likert scores could be calculated. Table 4 summarizes the results of the descriptive analysis with an interpretation of all results.

Table 4. Weighted averages for 5-point Likert scales.

Factors	Items	Mean	S.D.	Result interpretation
PU	7	1.3900	.49876	Very influential
PEOU	4	1.5733	.61942	Very influential
CULT	5	1.9997	.69224	Influential
PT	7	2.3586	.62882	Influential
SI	7	1.6516	.62692	Very influential
PCOM	2	1.5638	.66208	Very influential
AW	4	2.1763	.87356	Influential
CSQ	8	2.0852	.69808	Influential
SQ	7	1.8891	.54653	Influential
PM	3	1.5625	.57052	Very influential

5 Research Discussion

A descriptive analysis for each factor proposed in the MGAUM is given in order to explain their impact on citizen's' intention to adopt and use M-Government services in Saudi Arabia. Table 4 summarizes the results of the descriptive analysis with an interpretation of all results.

Perceived Usefulness (PU): The PU factor in the MGAUM model was measured by asking Saudi citizens (public users) seven questions (items); all were designed, to gather users' perceptions about the potential advantages and usefulness of using M-Government services.

It was important to determine what users' perceptions were about the usefulness of M-Government, the advantages that they would gain from using M-Government services and how this influenced their behavioural intention. Accordingly, these questions measured different aspects of usefulness and benefits including accomplishing transactions with the government more quickly, saving time, effort and money; whether M-Government makes communication between government agencies and citizens easier and the usefulness of reminders of important dates for conducting government transactions in sufficient time via text message, email and the mobile application.

The vast majority of participants (93.9%) agreed that using mobile government services would be useful in daily life. Moreover, (94.4% and 96.0% respectively) of participants believed that using mobile government services would enable them to accomplish government transactions more quickly as well as saving them time, money and effort and enable them to perform transactions when far from their location. Approximately 89.6% of participants believed that using M-Government services would make communication between a government agency and citizens easier through text message, applications and e-mail; and over 94.2% agreed that using mobile government services would remind them of important dates in order to conduct or receive government transactions in sufficient time or at the right time.

Table 4 summarises the results of the descriptive analysis with an interpretation of the result for the Perceived usefulness based on mean and standard deviation. The factor was interpreted as significantly influential on citizens' intention to adopt and use M-Government services; and that use of M-Government services would increase when users perceive their benefits. This indicated that governments should take into consideration the requirements and needs of users to be met before implementing any services. There many aspects to the advantage of using services via mobile devices especially applications; the first is that user experience will be better in terms of ease of use, saving time and effort and being easy to access. Secondly, using features on mobile devices that are not found on the website, such as reminders, location and camera add value to services.

The findings of this study are consistent with those reported in the literature, for example, Abdelghaffar and Magdy [55] empirically investigated factors that might affect the adoption of M-Government services in developing countries, especially in Egypt, another Arab nation. They found that perceived usefulness was a significant factor in predicting participants' intention to use M-Government. A study conducted in Taiwan by Hung et al. [3] also revealed that perceived usefulness was critical in the acceptance of M-Government services.

Perceived Ease of Use (PEOU): Four items (questions) were used to measure participants' perceptions about the ease of using M-Government services; and how PEOU would impact on users' intention to use these services. The vast majority of participants (93.7%) agreed that learning to use mobile government services would be easy for them. Moreover, 92% also believed that interactions with M-Government to access its services would be clear and understandable. Approximately 86.2% believed that using M-Government services does not require a lot of skill and effort as well as being easy to use.

The total score for the PEOU factor was 1.5733 (Table 4), which indicated that PEOU is very influential on users' intention to adopt and use M-Government services. The result suggests that the user experience is the first step in adoption; and if a user finds M-Government services easy to use and that it saves time and effort, then this impacts positively on his/her behavioural intention to adopt and use them. If services are easy to use, and people do not have to rely on asking for help from another person to use the application, the number of users will increase. Thus, PU and PEOU are essential factors in the MGAUM, and any theoretical framework which seeks to analyse intention, adoption and use of M-Government in the Saudi context or similar contexts in developing countries. The findings for this factor are with line with previous studies conducted by, Liu et al. [12] and Shanab and Haider [56]. These authors also found that PEOU is an important factor in determining intention to use.

Culture (CULT): The concept of culture is complex and multi-dimensional, and contains many different aspects, for example, religion, social structure, language, political institutions, education and economic philosophy [57]. The behavioural intentions of Arab users are very much influenced by social values, interpersonal relationships and other issues related to religion [58]. Therefore, in this research, we argue that many cultural aspects need to be investigated and analysed to see how culture impacts on users' intention to adopt and use M-Government services in Saudi Arabia. CULT was measured by five items relating to central cultural aspects including image, resistance to change and interpersonal social networks (wasta or connection or nepotism).

With respect to the influence of Image, participants were asked if they felt that using M-Government services would enhance their social status and make them feel more sophisticated; and a vast majority (82.2%) agreed that it would. Moreover, (85.2% and 87.9% respectively) of participants believed that using mobile government services would reduce the influence of interpersonal networks (wasta) and prevent any negative influence on their transaction by uncooperative employees.

Concerning resistance to change, participants were asked whether they preferred dealing with government agencies face-to-face rather than using M-Government services; and whether visiting agencies to track their transactions was better than tracking them online. The result showed 27.2% of participants agreed that face-to-face dealings were better, 17.4% of them were neutral, and 55.4% disagreed entirely. Furthermore, 21.8% of participants agreed that visiting agencies to track transactions was preferable to online tracking, while 64.4% disagreed and 13.8% were neutral. The composite of the CULT factor was 1.9997, a result that indicated that CULT is influential on users' intention to adopt and use of M-Government services (see Table 4).

The influence of cultural factors on intention to use corresponds with findings by other studies in the literature. For example, Alghamdi [28] revealed that social and cultural aspects were significant influences on Saudis' intention to adopt and use E-Government systems from both citizens' and employee's perspectives. Moreover, revealed that national culture HMBP [59] positively influenced the use of E-Government services. Naqvi and Al-Shihi [60] also revealed that one of the main barriers to Omanis adopting E-Government were cultural rather than technical issues.

Perceived Trust (PT): This factor was measured for Saudi citizens (public users) with seven items (questions) measuring different aspects of PT such as risks to privacy (sharing and storing personal information), security and trust.

Participants were asked if they felt that the Internet was not safe to be used for dealing with the government. More than a third of participants, 41.0% believed that the Internet was safe, while 33.3% believed it was not safe, and 25.7% were neutral. This indicates that participants did not know or were uncertain about whether the Internet was not safe to be used for dealing with the government. By contrast, 73.9% of participants agreed that mobile government services were a safe and trustworthy environment in which to conduct government transactions, 20.8% and 5.3% were neutral or disagreed respectively. This indicates that citizens' perceptions about the security and trust of M-Government services environment are highly positive, and this would possibly have a positive influence on citizens' intention to use M-Government services.

However, participants did not know or were uncertain about whether providing personal information was safe (42.6% agreed, 19.8% neutral and 37.6% disagreed) and whether their data could be misused when stored by M-Government systems (33.0% agreed, 24.3% were neutral and 42.8% disagreed). The total score for PT was 2.3586, indicating that PT is influential on intention to use M-Government. This finding is in line with numerous studies: Phonthanukitithaworn and Sellitto [61], Ahmad and Khalid [62] and Carter and Belanger [63] that have noted that perceived trust was a significant factor.

Social Influence (SI): Three items (questions) were used to measure how the SI factor in the MGAUM model influenced Saudi citizens (public users). This factor addresses users' perception of the effect of social influence and how this would encourage intention to adopt and use M-Government services. A large majority (80.5%) agreed that people important to them would think that they should use mobile government services, whereas 15.8% of them were neutral, and 3.7% disagreed.

Moreover, 89.3% of participants said they would be encouraged to use M-Government services by their families and friends. Furthermore, the vast majority of participants (92.3%) intended to use M-Government services because it was the current trend. The composite of the SI factor was 1.6516, which indicates that SI is very influential on users' adoption and use (Table 4). The results found by the social influence factor is consistent with previous studies revealed by Ahmad and Khalid [62] and Liu et al. [12]. This investigation demonstrates that in a context like Saudi Arabia, where communities are very close, SI is a very important factor to include in the MGAUM, interestingly the desire to be seen by significant others as 'following the trend' was revealed as a powerful incentive in this context.

Perceived Compatibility (PCOM): was measured by two items (questions) in this survey for citizens (public users). This factor focuses on how users perceive the compatibility of M-Government services with their lifestyle and behaviour, and how this affects and encourages their intention to use M-Government services.

The vast majority of participants believed that using M-Government services would fit well with their lifestyles as well as being the way they liked to conduct government transactions (91.4% and 89.7% respectively). The total score for PCOM was 1.5638 (Table 4), which indicates that this factor is very influential on users' intention to use. This indicates that a high level of compatibility with the innovation would increase users' intention to adopt and use it. This finding is in line with other studies in the literature that showed that a high level of compatibility with an innovation increased users' intention to adopt and use it Almuraqab [22] and Phonthanukitithaworn and Sellitto [61]. This study, which unlike other previous studies, included a high number of Saudi female participants, demonstrates how using M-Government is perceived as compatible to a lifestyle where using mobiles occurs daily. In a society where contact between sexes is sensitive related to religious and cultural reason, conducting government transactions on their phones arguably gives Saudi women both privacy and removes the need for any face-to-face interactions with male government officials.

Awareness (AW): is the first stage where user's experience a new service offered by the government. Four items (questions) were used to measure the impact of awareness on Saudi citizens' intention to use M-Government services. In addition, participants were asked about which advertising methods could affect citizens' awareness of M-Government services and encourage their intention to adopt and use. For this question, a 5-point Likert scale with the options 'Very influential' to 'Very uninfluential' was used.

Many participants (76.7%) believed that they had a good level of knowledge about the benefits, features and services of M-Government, 14.9% were neutral, and 8.4% did not. Almost 68.6% of participants agreed it was easy to find out if a government agency offered its services via mobile devices, 17.0% of participants were neutral and

14.4% disagreed. Furthermore, 68.8% of participants agreed with the statement: "I have received enough information and guidance on how to use mobile government services", while 14.9% disagreed and 16.3% were neutral. A similar result was obtained regarding whether participants were satisfied with the current awareness campaigns and advertising about M-Government services in Saudi Arabia; as 66.6% were satisfied, 16.4% were neutral and 17.0% were not satisfied.

As Table 4 shows, it is likely that AW positively influences citizens' intention to adopt and use M-Government services. These findings are consistent with those of previous studies Abdelghaffar and Magdy [55] and Al-Somali et al. [64]. A study by Shareef et al. [21] noted that the lack of awareness could increase the digital divide and lead to the failure of E-Government.

Public awareness could be enhanced in various ways including interactive advertising and social media campaigns as well as traditional advertising methods such as newspapers, brochures, TV, messages on public transport and in subways. Participants rated advertising methods (shown in Fig. 1) as follows: social media (73.3%), advertisements in public areas (69.7%), TV and radio channels (61.0%), government agencies' websites (54.5%), email and text messages (58.6%) and finally, newspapers and magazines (39.2%).

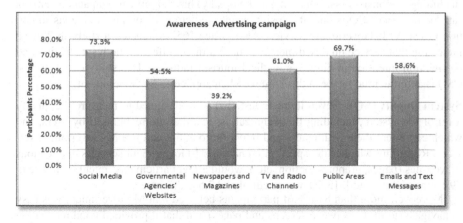

Fig. 1. Awareness of advertising campaigns

Therefore, our research results indicate that the government needs to raise awareness about the main goals of M-Government, the availability M-Government services and the advantages and benefits gained from the use of M-Government services to conduct various transactions. Public awareness could be enhanced in various ways including interactive advertising and social media campaigns as well as traditional advertising methods such as brochures and advertisements on TV, public transport and in newspapers. Current research suggests that increasing the awareness would significantly contribute to increasing citizens' willingness and intention to adopt and use M-Government services.

Citizen Service Quality (CSQ): Three main service quality dimensions were used to measure service quality in this study, i.e. reliability, responsiveness and empathy. Eight items (questions) were thus designed to measure customers' evaluation of the overall experience of services and go some way to explaining the difference between users' perceptions and their expectations of the services offered by the government. because delivering high-quality M-Government services by the government would help to achieve higher levels of citizen engagement, participation and willingness to use M-Government services.

Participants were asked to what extent that they believed that M-Government service providers give 'a prompt service with a good response'. Many participants, 75.6% agreed they did, 19.2% were neutral, and 5.2% disagreed. Similarly, most participants believed that M-Government service providers offered helpful assistance through SMS.

Moreover, the participants were asked whether they believed that information provided through M-Government services was accurate. 76.4% agreed it was, while 19.9% were neutral and 3.7% disagreed. Furthermore, 69.4% of participants believed that M-Government service providers showed a sincere interest in solving citizens' problems, whereas 24.8% were neutral, and 5.8% disagreed. The result indicates that CSQ is influential on users' intention to adopt and use M-Government services (Table 4). These findings echo those of Al-Hujran et al. [2] that the service quality dimension (including responsiveness, reliability, and empathy) have significant impacts on citizen satisfaction; and CSQ is one of the significant predictors of Jordanian citizens' intention to use an E-Government service. Also, Wang [65] conducted a study in Taiwan indicating that service quality dimensions have a direct effect on both satisfaction and behavioural intention in Taiwan's medical tourism industry. This study confirms that CSQ is an influential factor in this context when applied to M-Government.

System Quality (SQ): Seven items (questions) were designed to measure the quality level of the system, including the technical aspects that are recognised by users, and which can affect their willingness and intention to adopt and use M-Government services. Regarding whether the speed of launching M-Government services applications or websites (pages, graphics, option. etc.), would affect participants' intention to use it, 79.1% agreed it would, 13.5% were neutral and 7.5% disagreed.

Moreover, more than 81.6% of participants believed that M-Government was easy to navigate (to move between screens and pages) and that it provided good navigation functions; in contrast, 14.2% were neutral and only 4.2% disagreed. In respect to the existence of technical errors, such as applications crashing, links not working and unresponsiveness, (application/website), as well as the bad layout and unattractive interfaces of M-Government services 79.7% and 73.3% of participants respectively, agreed that these elements would reduce their willingness to use it. Regarding the compatibility of M-Government services with mobile devices such as GPS and camera, the vast majority 86.2% of participants agreed that services should be compatible. Furthermore, 80.2% and 76.8% respectively believed that M-Government services provided fast responses to their enquiries as well as up-to-date information. The composite of the SQ factor was 1.8897, which indicated that SQ is influential on users' intention to adopt and use M-Government services (Table 4).

The positive relationship between System Quality and intention to use services corresponds to findings in other studies in the literature, i.e. whenever the system quality of M-Government services increases, citizens' intention to adopt and use them will also increase. For example, Athmay et al. [66] revealed that system quality had a strong influence on the intention to use E-Government services; and Baabdullaha et al. [67] found that system quality was one of the main factors that significantly impacted on actual use behaviour.

Perceived Mobility (PM): This factor was measured by three items (questions). Participants were asked about their perceptions of the importance of accessing information and being able to use M-Government services whilst on the move. The result showed that the vast majority (89.8%) of participants expected to be able to use M-Government services anywhere and at any time when required. Almost the same percentage reported that they found mobile government services were easily accessible, portable and easy-to-use on different models of Smartphone. Participants were also asked if they considered it important to get critical alert notifications on their mobiles from government agencies via text or email regarding passport renewal, traffic penalties and emergency cases whilst they were on the move; and 94.6% agreed it was. The composite of the PM factor was 1.5651, which indicates that PM is a very influential factor influencing the intention to adopt and use M-Government services and show that citizens in Saudi Arabia value the ability to constantly access government services and information from any location. The findings for this factor are consistent with previous studies by Yen and Wu [69] and Wang [65], where they focused on Chinese citizens.

The statistical analysis and discussion above allow us to estimate the most influential factor for increase the intention to adopt and use M-Government services is Saudi Arabia.

6   Conclusion

Achieving a high rate of adoption and acceptance of M-Government services is considered as a challenge to a government because it faces several issues related to adoption, implementation and use; hence this research is introduced. The researchers constructed the MGAUM model to identify factors revealed by the literature and personal professional experience to be likely to influence Saudi citizens' intention to adopt and use M-Government services.

The result of descriptive analysis presented in this paper indicates that all the proposed factors in MGAUM model (PU, PEOU, CULT, SI, PCOM, PT, AW, CSQ, SQ and PM) were statistically significant factors in influencing Saudi citizens' intention to adopt and use M-Government services and when properly addressed could increase the adoption rate of M-Government services.

This study is part of on-going research, and thus, the results of this quantitative data study will be compared with the results of a qualitative data study in which managers in eight Saudi ministries were interviewed about their opinions and experiences of M-Government'; in order to expand understanding of the impact of the factors discussed.

We intend the results to provide a valuable insight into the main factors that influence citizen intention to adopt and use M-Government services in Saudi Arabia; which will be useful for researchers, the ICT industry and for policymakers who are keen to find strategies that result in quicker and more efficient take-up of such services.

This study added several contributions to theory and practice in the field of M-Government adoption and use. Firstly, this research developed the Mobile Government Adoption and Utilization Model (MGAUM) to analyse factors that affect users' adoption and use of M-Government. MGAUM integrates the Technology Acceptance Model with a number of social, cultural and technological factors, taken from other recognized theoretical acceptance models that have been identified as key factors in the literature. Secondly, the MGAUM is empirically tested and validated by collecting and analysing primary data from the citizens' perspectives. Thirdly, this is one of the first few studies investigating the adoption and utilization of M-Government in Saudi Arabia.

There are however limitations to this study due to issues of time available and distance of target population as well as lack of relevant literature and Saudi cultural issues involved in male researchers approaching female participants. For this reason, we recommend that further research is conducted into the relationships between the demographic data such as age, gender, education, income and experience of using mobile devices and the factors in the MGAUM in order to explore the influence of each on adoption and use of M-Government services. Female researchers would be better able to explore Saudi women's attitudes to M-Government adoption. The MGAUM could also be used to investigate attitudes to M-Government adoption in other Gulf countries or adapted to investigate and analyse factors that can impact Saudi citizens' adoption and usage of different interactive systems and electronic system such as m-banking, m-learning system, cloud computing services and m-commerce.

Appendix

See Table 5.

Table 5. Questionnaire items with associated codes and references [70].

Constructs	Items		Reference
	Code	Statement	Adopted from
Intention to Use	INT1	"I intend to use mobile government services in the future"	[26]
	INT2	"I intend to use mobile government services frequently"	
	INT3	"I will use mobile government services to perform governmental transactions"	
	INT4	"I would recommend that others use mobile government services"	

(*continued*)

Table 5. *(continued)*

Constructs	Items		Reference
	Code	Statement	Adopted from
Perceived Usefulness	PU1	"Using mobile government services would be useful in my daily life"	
	PU2	"Using mobile government services would enables me to accomplish governmental transactions more quickly"	
	PU3	"I think that using mobile government services save my time, money and effort and enables me to perform transactions that are not close in my location"	
	PU4	"Using m-government services would make the communication between a government agency and citizens more easy through text message, its applications and e-mail"	[28]
	PU5	"The ability to perform governmental transactions (24 h/7 days) will encourage me use m-government services more"	
	PU6	"I think using m-government services would save me multiple visits to different agencies when performing my transactions"	
	PU7	"I believe that using mobile government services will remind me of important dates for conducting government transactions in sufficient time or at the right time"	[25]
Perceived Ease of Use	PEOU1	"Learning to use mobile government services would be easy for me"	[26]
	PEOU2	"I believe my interaction with mobile government services to access government services would be clear and understandable"	
	PEOU3	"Using mobile government services does not require a lot of skills and efforts"	
	PEOU4	"I believe that mobile government services are easy to use"	
Social Influence	SI1	"People who are important to me would think that I should use mobile government services"	[30]
	SI2	"The use of my family members and my friends for mobile government services will encourage me to use it"	
	SI3	"It is the current trend to use mobile government services"	[31]

(continued)

Table 5. (*continued*)

Constructs	Items		Reference
	Code	Statement	Adopted from
Perceived Compatibility	COM1	"I believe that using mobile government services will fit well with my lifestyle"	[32]
	COM2	"I believe that using mobile government services will fit well with the way I like to conduct my governmental transactions"	
Perceived Trust	PT1	"I feel that the Internet is not safe to be used for dealing with government"	[28]
	PT2	"I feel that mobile government services is a safe environment and trustworthy to perform my governmental transactions"	
	PT3	"I would hesitate to provide personal information (such as my address, my income… etc.) through mobile government systems"	
	PT4	"I trust mobile government services to notify me of important information regarding the status of my governmental transactions, in sufficient time by text messages or through its applications"	[29]
	PT5	"I expect that mobile government services will not take advantage of me and will protect my privacy such as my personal information and address"	[28]
	PT6	I feel that my data that is stored in mobile government systems can be misused	
	PT7	"I think that government agencies in Saudi Arabia can be trusted to provide trustworthy mobile government services"	
Culture	CULT1	"Using mobile government services will make me feel more sophisticated and will enhance people's perception about me"	
	CULT2	"I believe that mobile government systems would reduce the influence of interpersonal networks (WASTA) on processing individuals' transactions"	
	CULT3	"I feel that dealing with the government agencies face to face is better than using mobile government services"	

(*continued*)

Table 5. (*continued*)

Constructs	Items		Reference
	Code	Statement	Adopted from
	CULT4	"I feel that visiting agencies to track my transactions is better than tracking them online"	
	CULT5	"Using mobile government would prevent the negative influence of some uncooperative employee on my transaction"	
Awareness	AW1	"I feel that I have a good knowledge about mobile government services benefits, features and services"	
	AW2	"I think it is easy to find out if government agency offered its services via mobile devices"	
	AW3	"I have received enough information and guidance of how to use mobile government services"	
	AW4	"In general, I am satisfied with the current awareness campaigns and advertising about mobile government services in Saudi Arabia"	
Perceived Mobility	PM1	"I expect that I would be able to use mobile government services at any time, and anywhere, when I need it"	[33]
	PM2	"I would find mobile government services to be easily accessible, portable and easy to use on different models of Smartphone's"	
	PM3	"It is important to me to get critical alert notification on my mobile from government agencies during mobility via text or email regarding passport renewal, traffic penalties and emergency cases"	
Citizens Service Quality	SERQ1RES1	"I believe that mobile government services providers give a prompt service with a good response"	[34]
	SERQ2RES2	"Mobile government services provider offers a helpful assistance through SMS"	
	SERQ3RES3	"I believe that mobile government services providers is always willing to help customers"	
	SERQ4REL1	"Mobile government services provider provides easy to use tools for checking on the status of an ordered service"	
	SERQ5REL2	"Mobile government services provider delivers on its undertaking to do certain things by a certain time"	

(continued)

Table 5. (*continued*)

Constructs	Items		Reference
	Code	Statement	Adopted from
	SERQ6REL3	"I believe that information provided through mobile government services is accurate"	
	SERQ7EMP1	"Mobile government services provider shows a sincere interest in solving some citizen problems"	
	SERQ8EMP2	"Mobile government services provider understand my specific needs"	
System Quality	SYSQU1	"The speed of launching the m-government services application m (pages, graphics, option…. etc.) will affect my willingness to use it"	[28]
	SYSQU2	"I believe that mobile government service (application/website) is easy to navigate "to move between screens and pages "and provides good navigation functions"	[35]
	SYSQU3	"The existence of technical errors while using mobile government service application/website would reduce my willingness to use it for my transactions. Such as crash application, links not working and unresponsive"	[28]
	SYSQU4	"Bad layout and unattractive interfaces of mobile government service (application/website) would reduce my willingness to use its services"	
	SYSQU5	"I think m-government services (applications/website) should be compatible with devices features such as GPS and camera"	[36]
	SYSQU6	"I think mobile government service (application/website) will provides fast responses to my inquiries"	[35]
	SYSQU7	"I think that mobile government service (application/website) provide up-to-date information"	[37]

References

1. Alghamdi, A., Beloff, N.: Towards a comprehensive model for e-government adoption and utilisation analysis: the case of Saudi Arabia. In: Maciaszek, L., Paprzycki, M. (eds.) Proceedings of the 2014 Federated Conference on Computer Science and Information Systems, pp. 1217–1225 (2014). https://doi.org/10.15439/2014f146
2. Al-Hujran, O., Al-Debei, M.M., Chatfield, A., Migdadi, M.: The imperative of influencing citizen attitude toward e-government adoption and use. Comput. Hum. Behav. **53**, 189–203 (2015). https://doi.org/10.1016/j.chb.2015.06.025
3. Hung, S.-Y., Chang, C.-M., Kuo, S.-R.: User acceptance of mobile e-government services: an empirical study. Gov. Inf. Q. **30**(1), 33–44 (2013). https://doi.org/10.1016/j.giq.2012.07.008
4. Kushchu, I., Kuscu, M.H.: From E-government to M-government: facing the inevitable. In: Proceeding of European Conference on E-Government (2003)
5. Scholl, H.J.: The mobility paradigm in electronic government theory and practice: a strategic framework. In: Euro Mobile Government (Euro mGov) Conference (2005)
6. Alotaibi, S.R.D., Roussinov, D.: Developing and validating an instrument for measuring mobile government adoption in Saudi Arabia. In: 18th International Conference on e-Business and E-Government (2016)
7. Ntaliani, M., Costopoulou, C., Karetsos, S.: Mobile government: a challenge for agriculture. Gov. Inf. Q. **25**(4), 699–716 (2008). https://doi.org/10.1016/j.giq.2007.04.010
8. Almarashdeh, I., Alsmadi, M.K.: How to make them use it? Citizens acceptance of m-government. Appl. Comput. Inf. **13**(2), 194–199 (2017). https://doi.org/10.1016/j.aci.2017.04.001
9. Serra, L.C., Carvalho, L.P., Ferreira, L.P., Vaz, J.B.S., Freire, A.P.: Accessibility evaluation of e-government mobile applications in Brazil. Procedia Comput. Sci. **67**, 348–357 (2015). https://doi.org/10.1016/j.procs.2015.09.279
10. Lallana, R.: E-government for development M-government: mobile/wireless applications (2004)
11. Alsenaidy, A., Ahmad, T.: A review of current state m-government in Saudi Arabia. Glob. Eng. Technol. Rev. **2**(5), 5–8 (2012)
12. Liu, Y., Li, H., Kostakos, V., Goncalves, J., Hosio, S., Hu, F.: An empirical investigation of mobile government adoption in rural China: a case study in Zhejiang province. Gov. Inf. Q. **31**(3), 432–442 (2014). https://doi.org/10.1016/j.giq.2014.02.008
13. Alonazi, M., Beloff, N., White, M.: MGAUM—towards a mobile government adoption and utilization model: the case of Saudi Arabia. Int. J. Bus. Hum. Soc. Sci. **12**(3), 459–466 (2018)
14. Alotaibi, R., Houghton, L., Sandhu, K.: Exploring the potential factors influencing the adoption of m-government services in Saudi Arabia: a qualitative analysis. Int. J. Bus. Manag. **11**(8), 56 (2016). https://doi.org/10.5539/ijbm.v11n8p56
15. Rana, N.P., Dwivedi, Y.K.: Citizen's adoption of an e-government system: validating extended social cognitive theory (SCT). Gov. Inf. Q. **32**(2), 172–181 (2015). https://doi.org/10.1016/j.giq.2015.02.002
16. Alotaibi, S., Roussinov, D.: A conceptual model for examining mobile government adoption in Saudi Arabia. In: Proceedings of the European Conference on E-Government, ECEG, vol. 2015-January, pp. 369–375 (2015)
17. Assar, K.: M-government in Saudi Arabia. Int. J. Adv. Res. Comput. Sci. Softw. Eng. **5**(1), 76–83 (2015)
18. Faziharudean, T.M., Li-Ly, T.: Consumers' behavioral intentions to use mobile data services in Malaysia. Afr. J. Bus. Manag. **5**(5), 1811–1821 (2011)
19. Alqahtani, M.A., Alroobaea, R.S., Mayhew, P.J.: Building a conceptual framework for mobile transaction in Saudi Arabia: a user's perspective. In: 2014 Science and Information Conference (2014). https://doi.org/10.1109/sai.2014.6918303

20. Al-Hadidi, A., Rezgui, Y.: Adoption and diffusion of m-government: challenges and future directions for research. In: Camarinha-Matos, L.M., Boucher, X., Afsarmanesh, H. (eds.) PRO-VE 2010. IAICT, vol. 336, pp. 88–94. Springer, Heidelberg (2010). https://doi.org/10. 1007/978-3-642-15961-9_9

21. Shareef, M.A., Dwivedi, Y.K., Laumer, S., Archer, N.: Citizens' adoption behavior of mobile government (mGov): a cross-cultural study. Inf. Syst. Manag. **33**(3), 268–283 (2016). https:// doi.org/10.1080/10580530.2016.1188573

22. Almuraqab, N.A.S.: M-government adoption factors in the UAE: a partial least squares approach. Int. J. Bus. Inf. **11**(4), 404–431 (2017)

23. Almuraqab, N.A.S., Jasimuddin, S.M.: Factors that influence end-users' adoption of smart government services in the UAE: a conceptual framework. Electron. J. Inf. Syst. Eval. **20**(1), 11–23 (2017)

24. Shareef, M.A., Kumar, V., Kumar, U., Dwivedi, Y.K.: E-government adoption model (GAM): differing service maturity levels. Gov. Inf. Q. **28**(1), 17–35 (2011). https://doi.org/10.1016/j. giq.2010.05.006

25. Davis, F.D., Bagozzi, R.P., Warshaw, P.R.: User acceptance of computer technology: a comparison of two theoretical models. Manag. Sci. **35**(8), 982–1003 (1989). https://doi.org/10. 1287/mnsc.35.8.982

26. Davis, F.D.: Perceived usefulness, perceived ease of use, and user acceptance of information technology. MIS Q. **13**(3), 319–340 (1989). https://doi.org/10.2307/249008

27. Shareef, M.A., Archer, N., Dwivedi, Y.K.: Examining adoption behavior of mobile government. J. Comput. Inf. Syst. **53**(2), 39–49 (2012). https://doi.org/10.1080/08874417.2012. 11645613

28. Alghamdi, S.A.: Key factors influencing the adoption and utilisation of e-government systems and services in Saudi Arabia. University of Sussex (2017)

29. Alloghani, M., Hussain, A., Al-Jumeily, D., Abuelmaatti, O.: Technology acceptance model for the use of m-health services among health related users in UAE. In: 2015 International Conference on Developments of E-Systems Engineering (DeSE) (2015). https://doi.org/10. 1109/dese.2015.58

30. Venkatesh, V., Thong, J.Y.L., Xin, X.: Consumer acceptance and use of information technology: extending the unified theory of acceptance and use of technology. MIS Q. **36**(1), 157–178 (2012). https://doi.org/10.2307/41410412

31. Chong, A.Y.-L., Chan, F.T.S., Ooi, K.-B.: Predicting consumer decisions to adopt mobile commerce: cross country empirical examination between China and Malaysia. Decis. Support Syst. **53**(1), 34–43 (2012). https://doi.org/10.1016/j.dss.2011.12.001

32. Moore, G.C., Benbasat, I.: Development of an instrument to measure the perceptions of adopting an information technology innovation. Inf. Syst. Res. **2**(3), 192–222 (1991). https:// doi.org/10.1287/isre.2.3.192

33. Hong, S.-J., Thong, J.Y.L., Moon, J.-Y., Tam, K.-Y.: Understanding the behavior of mobile data services consumers. Inf. Syst. Front. **10**(4), 431–445 (2008). https://doi.org/10.1007/ s10796-008-9096-1

34. Hujran, O., Aloudat, A., Ikhlas, A.: Factors influencing citizen adoption of e-government in developing countries: the case of Jordan. Int. J. Technol. Hum. Interact. **9**, 1–19 (2013). https://doi.org/10.4018/jthi.2013040101

35. Zhou, T.: Understanding users' initial trust in mobile banking: an elaboration likelihood perspective. Comput. Hum. Behav. **28**(4), 1518–1525 (2012). https://doi.org/10.1016/j.chb. 2012.03.021

36. Mahmood, Z. (ed.): E-Government Implementation and Practice in Developing Countries. IGI Global, Hershey (2013). https://doi.org/10.4018/978-1-4666-4090-0

37. Doll, W.J., Torkzadeh, G.: The measurement of end-user computing satisfaction. MIS Q. **12**(2), 259 (1988). https://doi.org/10.2307/248851

38. Blunch, N.J.: Introduction to Structural Equation Modeling Using IBM SPSS Statistics and AMOS. SAGE Publications, Thousand Oaks (2013). https://doi.org/10.4135/9781526402257
39. Sekaran, U., Bougie, R.: Research Methods for Business: A Skill Building Approach. Wiley, Hoboken (2013)
40. Eucharia, E., Nnadi, O.: Health Research Design and Methodology. Library of Congress. CRC Press, Boca Raton (1999)
41. Suhr, D., Shay, M.: Guidelines for Reliability, Confirmatory and Exploratory Factor Analysis. Western Users of SAS®Software (WUSS) (2008)
42. Bhattacharyya, D.K.: Cross-Cultural Management: Texts and Cases. Prentice Hall of India Private Ltd., New Delhi (2010)
43. Colton, D., Covert, R.W.: Designing and Constructing Instruments for Social Research and Evaluation. Jossey-Bass, San Francisco an imprint of Wiley (2007)
44. Nevo, B.: Face validity revisited. J. Educ. Meass. 22(4), 287–293 (1985). https://doi.org/10.1111/j.1745-3984.1985.tb01065.x
45. Khan, J.A.: Research Methodology. APH Publishing Corporation, New Delhi (2018)
46. Statistics, L.: SPSS Statistics Tutorials and Statistical Guides (2018). https://statistics.laerd.com/
47. Boone, H.N., Boone, D.A.: Analyzing Likert data. J. Ext. 50(2), 1–5 (2012). https://joe.org/joe/2012april/tt2.php
48. Viswanathan, M., Sudman, S., Johnson, M.: Maximum versus meaningful discrimination in scale response: implications for validity of measurement of consumer perceptions about products. J. Bus. Res. 57(2), 108–124 (2004). https://doi.org/10.1016/s0148-2963(01)00296-x
49. Venkatesh, V., Morris, M.G., Davis, G.B., Davis, F.D.: User acceptance of information technology: toward a unified view. MIS Q. 27(3), 425–478 (2003). https://doi.org/10.2307/30036540
50. Taylor, S., Todd, P.A.: Understanding information technology usage: a test of competing models. Inf. Syst. Res. 6(2), 144–176 (1995). https://doi.org/10.1287/isre.6.2.144
51. Bhattacherjee, A.: Understanding information systems continuance: an expectation-confirmation model. MIS Q. 25(3), 351–370 (2001). https://doi.org/10.2307/3250921
52. Clason, D.L., Dormody, T.J.: Analyzing data measured by individual Likert-type items. J. Agric. Educ. 35(4), 31–35 (1994). https://doi.org/10.5032/jae.1994.04031
53. Alfarra, W.A.: Analysing Questionnaires Data Using SPSS. Programs and Foreign Affairs Department, World Assembly of Muslim Youth, [Arabic source] (2009). https://www.kantakji.com/media/9166/edu.pdf
54. Nguli, J.: How to score a Likert scale. ResearchGate. https://www.researchgate.net/post/How_to_score_a_likert_Scale
55. Abdelghaffar, H., Magdy, Y.: The adoption of mobile government services in developing countries: the case of Egypt. Int. J. Inf. Commun. Technol. Res. 2, 333–341 (2012). https://pdfs.semanticscholar.org/03dd/ecb70373363604005a0d36d3a84c34098900.pdf
56. Shanab, E.A., Haider, S.: Major factors influencing the adoption of m-government in Jordan. Electron. Gov. Int. J. 11(4), 223–240 (2015). https://doi.org/10.1504/eg.2015.071394
57. Chang, L.: Cross-cultural differences in international management using Kluckhohn-Strodtbeck framework. J. Am. Acad. Bus. 2(1), 20–27 (2002)
58. Hu, P.J.-H., Al-Gahtani, S.S., Hu, H.: Arabian workers' acceptance of computer technology: a model comparison perspective. J. Glob. Inf. Manag. 22(2), 1–22 (2014). https://doi.org/10.4018/jgim.2014040101
59. Ranaweera, H.M.B.P.: Role of national culture on the use of e-government services in Sri Lanka. J. Bus. Financ. Aff. 5(2), 1–7 (2016). https://doi.org/10.4172/2167-0234.1000182
60. Naqvi, S., Al-Shihi, H.: M-government services initiatives in Oman. In: Proceedings of the 2009 InSITE Conference (2009). https://doi.org/10.28945/3389

61. Phonthanukitithaworn, C., Sellitto, C., Fong, M.W.L.: An investigation of mobile payment (m-payment) services in Thailand. Asia-Pacific J. Bus. Adm. **8**(1), 37–54 (2016). https://doi.org/10.1108/apjba-10-2014-0119

62. Ahmad, S.Z., Khalid, K.: The adoption of M-government services from the user's perspectives: empirical evidence from the United Arab Emirates. Int. J. Inf. Manag. **37**(5), 367–379 (2017). https://doi.org/10.1016/j.ijinfomgt.2017.03.008

63. Carter, L., Bélanger, F.: The utilization of e-government services: citizen trust, innovation and acceptance factors. Inf. Syst. J. **15**(1), 5–25 (2005). https://doi.org/10.1111/j.1365-2575.2005.00183.x

64. Al-Somali, S.A., Gholami, R., Clegg, B.: An investigation into the acceptance of online banking in Saudi Arabia. Technovation **29**(2), 130–141 (2009). https://doi.org/10.1016/j.technovation.2008.07.004

65. Wang, Y.: Expectation, service quality, satisfaction, and behavioral intention – evidence from Taiwan's medical tourism industry. Adv. Manag. Appl. Econ. **7**(1), 1–16 (2017). http://www.scienpress.com/Upload/AMAE/Vol%207_1_1.pdf

66. Al-Athmay, A.A.A.R.A., Fantazy, K.A., Kumar, V.: E-government adoption and user's satisfaction: an empirical investigation. EuroMed J. Bus. **11**(1), 57–83 (2016). https://doi.org/10.1108/emjb-05-2014-0016

67. Baabdullah, A.M., Alalwan, A.A., Rana, N.P., Kizgin, H., Patil, P.: Consumer use of mobile banking (M-Banking) in Saudi Arabia: towards an integrated model. Int. J. Inf. Manag. **44**, 38–52 (2019). https://doi.org/10.1016/j.ijinfomgt.2018.09.002

68. Yen, Y.-S., Wu, F.-S.: Predicting the adoption of mobile financial services: the impacts of perceived mobility and personal habit. Comput. Hum. Behav. **65**, 31–42 (2016). https://doi.org/10.1016/j.chb.2016.08.017

69. Wang, C.: Antecedents and consequences of perceived value in mobile government continuance use: an empirical research in China. Comput. Hum. Behav. **34**, 140–147 (2014). https://doi.org/10.1016/j.chb.2014.01.034

70. Alonazi, M.: MGAUM: a new framework for the mobile government service adoption in Saudi Arabia. University of Sussex (2019)

On Aspects of Internet and Mobile Marketing from Customer Perspective

Witold Chmielarz[1] (iD), Marek Zborowski[1](✉) (iD), and Mesut Atasever[2] (iD)

[1] Faculty of Management, University of Warsaw, 1/3 Szturmowa, 02-678 Warsaw, Poland
witold@chmielarz.eu, mzborowski@wz.uw.edu.pl
[2] School of Applied Sciences, Usak University, Ankara İzmir Yolu 8.Km Bir Eylül Kampüsü,
Merkez, Turkey
mesut.atasever@usak.edu.tr

Abstract. The main aim of this article is to identify customers' opinions concerning the place, role and influence of electronic marketing tools on making purchases on the Internet. The authors have applied the division of e-marketing into its traditional and electronic forms, on desktop computers and mobile devices, which was significant due to diversified opinions of clients concerning its use. The studies have been carried out with the application of a CAWI method examining a convenient, randomly selected sample of clients who are active in the Internet. The studies were aimed at evaluating specific e-marketing media and techniques which, in the customers' view, influenced shopping on the Internet. In particular, the respondents commented on the advantages, disadvantages and benefits resulting from the application of e-marketing on mobile devices. The conclusions and recommendations from the study may contribute to better use of these factors in order to facilitate consumers' purchases, not only in the Internet.

Keywords: i-marketing · m-marketing · Evaluation of electronic marketing

1 Introduction

The primary objective of this paper is to present the impact and significance of electronic marketing (e-marketing) in the purchasing process, based on the opinions of a selected group of potential clients. It is another study conducted as part of a series of research analysing a similar group of respondents in the situation where the opinions on e-marketing are largely diversified, and a dynamic development of mobile devices may be observed. Simultaneously, it should be noted that the study is of supplementary nature in relation to comprehensive studies undertaken by the authors examining the quality of websites and mobile applications.

Electronic marketing is understood in this paper as a combination of all components related to information technologies, especially the Internet, in order to increase the willingness of potential customers to make purchases [1]. It is associated with many tools which are mainly applied on the Internet [2] as well as new sales and payment techniques [3, 4]. It encompasses a wide range of themes connected with, for example, the evaluation of the possibilities of new devices (smartphones, tablets), users' response to new

© Springer Nature Switzerland AG 2020
E. Ziemba (Ed.): AITM 2019/ISM 2019, LNBIP 380, pp. 27–41, 2020.
https://doi.org/10.1007/978-3-030-43353-6_2

marketing forms and tools, the development of new e-marketing tools, etc. Kaznowski [5] believes that it is a significant part of the marketing strategy of an organisation. On the other hand, it is the result of a combination of modern marketing theories, use of information technologies [6] as well as the product of project management, in particular, change and risk management [7]. In order to create a marketing strategy related to the promotion of products and services via the Internet, it is necessary to carry out a project consisting in, among others, building an e-shopping website and devising marketing tools which would help to promote this website on the Internet. For a marketing strategy to be successful, we should collect and examine the opinions of potential clients regarding the media and marketing techniques. If we consider all the above comments, then electronic market will represent all the above-mentioned marketing activities aimed at meeting operational, tactical and strategic goals with the application of the Internet infrastructure [8, 9]. At this point it is important to note that currently the so-called mobility is one of the fastest developing phenomena. At present, mobile marketing is an essential part of electronic marketing. Due to the fact that it is perceived as all (advertising and promotional) activities using the functionalities of mobile devices [10, 11] it is difficult to distinguish between advertising available in browsers and special, dedicated smartphone mobile applications [12]. According to AMMA (The American Mobile Marketing Association), mobile marketing is understood as any form of marketing, advertising or promotional activity addressed to clients and transmitted via the mobile channel [13]. This definition of the phenomenon is the one applied in the present article. In addition, m-marketing offers basically unlimited possibilities of adapting the forms of promotion and communication to the needs of an individual recipient (far-reaching personalisation) [14]. This also means a significant reduction of the costs of organisations' activity [15].

In recent years we may observe a significant increase in - the company resources allocated to the activities related to e-marketing in Poland. According to an IAB and Internet - Standard reports [16–18] online advertising spending in 2017 increased by PLN 337 million and was higher by 9.3% compared to the dynamics of the previous year. A similar increase (8%) was recorded on the German market. The Turkish market located in the European ranking of the value of digital advertising just behind Poland increased by 16%. It is true that it is more than two times less than on the US market (21%), but it still puts Poland at high developmental thresholds. According to the IAB, spending on mobile advertising in 2017 reached PLN 890 million, and its share in all expenses increased to 23%. This market is growing so and more research should be devoted to it.

Electronic marketing was the object of many studies, both in the Polish and foreign markets, also from the point of view of a client [19–23] and new works analysing this field continue to appear. It is important to indicate that the majority of vital and relevant studies were published before the period of the most intense development of modern smartphones and tablets along with their dedicated applications.

The authors of this article aim to distinguish some of the basic tendencies related to these new phenomena as well as implications for the future development of electronic marketing, including mobile marketing. That is the reason why the authors have undertaken the present studies whose main aim is to analyse the use of e-marketing among the users of all kinds of computer devices used to access the Internet. The findings presented in this article, discussion and resultant conclusions constitute a report of the research involving a selected sample of Internet users in Poland at the beginning of 2019.

The structure of the article is adapted to achieve its main objective. The paper is split into sections. Section 1 is an introduction to the subject. Section 2 contains assumptions of methodology and sample presentation. Section 3 describes the research findings and discussion. Section 4 provides the conclusions, limitations and considerations for future investigative work.

2   Methodology and Study Sample

Following the previously conducted research [24], the authors adopted the verified research procedure which consists of the following stages:

- constructing the first version of the survey questionnaire, on the basis of previously conducted research, literature studies as well as experts' and own observations of the phenomena,
- verifying the questionnaire analysing the respondents' comprehension of the questions contained in the survey and the significance of the queries for the research, with the participation of randomly selected groups of respondents engaged in the pilot study,
- random selection of the groups of students for the study,
- making the verified and improved survey questionnaire available for the selected student groups (with the application of a CAWI – Computer Associated Web Interview method),
- analysis and discussion of the obtained findings,
- conclusions and possible directions for e-marketing development, on the basis of literature references and the authors' own studies.

In its final form, after eliminating the least significant questions and introducing changes aimed at clearer presentation of the remaining queries, the survey questionnaire included twenty-three substantive questions, divided into five groups and five questions related to the so-called demographics of the study sample. The detailed presentation of specific sets of survey questions is given below:

- electronic marketing environment – the frequency of using the Internet, the kinds of devices which are most frequently used in this type of communication, the place of accessing the Internet, the frequency of making purchases, the types of the most frequently used Internet websites,
- the effectiveness of electronic marketing – the level of effectiveness of electronic marketing, comparative evaluation of the effectiveness of electronic marketing and the traditional one as well as the reasons for the potential advantage of electronic marketing over its traditional form,
- evaluation of e-marketing as a source of information on products/services – the sources of obtaining information on products and services, sources of Internet-based information as well as aims of the application of the obtained information,

- evaluation of the distinguished e-marketing media and techniques – the evaluation of selected e-marketing media (with the application of the following scale: very good, good, satisfactory, non-satisfactory, no opinion); the approach of the respondents to selected e-marketing media (scale: I accept it, I ignore it, I don't accept it), ranking of selected e-marketing media; elements of e-marketing which respondents pay the most attention to; the respondents' approach to e-marketing in specific types of websites (scale: I like them, I don't care about them, they are boring, they are irritating); respondents' approach to e-marketing running on traditional and modern devices,
- respondent's approach towards marketing on mobile devices – the respondent's evaluation of m-marketing advantages, evaluation of the benefits of m-marketing, evaluation of m-marketing disadvantages, the kind of m-marketing which affects the respondent the most; the type of m-marketing which impacted the respondent's purchases the most in the last six months,
- demographics (age, gender, education, place of origin).

The presented study was carried out in mid-March 2019. The research sample was selected as a partially convenient and partially random sample among the students of the Faculty of Management at the University of Warsaw. An invitation to complete a survey questionnaire was distributed electronically among 356 students of BA and MA studies, both full-time and part-time courses, as randomly selected students' groups. 294 students completed survey questionnaires, which constitutes nearly 83% of the sample. This indicates nearly a threefold increase in the number of respondents from the same environment compared to the study of 2016 [5], which suggests increased interest in topics related to the possibilities of using the Internet for marketing purposes, especially in its mobile form. There was also a slight, less than 3%, increase in the number of respondents who completed an entire survey questionnaire correctly, in relation to the result recorded three years ago.

The selection of the sample consisting of students brought about certain limitations with regard to the possibility to interpret the findings. As the studies by Batorski and Płoszaja [25] indicate, the age group among which the studies have been carried out is a population which is most active in the Internet, most focused on innovation, and the one which is also the fastest to purchase and apply the latest technical solutions. Therefore, it is difficult to generalise the obtained results to be indicative of the entire society. On the other hand, it is a group which for the above-mentioned reasons is the most competent to evaluate the tools used in the internet and mobile marketing, because they spend the greatest amount of time in the Internet, not only to obtain information, but also to make purchases and communicate with the shops, using websites and mobile applications many times a day.

In the analysed sample, more than 95% of the respondents were representatives of this most active social group. The group included individuals who were 18–24 years old, with the average age of slightly over 21, where all survey participants had secondary education. Among the respondents, there were 57% of women and 43% of men, which reflects the present gender structure of UW students at the Faculty of Management. Three years ago, there were more students who were randomly selected from the groups of Accounting and Finance, where the percentage share of women was larger, which means that at present the participation of men increased by 8%. For the same reason, the number of working students who completed the survey questionnaire increased by 10% [9]. At present, in the examined study sample there were 55% of working students and 45% of students who were not professionally active. More than 52% of the respondents came from cities with over 500,000 residents, further 11% from towns with 100–500,000 inhabitants, 24% from the towns with 10–100,000 residents, less than 5% from small towns up to 100 inhabitants, and only 9% were from villages. In the present study, the share of students coming from large cities increased (rise of 16%), mainly at the expense of people coming from rural areas (drop by over 10%).

3   Findings and Discussion

The survey questionnaire was made available on the servers of the Faculty of Management at the University of Warsaw. The questions were divided into several groups, and the analysis of the responses with the discussion and comments are presented below.

The first group of questions was of introductory nature. Its goal was to identify the conditions of using electronic marketing. The queries concerned the frequency of using the Internet, the type of most frequently visited websites, devices used for this purpose as well as the place and frequency of doing online shopping. The response to the first question appears to confirm the findings of Batorski's study – all students use the Internet a few times a day. Undoubtedly, this was due to the popularity of mobile devices and – as it seems, a specific environmental culture of using them everywhere and at any time. This conclusion also results from the response to the following question, where over 23% of the respondents stated that it is the main and the only device which they use to connect with the Internet. Given that almost 12% of respondents use only a laptop and desktop computer for this purpose, this still confirms a clear advantage of this device over others. The greatest share of the sample – 44%, however, uses a combination of a laptop and a smartphone to connect with the Internet. As indicated in the comments section, the smartphone is mainly used to listen to music, communicate, obtain information and carry out small financial operations. Financial decisions which require careful consideration and extensive works or communications are usually associated with working on a laptop. Interestingly, fewer and fewer people use a tablet - 4% (nearly 3% less than three years ago) and a combination of a tablet with other devices (smartphone, desktop computer) – on average 3% (previously twice as many). Greater functionality, the decreasing size and weight of laptops cause a systematic replacement of a tablet with a laptop. In comparison with the situation from three years ago, the use of the smartphone as the only device to connect with the Internet declined (by nearly 10%), and the use of smartphone and laptop increased (by almost 11%).

The most frequently visited websites are social media websites (25%). Websites providing information/news are also popular - 12%. Thus, it emerges that the main and widely appreciated functions of the Internet are those which are associated with providing information or communicating. The use of search engines is also of primary importance with regard to providing information which the respondents require (18%). However, searching for a particular item is not always associated with purchasing it on the Internet: it is frequently only connected with looking for data concerning a given product or service. Nevertheless, e-shopping websites are most frequently visited by

19% of the respondents, and financial services by 21%. Thus, the area where electronic marketing might be applied is wide. The growing popularity of the use of mobile devices is demonstrated by the indicated places of accessing the Internet – nearly 93% of the respondents stated that they use it everywhere, and 13 times fewer people (7%) responded that they use it at work, at home or the university. The respondents are also a group which actively participated in making purchases, nearly 75% does shopping at least once a month, including an almost 10% share making purchases a few times a week or even several times a day. Only slightly over 24% claim that they do shopping rarely or never (less than 1%). Three years ago, the group of internet users who did online shopping rarely or never was twice as large.

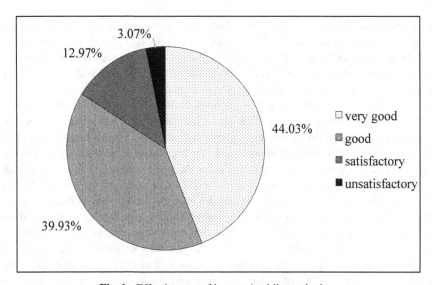

Fig. 1. Effectiveness of internet/mobile marketing.

The second part of the survey concerned the perception of the effectiveness of the application of electronic marketing by internet users: their subjective evaluation of the phenomenon of e-marketing, its comparison with traditional marketing and evaluation of the potential advantage of e-marketing over traditional marketing. The respondents assess internet marketing as good or very good in over 84%, and only over 15% perceive it as satisfactory or non-satisfactory (Fig. 1).

This is probably caused by the opinion that 24% of the respondents are convinced that internet and mobile marketing is better, and over 50% believe that the greatest effectiveness is achieved through a combination of electronic and traditional marketing. In turn, nearly 23% of survey participants think that the two types of marketing are difficult to compare because they are addressed to different target groups. In the case of almost a quarter of recipients, there exists a belief that the effectiveness of marketing depends on the age of the recipients and the most frequent use of media (smartphone versus laptop) associated with it (Fig. 2).

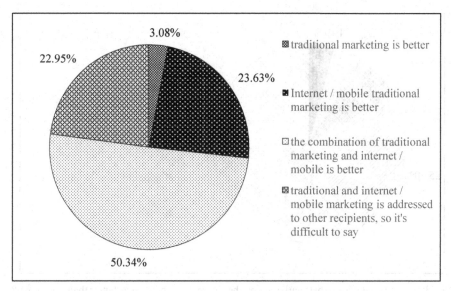

Fig. 2. Is internet/mobile marketing more effective than traditional?

The respondents regard continuous availability (33%, 25% in 2016) via mobile and remote or desktop devices and the possibility of buying items after clicking on the advertising field (via link) (nearly 26% as compared to 19% in 2016) to be the greatest sources of advantage of marketing in the Internet over traditional marketing. Also, the previously emphasised possibility to obtain more information about a product or service (25%) is of considerable importance. However, the possibilities of using comparison engines in e-marketing (only 8% of the respondents) and interactivity of internet advertising (5% of responded) were not greatly appreciated. The fact that the survey participants attach small importance to the possibility of selecting the cheapest item (possibly including the cost of transport) is surprising. It might seem that after many years of experience with this type of software and declarations included in other studies [9] related to the common use of comparison engines, in the customers' opinion, these factors tend to have more influence on a general positive evaluation of electronic marketing. Especially that in 2016 as many as 22% of the respondents indicated that it constitutes a significant advantage of internet marketing over its traditional form (Fig. 3).

The third part of the survey concerned issues related to the use of sources of obtaining information on products and services on the Internet and outside the Internet as well as its subsequent application. Among the analysed sample, the Internet proved to be an a decisively dominant medium (86% individuals) to access information about products and services (as compared to previous score at the level of 33%). In combination with the information obtained from a circle of friends and colleagues, this comprises over 98% of the places of obtaining commercial information. The importance of such media as television, radio, press, leaflets or paper information materials appears to be nearly nonexistent, which points to little interest in this form of marketing among the representatives of this social group. Comparison engines turned out to be the most common tool

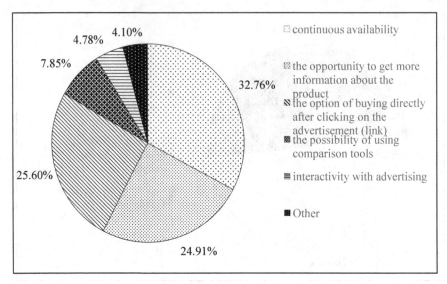

Fig. 3. What is the reason that marketing on the Internet can be seen as better than traditional?

(as it is believed by over 40% of the respondents) to search for information about products and services on the Internet. On the one hand, individuals are eager to use them, on the other hand, they do not perceive them as a tool which would be of crucial importance from the point of view of the effectiveness of e-marketing. The second place is taken by social media (nearly 31% share in the respondents' opinions). Even three years ago such an opinion would be encountered with disbelief; however, at present the influence of social media is becoming more and more important. This is also evidenced by the high, third place of blogs (15%). It is important to point out that even though a blog is in fact seen as a source of largely subjective information, it is still a medium which shapes consumers' tastes and views in certain sectors (e.g. fashion and cuisine). E-marketing offering different advertising forms contained on websites and carried out via emails is losing its importance (in total the score amounts to less than 9%). This form of advertising, which until recently was seen as dominant in this type of marketing, in a sense, is already regarded as a traditional form. According to 58% of the respondents, the information obtained on the Internet is used to make purchases in internet shops, and in the view of 38% of the survey participants - in traditional shops. It seems that the latter phenomenon deserves a more thorough examination, since the general conviction is that searching for information in the Internet is associated with shopping in internet shops. In view of the recorded statistics [18] of the values of over 2/3 of Allegro sales revenues, the information about using the information to make purchases at internet auctions (4%) also appears to be underestimated.

In the fourth part of the survey the respondents were asked to evaluate particular media and e-marketing techniques: the effectiveness of the applications of the media, approach towards selected e-marketing techniques, places in the ranking of products which induce consumers to make purchases, elements which respondents pay particular attention to and those which attract them the most as well as the evaluation of the respondent's approach to placing particular elements of e-marketing in marketing media and on various types of devices (both traditional and modern ones).

The evaluation of the effectiveness of selected electronic marketing media was based on a four-point scale from: unsatisfactory, satisfactory, good and very good. The highest rated techniques were: presence in social media (26% of very good scores), clarity and attractiveness of a website (24% of very good scores) as well as the presence in mobile solutions (20%). The highest number of good scores were obtained by positioning (18%) and sponsored links (15%). In the latter case, the opinions were divided because slightly more people (18%) evaluated them only at a satisfactory level. Banners, links to other websites (19% and 18% respectively) and newsletters (21%) were evaluated at the border between satisfactory and unsatisfactory. The most unsatisfactory technique was related to advertising mailing messages (43% of unsatisfactory scores).

The evaluation of the effectiveness of the phenomenon is affected by the respondents' attitude towards selected e-marketing techniques. The most widely acceptable among e-marketing techniques are clarity and attractiveness of a website (14% of accepting opinions), presence in social media (13%) and positioning (11%). The remaining techniques which are approved of by the survey participants are: replacing of advertising videos, music or texts, etc. as well as the appearance of a company logo on a website. Advertising presented on blogs or sponsored blogs is usually ignored (11% each), similarly to sponsored links and banners (10% each). Banners are not acceptable for a 10% share of respondents. The most unacceptable appear to be pop-up windows (30% of responses – I don't like it), advertising e-mails (14%) as well as advertising in posts in internet forums (10%).

This survey section was also aimed at creating a specific ranking of factors which motivate clients to make purchases. In this ranking, the first place among the responses was taken by the clarity and attractiveness of a website (33% of views). The second position was occupied by the presence in social media (22% of opinions). The subsequent places were taken by factors such as discounts after exceeding a specific value of the purchase (17% responses) and positioning (11%). The last positions in the assessment were taken by pop-up windows (43% in the last position), e-mailing advertisements (20% in the penultimate position). The obtained findings confirm earlier responses' opinions concerning particular media and advertising techniques.

According to respondents' opinions, clients pay the most attention to graphic elements (34%) as well as the innovativeness and attractiveness of the presentation (29%). They pay the least attention to technical elements of e-marketing such as: text (8% of the surveyed students believe it is the case) or the sound and music (14% of responses). So, what would attract them to visit the website? In the views of the study participants, at present, the most efficient in this regard are elements such as short videos (28%) and large graphic banners between a logo and the content (16%). The least effective are: buttons (5%) and pop-up windows (8%). The above ranking shows a specific transition of the existing clients to more modern technical elements of e-marketing and "fatigue" with the forms which are frequently encountered in the current practice of using the Internet.

From the point of view of a client, the greatest acceptance for placing e-marketing in selected marketing media was recorded in the case of e-shopping websites (23% of responses), social media websites (20%) as well as company and news websites (15% and 16% respectively). Nearly the same number of respondents ignore e-marketing elements on company websites. These items also do not disturb respondents while visiting company blogs (20%), private blogs (15%) and mobile media (14%). Perhaps it is the case because the survey participants view them as boring, irritating and irrelevant with regard to clients' knowledge about a product or service. As far as clients' using Internet tools is concerned, however, the most irritating and disturbing elements of e-marketing are contained in mailings (39% of the responses). At the same time, 17% of the sample consider them boring.

Over 28% of survey participants do not notice any difference with regard to what type of device they use: a traditional or a modern one. They accept e-marketing elements and tools on any device. Only 10% of the sample state that they dislike e-marketing in general. While, at the same time, nearly 26% of respondents declared that they like e-marketing on modern devices (smartphone, tablet), and only 6% like it using traditional devices (laptop, desktop computer).

The last group of survey questions concerned the respondents' approach to the phenomenon of marketing on mobile devices, namely: advantages and disadvantages of m-marketing, benefits of m-marketing and the effectiveness of m-marketing techniques in relation to the client. Among the greatest advantages of m-marketing, the respondents mainly distinguished the fact that it is available at all times and everywhere (24%) and it can apply a personalised advertising message (21%). The last positions were taken by the high effectiveness of this medium (8%) as well as the fact that it can be treated as a determinant of modernity (10%). The advantages of m-marketing are presented in Fig. 4.

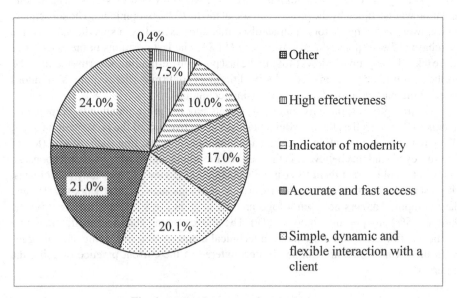

Fig. 4. Main advantages of m-marketing.

The advantages of m-marketing bring direct benefits for the client. Among the selected benefits, the most important factor (37% of the responses) was the use of NFC technique (e.g. Near Field Communication – Tatrzański Park Narodowy/Tatra National Park guide) or QR codes (e.g. train tickets). According to the survey participants, the second significant benefit was geolocation and mobile navigation (31%). The subsequent positions were taken by the possibility to create mobile websites (13%) and SMS marketing (9%).

The biggest disadvantage of m-marketing is the necessity of longer screen scrolling (34% of respondents believe it is the case) and increasing difficulty of getting rid of advertising messages (33%). Another negative factor is the fact that they take too much space on a screen which is already rather small (20%). The smallest number of people believe that advertising on mobile devices is too general and the graphic presentation is of lower quality (3–4%). The disadvantages of m-marketing are presented in Fig. 5.

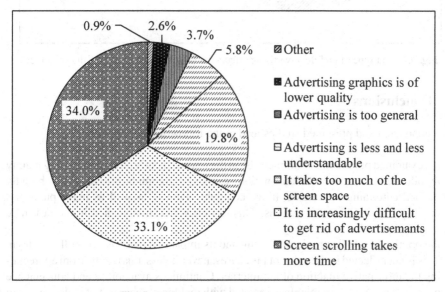

Fig. 5. Main disadvantages of m-marketing.

According to the survey participants, the greatest influence is indicated in the case of graphic advertising elements (66%). The next place is taken by the video advertising of the application (17%) and graphic advertising of the application (11%). The last one is text ads (0,68%). This findings are shown in Fig. 6.

The remaining kinds of mobile advertising are of limited importance, namely, they constitute only 5%. In the last six months, the aspects which had the greatest impact on respondents' purchases included: the use of mobile applications (44%), using geolocation and mobile navigation (17%) as well as SMS marketing (14%). The remaining m-marketing techniques did not exert any significant influence on the purchases made by the respondents in the last six months.

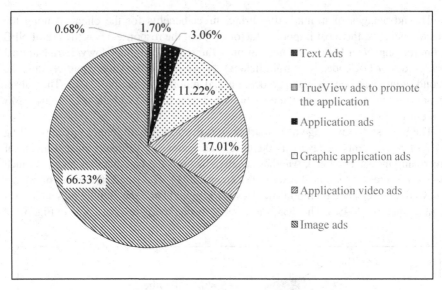

0.68%   1.70%   3.06%

11.22%

17.01%

66.33%

■ Text Ads

▦ TrueView ads to promote the application

■ Application ads

☐ Graphic application ads

▨ Application video ads

▧ Image ads

Fig. 6. What type of mobile advertising affects the most effectively affects the customer?

4   Conclusions

The conducted and presented studies lead to the following conclusions:

- the examined population is "immersed" in the Internet nearly all the time, using mainly mobile devices to search information, exchange communications, enjoy broadly defined entertainment (music, films, computer games), as well as make purchases or carry out financial transactions. This tendency has strengthened in the last three years,
- the opinion about electronic marketing and its impact on purchases is still very high. This is not reflected in the value of purchases; nevertheless, this results from appreciating the informative function of the Internet. Continuous availability and convenience of the use is not only or mainly associated with making purchases, but it also serves to obtain information about a product or service. The decisions concerning the purchase and the way this operation is being carried out (via the Internet or traditionally) are taken later,
- the attitude of the respondents towards comparison engines is unclear. On the one hand, nearly everyone uses them; on the other, clients do not perceive them as the most important tool which might be seen as a specific advantage of e-marketing over traditional marketing. A question arises: are the tools so commonplace that its use is treated as real, or the opinions about the products and services are primarily sought in the social media?
- at present, information acquired online is used mainly for shopping on the Internet, and to a slightly lower extent for purchases in traditional shops,
- the effectiveness of e-marketing media, in the respondents' opinion, depends mainly on the presence in the social media and characteristic features of the website (its

clarity and attractiveness); in the ranking of the factors inducing consumers to make purchases, apart from the above aspects, the respondents list also discounts offered after exceeding a certain amount of money,

- pop-up windows and spam mailing are the two most disliked elements in e-marketing,
- the respondents mainly pay attention to such technical elements of e-marketing, like graphic elements, in particular, short videos, appearing mainly on social media websites,
- the irritation associated with excessive advertising in mailings is growing; while the degree of acceptance of e-marketing received via traditional and modern devices is rather high (28%). The studies concerning this very phenomenon in relation to websites [e.g.] show that this solution appears to be the most undesirable with regard to the evaluation of the website quality. The greatest level of acceptance for video marketing on mobile devices undoubtedly also plays an important role in this respect,
- we may also observe a phenomenon of a specific shift of the interaction with the Internet from traditional to mobile devices and more and more common blurring of the boundaries between mobile laptops and tablets due to the greater universal use of laptops. The dominating position of smartphones in everyday life also has more and more influence on the evaluation of e-marketing in its mobile form,
- there occurs a specific shift in communication between individuals (so far more in the private sphere) from traditional mailing towards social media and messengers,
- the advantages of m-marketing result from its continuous availability and a possibility to personalise the message; the disadvantages mainly consist in the fact that it occupies a large part of the screen and its related necessity of longer scrolling or the fact that such an advertisement is more and more difficult to remove from the screen,
- it emerges that the aspects which have the greatest influence on the client are graphic and video advertisements in the applications.

The limitation of the study was the fact that it was carried out among a rather uniform sample of respondents coming from academic environment. As previously mentioned, this was the most active group with regard to new technologies, and the obtained findings tend to present a somewhat idealised view of the clients' relation towards both the technologies themselves as well as the operating media of electronic advertising. The study should be extended to include also other social groups which do not use the Internet to such an extent, both in their private life and economic activity. This would allow for a more comprehensive, holistic view of the possibilities of e-marketing applications. On the other hand, international and intercultural studies seem to be a very interesting direction for further studies, which would allow for specific universalisation of the obtained findings.

The study is useful and important for researchers and practitioners. Researchers may use described methodology for undertake similar analysis in the other countries or environment (different sample groups) or maybe in context of international comparisons. For practitioners, the findings of the research would be used to improve all activities connecting with implementation of i-marketing and m-marketing in their business. Especially, it will help them to understand what are the customers' expectations in the relation to e-marketing tools.

References

1. Meng, X.: Developing model of E-commerce E-marketing. In: Huangshan, P. R. (ed.) Proceedings of the 2009 International Symposium on Information Processing (ISIP 2009), China, 21–23 August 2009, pp. 225 –228 (2009)
2. Sznajder, A.: Marketing Wirtualny (Virtual Marketing). Oficyna Ekonomiczna, Cracow (2002)
3. Zarańska, K., Zborowski, M.: Charakterystyka Bankowości Elektronicznej. (Electronic Banking Characteristics). In: Gospodarowicz, A. (ed.) Bankowość elektroniczna. Istota i innowacje (Electronic Banking. Essence and Innovations), pp. 11–61. Wydawnictwo C.H. Beck, Warszawa (2018)
4. Frąckiewicz, E.: Marketing Internetowy (Internet Marketing). Wydawnictwo Naukowe PWN, Warsaw (2006)
5. Kaznowski, D.: Nowy Marketing w Internecie (New Marketing in Internet). Difin, Warsaw (2007)
6. Sun, S.: Innovation mode and strategy research on small and medium-sized enterprise E-marketing in post financing crisis. Contemp. Logist. **04**, 13 (2011). https://doi.org/10.5503/J.CL.2011.04.003
7. Hasan, J.: Analysis of E-marketing strategies. Studia commercialia Bratislavensia **14**(14), 201–208 (2011). https://doi.org/10.2478/v10151-011-0006-z
8. Chmielarz, W.: Study of smartphones usage from the customer's point of view. Procedia Comput. Sci. **65**, 1085–1094 (2015). https://doi.org/10.1016/j.procs.2015.09.045
9. Chmielarz, W., Zborowski, M.: Aspects of mobility in e-marketing from the perspective of a customer. In: Ganzha, M., Maciaszek, L., Paprzycki, M. (eds.) Proceedings of the 2016 Federated Conference on Computer Science and Information Systems, pp. 1329–1333. PTI, Warsaw (2016). https://doi.org/10.15439/2016F112
10. Hovancakova, D.: Mobile Marketing. Studia commercialia Bratislavensia **4**(14), 211–225 (2011). https://doi.org/10.2478/v10151-011-0007-y
11. Bernauer, D.: Mobile Internet - Grundlagen. Erfolgsfaktoren und Praxisbeispiele. Vdm Verlag Dr, Müller (2008)
12. Hatalska, N. (2016). http://hatalska.com/slangoskop/marketing-mobilny/. Accessed 30 Mar 2016
13. Salo, J., Sinisalo, J., Karjaluto, H.: Intentionally developed business network for mobile marketing: a case study from Finland. J. Bus. Ind. Mark. **23**(7), 497–506 (2008). https://doi.org/10.1108/08858620810901257
14. Konkol, S.: Marketing Mobilny (Mobile Marketing). Helion, Gliwice (2010)
15. Sznajder, A.: Technologie mobilne w marketingu (Mobile Technology in Marketing). Wolters Kluwer, Warsaw (2014)
16. IAB Raport (2018). https://iab.org.pl/wp-content/uploads/2018/06/HBRP-raport-IAB-04-18.pdf. Accessed 10 Apr 2018
17. InterStandard (2019). https://www.internetstandard.pl/whitepapers. Accessed 10 Apr 2019
18. Meeker, M.: Internet trends 2018 report. In: Code Conference May 30th, 2018 (2018). https://www.slideshare.net/kleinerperkins/internet-trends-report-2018-99574140. Accessed 10 Apr 2019
19. Roach, G.: Consumer perceptions of mobile phone marketing a direct marketing innovation. Direct Mark. Int. J. **3**(2), 124–138 (2009)
20. Gao, T., Sultan, F., Rohm, A.J.: Factors influencing Chinese youth consumers' acceptance of mobile marketing. J. Consum. Mark. **27**(7), 574–583 (2010). https://doi.org/10.1108/07363761011086326

21. Świerczyńska-Kaczor, U.: e-Marketing przedsiębiorstwa w społeczności wirtualnej (e-Marketing of Company in Virtual Society). Difin, Warsaw (2012)
22. Wielki, J.: Modele wpływu przestrzeni elektronicznej na organizacje gospodarcze (Models of Virtual Space Impact on Economic Organizations). Wydawnictwo Uniwersytetu Ekonomicznego we Wrocławiu, Wrocław (2012)
23. Kiba-Janiak, M.: The use of mobile phones by customers in retail stores: a case of Poland. Econ. Sociol. **7**(1), 116–130 (2014). https://doi.org/10.14254/2071-789X.2014/7-1/11
24. Chmielarz, W., Zborowski, M.: The application of a conversion method in a confrontational pattern-based design method used for the evaluation of IT systems. In: Ganzha, M., Maciaszek, L., Paprzycki, M. (eds.) Proceedings of the 2014 Federated Conference on Computer Science and Information Systems, pp. 1227–1234. PTI, Warsaw (2014). https://doi.org/10.15439/2014F198
25. Batorski, D., Płoszaj, A.: Diagnoza i rekomendacje w obszarze kompetencji cyfrowych społeczeństwa kompetencji cyfrowych społeczeństwa kompetencji cyfrowych społeczeństwa kompetencji cyfrowych społeczeństwa i przeciwdziałania wykluczeniu cyfrowemu i przeciwdziałania wykluczeniu cyfrowemu i przeciwdziałania wykluczeniu cyfrowemu i przeciwdziałania wykluczeniu cyfrowemu w kontekście zaprogramowania wsparcia w latach 2014-2020. (Diagnosis and recommendations in the area of digital competence society digital competence society digital competence society digital competence society and counteracting digital exclusion and counteracting digital exclusion and counteracting digital exclusion and counteracting digital exclusion in the context of programming support in 2014–2020). Warsaw (2012). http://www.euroreg.uw.edu.pl/dane/web_euroreg_publications_files/3513/ekspertyza_mrr_kompetencjecyfrowe_2014–2020.pdf. Accessed 29 Mar 2019

Drivers and Challenges for Digital Transformation in the South African Retail Industry

Rion van Dyk and Jean-Paul Van Belle[✉] [iD]

University of Cape Town, Private Bag, Rondebosch, South Africa
jean-paul.vanbelle@uct.ac.za

Abstract. Markets are driving organisations worldwide towards digital transformation. This research investigates this phenomenon in a particular environment by looking at what drives and inhibits South African (SA) retail organisations to adopt digital transformation. It also looks at the proposed use cases in retail for selected digital technologies. Given the relative scarcity of academic research and available theory on the topic, a case study approach was adopted. The analytic framework used was the Technology, Organisational, and Environmental (TOE) framework, which proved a suitable way to systematically categorize the perceived drivers and challenges. The most prominent digital transformation initiatives in the SA retail industry were the adoption of cloud technologies and data analytics. The factors and use cases which were uncovered, as well as their relative importance, could inform other retailers in their decision-making process concerning digital transformation.

Keywords: Digital transformation · Digital technologies · Strategy · South African retail organisations · Technology adoption · TOE · Perceptions · Understanding · Technology drivers

1 Introduction

Customer-facing organisations, especially in the retail sector, are required to become more responsive to customer demand; this competitive pressure has forced them to embark on a digital transformation process [1]. Digital transformation refers to the strategy that changes an enterprise business model to provide customers with enhanced products or services by taking advantage of new or existing digital technologies [2]. Business digitalization changes the competitive landscape by threatening digital disruption from new market entrants, while digitally savvy customers are demanding more from the enterprise [3]. Digital transformation affects every enterprise and sector as the market-changing potential of digital technologies is often wider than sales channels, supply chains, products and business processes [4].

One of the biggest challenges enterprises currently face is integrating and exploiting new digital technologies [4]. Digital technologies are tools that enterprises must make use of to get closer to their customers, transform their business processes and empower

© Springer Nature Switzerland AG 2020
E. Ziemba (Ed.): AITM 2019/ISM 2019, LNBIP 380, pp. 42–62, 2020.
https://doi.org/10.1007/978-3-030-43353-6_3

their employees [5]. Current new digital technologies include cloud computing, mobile, analytics, social media, robotics and Internet of Things (IoT) technologies [6]. These digital technologies can present the enterprise with game-changing opportunities if they are combined with accessibility of enterprise data to enrich their products, services and customer relationships [7].

There is a lack of information around digital transformation, its perceptions and use cases in the SA retail industry to aid its adoption. The main objective of this study was to understand and examine the current perceptions and status of digital transformation within a SA retail organisation. Furthermore, the study aimed to identify factors influencing the intended adoption of digital transformation within the SA retail organisation. This will provide the information and knowledge needed for the retail industry to make informed decisions about the potential future use of digital technologies and how to overcome adoption barriers.

Two propositions are posed to relate the research findings to existing theories and models identified in the literature review.

- **Proposition 1**: Digital transformation by SA retail organisations is driven by specific TOE (Technology, Organisational, & Environmental) factors.
- **Propostion 2**: SA retail industry organisations have identified specific core technologies driving digital transformation.

It is important to study the factors influencing the intended adoption of digital transformation so that enterprises can understand the challenges and address them. Addressing these challenges will be beneficial to the enterprise as it will assist it to create a clear and coherent digital strategy, lead to retaining and attracting top talent, and create a company culture where employees can be innovative and creative. Ultimately, a digitally transformed enterprise will be able to easily adapt taking advantage of new opportunities and have a competitive advantage over their competition.

The next section of the paper includes a literature review defining digital transformation, the main digital technologies transforming the retail industry, factors influencing digital transformation and introducing the TOE theoretical framework used in the research. It then introduces the research methodology and design used for the study. The research analysis and findings section is structured using the TOE factor groupings: technology, organisation and environment to address the first proposition; this is followed by an overview of the technologies identified by the interviewees perceived to be riving digital transformation in South African retail to address the second research proposition. The discussion section revisits the propositions and reflects on the validity and reliability of the findings. Finally the conclusion identifies some of the major limitations and possible avenues for future research.

2 Literature Review

2.1 Defining Digital Transformation

Digital transformation refers to an enterprise business model that applies new or existing digital technologies and products or services into digital variants to offer a tangible product to their customers [2]. Digital transformation is not only about technology, but it also requires a new way of thinking and strategy by enterprise executives. *"Digital transformation is the profound transformation of business and organisational activities, processes, competencies and models to fully leverage the changes and opportunities of a mix of digital technologies and their accelerating impact across society in a strategic and prioritized way, with present and future shifts in mind"* [1]. Enterprise digital transformation strategies should include the application of digital technologies to enterprise processes, products and assets to enhance customer value, uncover new monetization opportunities, improve efficiencies and manage risk across the enterprise [8, 9].

2.2 Core Digital Technologies Affecting the Retail Industry

New digital technologies (social, mobile, analytics, cloud computing and Internet of Things [IoT] technologies) could present the enterprise with game-changing opportunities and existential threats. Leaders in digital transformation apply new digital technologies and related technologies in conjunction with the accessibility of enterprise data to enrich their products, services and customer relationships [7].

Social Media. The phenomenal and exponential growth of social media and mobile has resulted in many organisations realizing that an online presence is required to reach out and connect with their digital savvy customers [10]. Capturing data from tools such as Facebook, LinkedIn and blogs is essential to integrate the information into the sales process [11]. Digital savvy customers follow brands on social media and expect to be able to view store inventory online to enable them to do "showroom" shopping before going into a physical store [10].

Mobility. Digital technologies have enabled enterprises to make use of mobility and ubiquitous connectivity features providing the enterprise with immediate interaction and access to a wide range of data and computing power thereby enabling enterprises to analyse their data and make decisions in real time [12]. Mobile connectivity meant that tech-savvy customers across all facets of society completely changed their behaviours, expectations and the way they interact with enterprises [4]. Mobile phone penetration throughout Africa, -considered the least digitally populated continent, has reached 70% of its one billion inhabitants, with a fast-growing proportion having internet access. Mobile technology advances allow for the capture of geographical and contextual data that was previously not possible [13]. Digitalization experienced a significant boost with the introduction of smart mobile devices and the applications that run on them [14]. Furthermore, the declining cost of mobile technologies has broadened their potential for worldwide use [13].

Analytics. Digital analytical tools coupled with computer-enabled techniques can yield insight to enterprise executives from massive multidimensional datasets enabling them to make use of analytics to make strategic enterprise decisions [13]. About 90% of the data available today has been produced in the last two years. This data explosion has been driven by new data sources such as digital transactions, mobile devices, embedded sensors and the growing use of social media by the global population. Enterprises can benefit from learning how to capture, absorb, store and analyse their data and turn their data into a valuable asset [14]. Data analytics should be incorporated into new digital products for personalisation reasons, but also to inform other enterprise departments like product development, sales and marketing [15]. Using an analytical-based approach allows organisations to personalise their service and marketing to the need of each of their individual customers by constantly innovating, improving their processes, launching new service-based, data-driven applications and capabilities [16].

Cloud Computing. This can be defined as "a model for enabling ubiquitous, convenient, on-demand network access to a shared pool of configurable computing resources (e.g., networks, servers, storage, applications, and services) that can be rapidly provisioned and released with minimal management effort or service provider interaction" [17]. Cloud computing technologies enable enterprises to outsource some elements of the IT value chain with benefits for enterprises such as reduced costs, scalability, flexibility, capacity utilisation, higher efficiencies and mobility [18].

The Internet of Things (IoT). This refers to a type of network that enables any device to connect to the internet based on stipulated protocols through information sensing equipment to conduct communication and information exchange. The IoT concept has become more practical in recent years due to the exponential growth of the use of smart mobile devices, the growth of data analytics and cloud computing. IoT enables things to be connected at anytime, anywhere, with anything and with anyone ideally using any network, path or service [19]. IoT will force enterprises to digitally transform and will bring fundamental changes to individuals' and society's expectation and perspectives on how technologies and applications work in the world [20].

2.3 Factors Influencing Digital Transformation

"Digital transformation is a highly complex company-wide endeavour which requires a systematic approach by enterprise executives to formulate a digital transformation strategy which is crucial for successful digital transformation initiatives" [21]. Enterprises could gain a competitive advantage over competitors by making use of new digital technologies which include cloud computing, mobile, social, analytics and Internet of Things. Furthermore, enterprises could enrich their current products, services and customer relationships through new digital technologies [7].

It is of utmost importance that enterprises address the most common factors influencing the intended adoption of digital transformation before embarking on digital transformation projects. These factors include:

- Ensuring the enterprise leadership has the ability to steer digital transformation by setting direction, building momentum and ensuring the enterprise follows [5].
- Formulating a clear and coherent digital strategy that integrates leadership and company culture to transform their enterprise and the way they work [9].
- Committed leadership that drives digital transformation from the top-down setting direction, building momentum and ensuring the enterprise follows through on digital strategies [5].

- Employing, retaining and developing talent to ensure the enterprise has the "right employees in the right place" to allow the enterprise to quickly adapt to change, make adjustments and create new opportunities [9].
- Ensuring the enterprise has to rapidly self-organise [13].
- Fostering a culture where employees are encouraged to take risks, innovate, be creative and create a collaborative work environment [22].
- Embracing Business Intelligence and analytics to ensure executives make better decisions by managing by numbers and facts [23].
- Ensuring that the correct enterprise architecture is in place to enable flexibility and agility in order to quickly adapt to new business demands [24].
- Creating an omni-channel retail environment to satisfy the changing customer search and buying process [25].

Executives should be guided by the enterprise digital strategy in their efforts to create competitive advantage, value and customer satisfaction by combining existing technology with capabilities of other digital technologies [7].

2.4 Technology, Organisation, Environment Framework (TOE)

The TOE framework looking at factors that drive decision making relating to the adoption and implementation of technology innovations and classifies these into three broad categories (Fig. 1) [26].

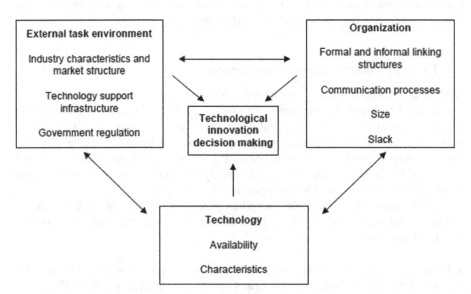

Fig. 1. The TOE (Technology, Organisation, and Environment) framework [26]

The **technology** aspect include all technologies that might be applicable to the enterprise including technologies currently being used by the enterprise, technologies that are available to the enterprise but are not being used and innovative technologies that might enable the enterprise to evolve and adapt [26, 27]. The **organisational** aspect of the TOE framework relates to all descriptive measures and resources of the enterprise (e.g. the number of employees and communication protocols) which may affect executive management decisions with regards to adoption and implementation [26]. Finally, the **environmental** aspect of the TOE framework includes elements, such as the structure of the retail industry in SA, which might affect the adoption of technology within an enterprise [26].

3   Research Approach and Design

Two core research questions drove the research:

RQ1:   What are the key drivers and inhibitors for digital transformation within the retail organisation?

RQ2:   What digital technologies are perceived to drive digital transformation in SA retail?

A case study approach was chosen as an appropriate strategy to conduct this qualitative study [28]. The research was conducted within a leading African retailer which is part of a retail group with currently more than 4950 stores in 12 African countries. The retailer, used for the case study, currently has 2164 stores across Southern Africa and employs more than 15000 staff. The researchers chose the retailer's head office, in the Western Cape region of SA, as the case site for this study. One of the researchers understands the company culture as he has been employed by the retail group for more than 7 years. Brands within the retail group are well-known household names in Southern Africa. The company has a strong customer focus and their core revenue comes from product sales through their stores to clientele.

The researchers actively solicited company documentation before and during interviews which were analysed to support the research. Twelve highly experienced interviewees, across a number of relevant but varied organisational roles, participated in the research. A semi-structured interview protocol was followed. As shown in Fig. 2, the theme saturation point occurred from the ninth interview as no new themes emerged in the subsequent three interviews. Therefore, the sample size can be deemed to be sufficient.

The interviewees are listed in Table 1 (but note that the Participant number in Table 1 does not necessarily correspond directly with the Interview number in Fig. 2). All interviewees had degrees or diplomas. The gender split, 9 males and 3 females, is a fair reflection of the demographics found in the retail industry population. The sample population has vast IT retail experience (averaging 24 years) and had seen multiple IT strategies and technologies change over the past two decades. P-8 to P-12 can be seen to represent the executive viewpoint.

The researchers used a thematic approach to analyse the company documentation provided and the interview data collected during the research. The NVivo qualitative analysis software was used to assist then analysis.

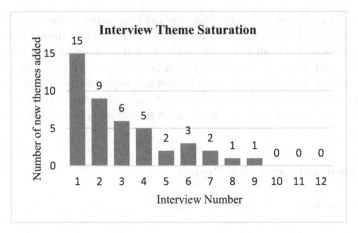

Fig. 2. Interview thematic saturation

Table 1. Interviewee sample

#	Position	Gender	Experience
P-1	Team leader	Male	24 Years
P-2	Team leader	Male	18 Years
P-3	Team leader	Male	15 Years
P-4	Team leader	Male	21 Years
P-5	DevOps	Male	10 Years
P-6	Enterprise architect	Male	23 Years
P-7	Enterprise architect	Female	25 Years
P-8	Director	Male	29 Years
P-9	Director	Female	26 Years
P-10	Director	Female	30 Years
P-11	Director	Male	32 Years
P-12	CIO	Male	35 Years

4   Research Analysis and Findings

As an initial exploratory overview analysis, a wordcloud on the basis of the word frequencies in the interview transcriptions was created (Fig. 3 – left). Following this, a *cluster analysis* on the co-occurrence of the 50 top words was performed. A subset of the most pertinent portion of the dendrogram is given in Fig. 3 (right).

Some interesting word clusters are *transformation* with both *potential* and *want,* indicating both the desire and perceived opportunity of the interviewees. Interestingly, *digital* was paired most often with *organisation,* referring to the need to move to a digital organisation, whereas *technologies* was most frequently used in combination with the term *business,* speaking to IT-business alignment. Finally, it is interesting to note that *IoT* was associated most often with *cloud;* whereas *data* was almost invariably linked to *use.*

In what follows, the focus will be on the actual drivers of digital transformation, as perceived by the respondents. These drivers are grouped and discussed according to the three headings as posited by the TOE research framework: technological, organisational and environmental factors.

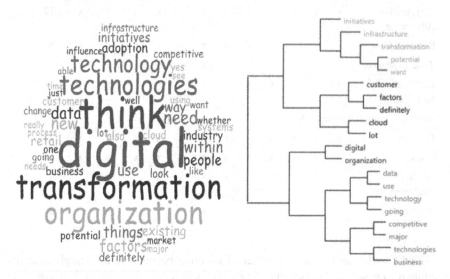

Fig. 3. Relative word frequency word cloud (L) and word clusters dendogram (subset) (R)

4.1 Technology

A total of three factors were identified under the technology theme of which the two most significant were "perceived challenges" and "relative advantage", refer to Table 3 (the second column shows number of interviewees mentioning the theme). All participants perceived there to be both relative advantages and challenges by the adoption of digital transformation within the retail industry. The advantages and challenges could have a positive or negative effect on the adoption. They also indicated the core available technologies. The technology theme was broken down into subthemes and discussed below.

Table 2. Technology sub-themes

Participant:	1	2	3	4	5	6	7	8	9	10	11	12	Count
Perceived Challenges													
Infrastructure Impact	x	x	x	x	x	x	x	x	x	x	x	x	**12**
Security		x			x	x	x	x	x	x	x	x	**10**
Talent/Technical Skills		x				x				x	x		**4**
Relative Advantage													
Competitive Advantage	x	x	x	x	x	x	x	x	x	x	x	x	**12**
Reduced Cost		x			x	x	x	x	x		x	x	**8**
Time to Market		x				x	x	x	x			x	**6**
Customer Satisfaction	x			x	x					x	x	x	**6**
Available Digital Technologies													
G-Suite	x	x	x	x	x	x	x	x	x	x	x	x	**12**
Cloud	x	x	x	x	x	x	x	x	x	x	x	x	**12**
Artificial Intelligence						x	x	x	x				**4**
Machine Learning						x	x						**2**

Perceived Challenges (+/−). A number of adoption barriers were highlighted in the literature review such as the lack of a clear and coherent digital strategy, talent, company culture, IT function transformation and Omni Channel retail capabilities. This was consistent with the responses from the participants with issues around security, workforce talent and resistance to change coming up the most.

It should be highlighted that despite digital strategy being highlighted during the Literature Review as one of the major challenges affecting the adoption of digital transformation, none of the participants mentioned this as a challenge.

Infrastructure Impact (+). Several concerns were raised by participants around how the adoption of digital technologies, specifically cloud technology adoption, would impact their organisation's infrastructure and thus would have a positive impact on digital transformation adoption. Most participants mentioned that the enterprise is currently busy with multiple projects to facilitate cloud adoption and that this will most certainly have a major impact on the existing infrastructure and data centres of the enterprise as P-3 stated "...*we are in the process of digital transformation and part of it is moving from our own on premise infrastructure to hosted cloud-based infrastructure*". All participants thought that adopting cloud technologies will result in a saving for the enterprise as maintenance of the on-premise hardware will decrease significantly.

Another infrastructural concern that was raised was the need for high-speed low latency connectivity. P-6: *"...with our cloud deployment as our need on high-speed low latency connectivity, for instance, is an infrastructure component that is important to improve on"*.

Security (−). Most participants highlighted that there is a security risk that must be considered with the adoption of cloud technologies as part of digital transformation: *"You are moving outside the boundaries of your corporate network so that is a security risk."* (P-7). This respondent is also of the opinion that data is an organisation's currency and the organisation should protect that intellectual property (IP) at all cost. P-8 also raised the concern for data protection by stating *"...so by making us connected to everything at all times we have to make sure that we've got the bases in place to still protect a corporate organisation like we are"*. P-2 further solidifies the security concern by stating *"You're ultimately putting everything into one place out there in the world, so security really needs to become a top priority"*.

Further concerns were raised about SA's Protection of Personal Information Act (POPI) and payment card information (PCI) compliance. PP-2 states that *"...the personal information act POPI requires information to be stored in a certain way with security applied. This actually becomes more important with cloud storage. Also, their payment card information also strict compliance rules that need to be adhered to..."*. Although enterprises must take regulatory compliance into consideration, it's not necessarily a factor that would influence the choice of technology but rather the data generated by the technology as stated by P-11 *"...I don't think it necessarily influences the technologies that use but it certainly influences what you do with the data that technology generates"*.

Talent - Technical Skills (+/−). As mentioned in the literature review, one of the most important critical success factors of digital transformation is to hire new digital talent to compliment or replace the existing workforce to ensure that the enterprise has the *"right employees in the right place"* [15].

Interviewees gave mixed responses when prompted to comment if the organisation possesses the necessary technical skills to implement digital technologies as part of their digital transformation strategy. Eight participants felt that technical skills within the organisation should not be an adoption barrier in today's fast-changing IT environment: *"...it's not technical skills that will stand in our way"* [P-8]. P-7 is of the opinion that the organisation could partner with an expert external third party to overcome any technology challenge by stating *"We would have to partner with specialized partners in certain areas to take us on the journey. So, if we partner with the right people, I don't think our technical skills will play such a big role"*. However, P-2 felt that employees might fear new technologies and that new talent will be required to upskill existing employees by stating *"Yes absolutely - the lack of technical skills as far as I can see brings about it a fear. New talent will be required for training of existing employees"*.

Relative Advantage (+). During the data analysis "Relative advantage" emerged as the second biggest factor under the technology major theme and having a positive impact on its adoption. Participants identified a number of perceived benefits (Table 2), with customer satisfaction, competitive advantage and reduced cost being cited the most (second column = number of interviewees mentioning the theme).

All participants in the study highlighted that digital transformation would have a positive impact on customer satisfaction, ultimately providing the enterprise with a competitive advantage. Furthermore, by leveraging digital technologies, enterprises can collect data on customers and use data analysis techniques to offer customers specific goods and services as highlighted by P-12 *"...that if you start knowing your customer better, you can offer him things that are very specific to him"*.

Available Digital Technologies (+). Availability of digital technologies emerged as the third biggest factor under the technology major theme. An important factor pertaining to technology adoption is the availability of technological innovation [26]. It was important to identify the different digital technologies available as one of the objectives of this study was to identify potential use cases for digital transformation within the SA retail industry.

Google Suite (G Suite) (+). G Suite is a set of Google applications that brings together essential services to help businesses. This is a hosted service that lets businesses, schools, and institutions use a variety of Google products including Email, Google Docs, and Google Calendar. The adoption of Google Suite to replace Microsoft Office was highlighted by multiple participants as an important step towards digital transformation. P-2 highlighted the benefit of multiple employees working on the same Google Doc from different locations while having a conference call by stating, *"I mean it would it's nice to be able to sit and work on a document simultaneously with someone in Durban and Johannesburg while having a conference call"*.

Cloud (+). The majority of participants stated that the use of cloud technologies plays a significant role towards the adoption of digital transformation. *"The cloud technology is one of the key technologies to enabled transformation. We are implementing Google cloud platform as our data lake option and we will leverage technologies such as AI in that platform"* [P-7]. The importance of providing the retailers and customers with close to real-time information on products and services was highlighted: *"...close to real-time share information so that our feedback cycle from what we observe in our sales activity in the store can feedback all the way to our planning, manufacture, logistics and merchandising to close that loop so that that becomes more efficient"* [P-6].

Artificial Intelligence (AI) (+). AI refers to the ability of a digital computer, computer-controlled robot or systems to perform tasks commonly associated with intelligent beings, like the ability to reason, discover meaning, generalize, or learn from past experience. The organisation will be leveraging their data in the cloud together with AI technologies to generate new valuable insights. P-7 states *"Put all of the data together in the cloud and then use the AI technologies to generate new insights for us. I think that there is a huge competitive advantage in machine learning and AI calls that technology will be able to derive insights way faster than a human will possibly be able to on volumes of data"*.

Machine Learning (MI) (+). P-8 explained that the organisation already makes use of machine learning technologies to track if employee's email has been infected by a virus. P-7's personal view is that the organisation's data in the cloud together with machine learning will be of great benefit to the enterprise in the future.

4.2 Organisation

A total of nine factors were identified under the organisation theme during the semi-structured interviews. This made it the most populated super-theme (Table 3).

Table 3. Organisational sub-themes

Participant:	1	2	3	4	5	6	7	8	9	10	11	12	Count
Resistance to Change	x	x	x	x	x	x	x	x	x	x	x	x	12
Financial Resources				x			x	x	x	x	x	x	7
Big data & Analytics		x			x	x	x	x	x	x			7
Technology Readiness	x				x	x	x		x		x		6
Collaboration		x						x	x	x		x	5
Digital Strategy						x			x		x	x	4
Company Culture	x					x	x					x	4
Compatibility		x					x			x			3
Trialability						x		x				x	3

The high number of factors identified by the participants suggested that organisational factors were dominant in their opinion when considering the adoption of digital transformation within the retail industry. The researchers will discuss these factors in the next subsections.

Resistance to Change (+/−). The most cited factor under the organisation theme was resistance to change. Most participants highlighted that some employees have been working at the organisation for many years and are used to doing things a certain way: "...we always has employees that are resistant to change so we might be leaving people behind if we don't put in a lot of effort to bring them on board and to take them with us on the journey. One of the factors is that people often say it's always been done in the same way that it's historically resistant to change" [P-8]. P-6 highlighted the fact that before you can address resistance to change, you must clearly define the scope of the project: "... you need a clear definition of what your digital transformation is". Communication challenges can be addressed by a clear and well-defined scope which is clearly communicated to all employees. P-5 highlighted that as part of addressing the resistance to change within the organisation, you may have to address issues with current processes. P-2 mentioned that change management is a very important factor: "...change management is such a big thing. If you don't handle it correctly, they won't adopt it, well not easily at least".

Digital Technology Readiness (+). Some participants stated that the organisation needs to be prepared to adopt digital technologies. Preparing the organisation for digital technologies so that they are ready and willing to adopt new technologies will have a positive impact. P-7 stated that the organisation currently "...*rely heavily on the Gartner hype cycle, specifically the one for emerging technologies and retail technologies*" to ensure the organisation is kept up to date with technology. Technologies that could present business value are proposed to the retailers to assess the retailers' appetite to adopt the technology. P-1 stated that each new technology is evaluated by a technical forum. The technology is assessed in a "sandbox" environment before testing it as a proof of concept (POC). Technologies are only approved for implementation after a rigorous evaluation process. P-5, who is part of the technical forum, states that each technology is assessed based on the organisation's requirement matrix and "...*based on the requirements and our future requirements that we can think of we would select the technology that best fits our area and our vision*".

Financial Resources (−). Factors relating to financial resources in an organisation such as the cost of adopting new technologies or cost of changing existing technologies have a negative impact on whether an organisation will decide to proceed with implementing technology changes. Return on investment (ROI) plays a major part from the beginning when organisations decide on which technology projects will be implemented: "... *if the return on investment is good enough then that's how I would motivate the use of new technology.*" [P-9]. ROI is very important in retail: "*as low cost the retailer we are always striving to find more competitive ways to do things to be more cost-efficient*" [P-9]. P-7 highlights the fact in some industries it is more difficult to secure funding for projects than in others by stating "...*the retailers are very reluctant. In the banking and insurance sector, money for major key investments is not such a big issue. In retail, you know the retailers are very reluctant to fork out the chequebook to buy these big investment items that are going to transform the companies*".

Big Data & Analytics (+). Data is being generated by a magnitude of sources within the organisation. The organisation harvests as much of the generated data as possible and stores it in the cloud to use digital technology to generate new valuable insights for the business. P-7 stated that the organisation "...*put[s] all of the data together in the cloud and then use[s] the AI technologies to generate new insights for us*". The organisation benefited from the big data and analytics strategy in a number of ways. The organisation was "*able to derive insights way faster than a human will possibly be able to on volumes of data*" [P-7]. The sharing of information became easier: "...*which then makes sharing information processes accessible to staff internally, external parties*" [P-6]. Another benefit highlighted was that the adoption of cloud, analytics and the leveraging of big data gave the organisation the ability to better understand and know their customer. Marketing certain products to certain customers improved significantly as more information about the customer where collected, stored and analysed: "...*if you can understand your customer you can better fulfil their needs and the only way to do that is with big data and data analysis*" [P-2].

Trialability (+). "*Trialability is the degree to which an innovation may be experimented with on a limited basis...*" [29]. A trial or test of the capabilities of digital technologies, in the form of a proof of concept (POC), is a way for an organisation to stifle any doubt or negative perceptions they may have about certain digital technologies and is a positive enabler of adoption. P-6 highlighted the fact that organisations don't always have to be the first to adopt new technologies, especially without proving that the adoption of new technologies will add value: *"...you don't need to be the guinea pig and embark on new technology trends without proving that for yourself first. You don't want to go big bang on new stuff, you always want to take baby steps, always have POC's, test it out, monitor if you are achieving your goals and benefits you have set yourself and over time commit to more of that as you see that actually working within the organisation"*.

Compatibility (+). *"Compatibility is the degree of how consistent an innovation is perceived to be within an organisation and is affected by internal structures, strategy, values, experience and the needs of the business"* [30]. P-7 confirmed that the retail organisation must investigate and demonstrate to the business that new digital technologies will add business value by stating that the organisation must *"...determine what business value that is technologies will actually have for our retailers and also the appetite of the retailer to actually adopt that technology"*.

Company Culture (+/−). Company culture can have a positive or negative effect on the adoption of digital transformation within the retail industry: *"...if the culture is not ready or your culture is not very open to change, then that could be a barrier for you in terms of digital transformation"* [P-7]. Experienced employees might see change as a risk to their careers. It is of utmost importance that the expectation of all employees are managed well, before, during and after embarking on a digital transformation journey as highlighted by P-6 *"as people get a bit older, for them, it becomes a risk towards their career where the younger people are more eager to change. I think you need to balance that as well"*.

Digital Strategy (+/−). The lack of a clear and coherent digital transformation strategy driven top-down by top management can be a negative factor adoption factor: *"...you need a clear definition of what your digital transformation is. You do need to scope what you mean by that clearly. There is a risk that people might misunderstand what the context is and in terms of that there could be communication challenges"* [P-6]. The need for a clear and coherent digital transformation strategy was emphasized by P-5: *"...if traditional brick-and-mortar retailers want to survive they will need to transform and grow their e-commerce divisions."* Their vision for digital transformation is clearly communicated to the entire organisation and is driven top-down by executives: *"I think the way the project is approached and communicated and the benefits explained to people will have a big impact on how positive the transformation will be accepted and how successful it will be"* [P-9].

Collaboration (+). Multiple participants highlighted that collaboration between employees within the organisation will have a positive impact on the adoption of digital transformation. P-8 stated that collaboration must be done between employees and clients to determine the scope for a project by saying *"...collaborates with the clients at the highest level. Collaborate with what it is that they're trying to achieve"*. The need to have communication tools available in an organisation with a distributed workforce was highlighted by P-2: *"...we are a large group of people with the distributed management team across SA, there's definitely a need for communication tools that bring us together"*.

4.3 Environment

Only four factors were identified under the environment theme (Table 4). The retail customer was by far the most cited factor emphasizing its importance and customer-orientation.

Table 4. Environmental sub-themes

Participant:	1	2	3	4	5	6	7	8	9	10	11	12	Count
Customer	x	x	x	x	x	x	x	x	x	x	x	X	**12**
Competition/Competitive Advantage						x	x		x		x	x	**5**
Time to Market		x					x		x		x	x	**5**
Connectivity			x		x								**2**

Customer (+). The retailer customer was highlighted by most as one of the biggest driving factors of digital transformation within the SA retail industry, thus having a positive influence on adoption. The SA retail customer's behaviour when shopping and doing research before and during shopping is changing: *"More and more customers are expecting digital transformation with buying online as well as doing online research and just the convenience of shopping anytime anywhere"* [P-9]. Customers want to use their smart devices while shopping and expect information on products as and when needed: *"...the customer has changed. The customer wants things and information at their fingertips; the customer wants to use new devices and in order to use their device of choice"* [P-7].

Retail organisations must adapt and adopt digital technologies to ensure they cater for the needs of the changing customer by enriching the customer experience: [referring to the adoption of digital technologies to enrich the customer's shopping experience] *"...it needs to add customer value, it needs to improve the experience, it needs to reduce cost & risk, it needs to improve quality"* [P-6].

Competition/Competitive Advantage (+). Organisations have to change, adapt, transform and adopt digital technologies to stay competitive in the SA retail environment: *"you will have to adapt and transform to stay competitive"* [P-9]. A close eye is kept on what the competition is doing in the market, especially regarding digital technologies, to ensure sales and market share does not decline: *"...if our competitor is gaining market share or we are losing sales or whatever because of a competitor employing digital technologies it's definitely something that we will look at"* [P-7]. Furthermore, the organisation is more reactive to externally visible digital technology innovations that could affect the customer's shopping behaviour: *"When the customer's perception of innovation is positively affected by something that's clearly externally visible I do think that forces the organisation to adopt. You need to be more reactive in terms of an external visible technology influence than an internal one"* [P-6].

Time to Market (+). Time to market is a very important factor in the very competitive SA retail market. The perception arose during the semi-structured interview that digital technologies would improve time to market of products, thus having a positive impact on the adoption of digital transformation. Digital transformation coupled with improved business processes and activities will most definitely result in an reduced time to market and cost, increased market share and profit as mentioned by P-2 *"...improve our processes and activities if we get this recipe right we will most definitely improve our time to market reduce our costs and increase our market share and hopefully this all leads to increase profits"*.

Connectivity (−). The retail group has a wide footprint of brick and mortar stores throughout Africa requiring an internet connection to trade and be operational. The lack of connectivity throughout Africa was raised as a factor that would negatively impact the adoption of digital transformation when P-3 stated *"...I think connectivity is a massive issue given our big footprint and widespread brick-and-mortar stores connectivity is not consistently available everywhere"*.

4.4   Which Technologies Are Driving Digital Transformation in Retail?

The combined analysis from the Literature Review and semi-structured interviews revealed nine core technologies as driving the digital transformation within the SA retail industry. Table 5 lists these, ordered by the combined number of participant responses per use case.

Table 5. Technologies driving digital transformation

e-Commerce solutions	12
Big Data & Analytics	9
Cloud	9
Artificial Intelligence	5
Bots	4
Machine Learning	3
Facial Recognition	3
Self-Checkout	2
RFID	2

The most cited technology across the board was to provide the retail group with an e-Commerce solution. Big data, analytics, and cloud computing were also identified by three-quarters of the respondents, as being crucial to digital transformation. Not surprisingly, artificial intelligence, and the associated technologies such as bots, machine learning and facial recognition, also featured but were, perhaps surprisingly, mentioned by only about one-quarter of the respondents. This reflects either a perceived lack of maturity of the technologies themselves, or perhaps a lack of capability/readiness of the organisation to adopt these technologies. Attitudes around self-checkout appear to be still in their infancy in South Africa. Although RFID is already used in the organisation's supply chain and RFID chips are embedded in high-value items for security purposes, this technology was surprisingly not seen as driving digital transformation since it was only mentioned by 2 respondents. Perhaps the reason for this is that the technology is already in use and therefore not considered to be a prospective transformative technology.

5   Discussion

The findings can be used to answer and discuss the research questions.

5.1   Drivers and Inhibitors for Digital Transformation

The principal goal of the study was to identified adoption factors, during the Literature Review and research strategy, and to provide the knowledge and information needed to the SA retail industry to ensure informed decision are made regarding potential future use. Several positive (driving) and negative (inhibiting) factors were identified across the Technology, Organisational and Environmental organising super-themes.

Perceived challenges were highlighted as the biggest negative factor of the **Technological** theme, while relative advantage was highlighted as the biggest positive factor in the adoption of digital transformation. Data security when implementing cloud technologies was highlighted as a major concern/negative adoption factor while the adoption of cloud technologies and reduced onsite hardware was seen as a major benefit and stepping-stone to becoming digitally transformed. The most adoption factors identified fell under the **Organisational** organising theme. It became clear that resistance to change would be the biggest organisational barrier to overcome when undertaking digital transformation initiatives. Furthermore, it was highlighted that the cost of implementing digital technologies will play a big role, and ultimately return on investment will be a deciding factor. Three new negative factors were identified during the semi-structured interviews around resistance to change, data security of cloud technologies and financial resources to fund digital initiatives. One of the most important findings that emerged from the **Environment** major theme was that the retail customer basically drives digital transformation. The changing customer, their needs and the change in how they shop was highlighted by all participants. Thus customer-orientation rather than competitor analysis should drive the adoption of digital transformation in the SA retail sector.

5.2 Technologies Driving Digital Transformation

Participants identified nine technologies as driving digital transformation within the retail industry. Apart from e-Commerce platforms, cloud technologies and data analytics (including big data) were the most frequently cited and were the ones which the participants indented implementing. AI and associated technologies were only seen by a quarter of the respondents as digital transformation use cases, testifying to either a perceived technology immaturity, a lack of demonstrated benefits or a laggard adoption attitude. Specific benefits of these technologies include satisfying changing customer needs, decreasing time to market, and increasing customer value, which could be achieved by implementing digital transformation initiatives. Due to the agreement about the specific technologies and benefits identified, this proposition is strongly supported.

5.3 Validity and Reliability of Findings

As mentioned in the research design section, the researchers selected the case study approach as the most appropriate strategy to conduct this qualitative study. The researchers used a single case study to allow in-depth investigation and understanding of the factors influencing the intended adoption of digital transformation within the organisation. Overall there was a consistency between the factors influencing the indented adoption of digital transformation identified during the Literature Review and the findings from the research strategy. Contradictions arose around the main factor that influences the intended adoption of digital transformation. The Literature Review highlighted that the main factor is a clear and coherent digital strategy which is actively driven top-down by executive management while the research strategy revealed that the main factor is resistance to change. This could be due to the fact that the case site is currently busy with digital transformation projects which are actively driven by top management, thus not an important factor in this specific organisation.

6 Conclusion, Limitations and Future Research

The research identified 22 drivers that affected the adoption of digital transformation within the SA retail sector. These were grouped using the TOE framework. **Technological** factors identified include the imperative to address technical challenges including securing a sound infrastructure (e.g. move into the cloud and secure a high-speed, low-latency connection ideally through a locally based cloud vendor); security risks include protection of IP as well as customer privacy; and hire the correct technical skills. The relative advantages obtained include not only competitive advantage but also reduced costs, reduced time to market and improved customer satisfaction. The most prominent **organisational** issue identified was resistance to change, emphasizing the need for change management and a corporate culture embracing transformation and collaboration. Enterprises that add specialized digital change agents to their workforce to assist current employees through the digital transformation process will increase their success rate. Assessing the organisation's readiness, possibly through proof of concept sandbox testing is also important – these include aspects of the technology's trialability and organisational compatibility. Digitally mature enterprises must attract and recruit to ensure they don't have skills gaps. Ensuring that big data and effective data analytics are in place is also rated as a crucial step in digital transformation. A clear digital strategy which includes scope and objectives and is driven from the top down rounds off the organisational factors. The crucial **environmental** factor was, not unsurprising, a focussed customer-orientation for any technologies that are introduced i.e. does it help or add value for the customer as opposed to a knee-jerk competitor-driven response. Ultimately, enterprises must analyse the customer's behaviour through their entire shopping experience by making use of big data and analytics.

Among the core technologies mentioned by participants as driving digital transformation in the retail industry, e-Commerce solutions, big data, analytics, and cloud adoption were mentioned the most.

The extent to which these findings can be generalized to other countries depends on the structural and environmental similarity of the retail industry with the South African one which operates in a first world/third world context: infrastructure and scarce skills considerations may be more specific, but overall skills, readiness, corporate culture, change management, relative advantage and others are likely to be generalizable to many other country contexts.

Some limitations must be considered when interpreting the results of this study. The study provided a narrow focus on one large retail group, while the retail industry is made up of organisations of varying sizes. The seniority and the position that some of the interviewees fulfil in the case site enterprise limited the time they had available for interviews. Also, the interviewee base was quite small but thematic saturation was reached after the ninth interview.

Future studies around the adoption of digital transformation in the retail sector could be conducted to identify new factors that might impact adoption. The research has identified the need for a study to be conducted across the SA retail industry in order to access a national view on digital transformation in different size retail organisations. That way a more in-depth view of drivers and inhibitors influencing the digital transformation and more potential use cases could be identified.

References

1. Henriette, E., Feki, M., Boughzala, I.: The shape of digital transformation: a systematic literature review. In: MCIS 2015 Proceedings, pp. 431–443 (2015)
2. Gassmann, O., Frankenberger, K., Csik, M.: The Business Model Navigator: 55 Models that will Revolutionise your Business. Pearson, Cambridge (2014). https://doi.org/10.3139/9783446437654.003
3. Sia, S.K., Soh, C., Weill, P.: How DBS bank pursued a digital business strategy. MIS Q. **15**(2), 105–121 (2016)
4. Hudson, L., Ozanne, J.: Alternative ways of seeking knowledge in consumer research. J. Consum. Res. **14**(4), 508–521 (1988). https://doi.org/10.1086/209132
5. Westerman, G., Tannou, M., Bonnet, D., Ferraris, P., McAfee, A.: Leading Digital: Turning Technology into Business transformation. Harvard Business Press, Massachusetts (2014)
6. Dery, K., Sebastian, I.M., van der Meulen, N.: The digital workplace is key to digital innovation. MIS Q. **16**(2), 135–152 (2017)

7. Sebastian, I.M., Ross, J.W., Beath, C., Mocker, M., Moloney, K.G., Fonstad, N.O.: How big old companies navigate digital transformation. MIS Q. Exec. **16**(3), 197–213 (2017)
8. Rodgers, E.M.: Diffusion of Innovations, 4th edn. Free Press, New York (1995)
9. Kane, G.C., Palmer, D., Phillips, A.N., Kiron, D., Buckley, N.: Winning the digital war for talent. MIT Sloan Manage. Rev. **58**(2), 17–19 (2017)
10. Hansen, R., Sia, S.K.: Hummel's digital transformation toward omni-channel retailing: key lessons learned. MIS Q. **14**(2), 132–149 (2015)
11. Rogers, D.L.: The Digital Transformation Playbook: Rethink Your Business for the Digital Age. Columbia University Press, Columbia (2016). https://doi.org/10.7312/roge17544
12. Ismail, M.H., Khater, M., Zaki, M.: Digital Business Transformation and Strategy: What Do We Know So Far? University of Cambridge, Cambridge Service Alliance, November 2017
13. Soule, D. L., Carrier, N., Bonnet, D., Westerman, G. F.: Organizing for a Digital Future: Opportunities and Challenges. MIT Center for Digital Business and Capgemini Consulting (2014). Working Paper. https://doi.org/10.2139/ssrn.2698379
14. Gimpel, H., Hosseini, S., Huber, R., Probst, L., Röglinger, M., Faisst, U.: Structuring digital transformation: a framework of action fields and its application at ZEISS. J. Inf. Technol. Theory Appl. **19**(1), 32–54 (2018)
15. Hess, T., Matt, C., Benlian, A., Wiesböck, F.: Options for formulating a digital transformation strategy. MIS Q. **15**(2), 123–139 (2016)
16. Ghasemkhani, H., Soule, D.L., Westerman, G.F.: Competitive Advantage in a Digital World: Toward an Information-Based View of the Firm. MIT Center of Digital Business, Working Paper (2014). https://doi.org/10.2139/ssrn.2698775
17. Lane, M., Shrestha, A., Ali, O.: Managing the Risks of Data Security and Privacy in the Cloud: a Shared Responsibility Between the Cloud Service Provider and the Client Organisation. The Bright Internet Global Summit, Seoul (2017)
18. Carroll, M., Van Der Merwe, A., Kotze, P.: Secure cloud computing: Benefits, risks and controls. Information Security South Africa, pp. 1–9. IEEE (2011). https://doi.org/10.1109/ISSA.2011.6027519
19. Patel, K.K., Patel, S.M., Professor, P.S.A.: Internet of Things-IOT: definition, characteristics, architecture, enabling technologies, application & future challenges. Int. J. Eng. Sci. Comput. **6**(5), 6122–6123 (2016)
20. Vermesan, O., Bacquet, J.: Cognitive Hyperconnected Digital Transformation: Internet of Things Intelligence Evolution. River Publishers, Denmark (2017). https://doi.org/10.13052/rp-9788793609105
21. Singh, A., Hess, T.: How chief digital officers promote the digital transformation of their companies. MIS Q. Exec. **16**(1), 1–17 (2017)
22. Westerman, G., Bonnet, D., McAfee, A.: Leading Digital: Turning Technology into Business Transformation. Harvard Business Press, Massachusetts (2014)
23. Sawy, O.A., Kræmmergaard, P., Amsinck, H., Vinther, A.L.: How LEGO built the foundations and enterprise capabilities for digital leadership. MIS Q. Exec. **15**(2), 141–166 (2015)
24. Zimmermann, A., Schmidt, R., Sandkuhl, K., Wißotzki, M., Jugel, D., Möhring, M.: Digital enterprise architecture-transformation for the internet of things. In: IEEE 19th Enterprise Distributed Object Computing Workshop (EDOCW), pp. 130–138. IEEE (2105)
25. Verhoef, P.C., Kannan, P.K., Inman, J.J.: From multi-channel retailing to Omni- channel retailing: introduction to the special issue on multi-channel retailing. J. Retail. **91**(2), 174–181 (2015). https://doi.org/10.1016/j.jretai.2015.02.005
26. DePietro, R., Wiarda, E., Fleischer, M.: Processes of Technological Innovation. Lexington Books, Massachusetts (1990)
27. Baker, J.: The technology–organization–environment framework. In: Dwivedi, Y., Wade, M., Schneberger, S. (eds.) Schneberger. Integrated Series in Information Systems, vol. 28, pp. 231–245. Springer, New York (2012). https://doi.org/10.1007/978-1-4419-6108-2_12

28. Benbasat, I., Goldstein, D.K., Mead, M.: The case research strategy in studies of information systems. MIS Q. **11**, 369–386 (1987). https://doi.org/10.2307/248684
29. Rodriguez, M., Peterson, R.M., Ajjan, H.: CRM/social media technology: impact on customer orientation process and organizational sales performance. In: Kubacki, K. (ed.) Ideas in Marketing: Finding the New and Polishing the Old. Developments in Marketing Science: Proceedings of the Academy of Marketing, pp. 636–638. Springer, Cham (2015). https://doi.org/10.1007/978-3-319-10951-0_233
30. Lin, A., Chen, N.C.: Cloud computing as an innovation: perception, attitude, and adoption. Int. J. Inf. Manage. **32**(6), 533–540 (2012). https://doi.org/10.1016/j.ijinfomgt.2012.04.001

Using Heuristics for Assessing the Usability of the Public Information Bulletins in Poland

Łukasz Krawiec(✉) and Helena Dudycz

Wroclaw University of Economics and Business, Wrocław, Poland
{lukasz.krawiec,helena.dudycz}@ue.wroc.pl

Abstract. Increasing attention is being paid to the usability of public administration websites. Websites of this kind should offer appropriate functionality as well as being accessible to their users. This, among other things, is due to the many regulations introduced by countries' governments. The aim of this paper is to present the most common usability errors identified on the websites of public administration units and the preliminary results of the assessment of the usability of Polish twenty largest cities' Public Information Bulletin websites with the use of the heuristic evaluation. The study was conducted according to the heuristics method proposed by J. Nielsen. The main groups of errors affecting the usability of such websites were identified. Each of the error groups was assessed by an expert in terms of its importance for the overall assessment of the website's usefulness. On this basis, the categories were assigned ranks from 1 to 5. This enabled indicating errors on the websites under study, as well as performing a comparison of the websites of the Public Information Bulletin of selected cities. The contribution of the article consists in the proposal of fourteen categories of heuristics for testing the usability and accessibility of public administration websites. The article presents a survey of public administration websites (on the example of the Public Information Bulletin in Poland) using the proposed heuristics.

Keywords: Web usability · Web accessibility · Web usability study · Heuristic evaluation · Human-Computer interaction · Public administration unit

1 Introduction

The high quality of a website depends to a large extent on features such as usability [1]. Without it, even very valuable content might never reach the audience, which – for many reasons including commercial viability – is usually a significant factor from the website developer's viewpoint. From the perspective of the public interest, especially in the age of the information society, all websites should offer features such as usability and accessibility [2]. Regardless of the motives of designers or clients – the purpose of websites mainly comes down to the effective presentation of their content and efficient conveyance of information (usefulness) to the largest possible audience (accessibility) [3]. This means that it is important to ensure that both healthy and disabled people are able to effectively familiarize themselves with the information provided on the website and take advantage of its functionalities. Accessibility problems are most common among

© Springer Nature Switzerland AG 2020
E. Ziemba (Ed.): AITM 2019/ISM 2019, LNBIP 380, pp. 63–75, 2020.
https://doi.org/10.1007/978-3-030-43353-6_4

users with reduced mobility, hearing or vision, including those with cognitive disorders. Accessibility is now seen more broadly, i.e. the aim is to make the website accessible to as many people as possible, including the elderly, people with disabilities, people with low bandwidth internet access, and people using older devices, which are usually slower than modern ones [4].

As far as creating useful and accessible websites of public administration units is concerned, it is necessary to conduct continuous research and usability tests, perceiving it as one of the basic activities in the process of developing such websites. The aim of such activities is to prevent dissatisfaction among users (i.e. citizens) and to provide a place where they can find the information they need quickly and efficiently. This is particularly important in the case of public administration units' websites, which is why many countries are implementing recommendations and legal requirements to ensure the quality of public websites containing information and content of particular interest to the general public.

In Poland, the 61st article of the Constitution of the Republic of Poland of 1997 indicates that citizens have the right to obtain information including access to documents [5]. Due to the universality of documents in electronic form and the enormous role of the Internet, the Act on access to public information was drawn up [6] in 2001 based on the indicated fragment of the Constitution. The term Public Information Bulletin (PIB; Polish name: Biuletyn Informacji Publicznej) appears many times in its content, starting from article 7. PIB constitutes a unified system of Internet services ensuring free-of-charge and universal access to public information in Poland.

The aim of this paper is to present the use of the identified fourteen heuristics for the research into the usability of the websites of public administration, providing the example of the Public Information Bulletin websites of the largest cities in Poland. The structure of the paper is outlined below. First, the importance of the usability of websites is presented. The next section describes the research conducted and the results obtained. Finally, a summary of the paper is provided.

2   Theoretical Background

2.1   Web Usability Study

A website (a World Wide Web site) is an element of the Internet, usually dedicated to a single domain and consisting of a homepage (start page) and a number of related documents. It is a document in a multimedia format using hyperlinks, i.e. links to other Internet resources, such as related websites, graphic documents, text documents, and audio files. In other words, a web page is a result of a web browser's reading an HTML document. It may contain structured elements such as text, images, animations, sounds, films, and links to other pages or places in the same document [7].

Given the technical and visual diversity of websites developed in recent years, developing a comprehensive listing of all principles of good design practices becomes an extremely difficult task. However, it is possible to sort these rules and indicate websites' most important features. These are web visibility, web benefit, web usability, and web accessibility [8]. As noted above, the last two parameters are of particular importance and strongly interrelated. Each of them is fundamental in terms of experience quality and the effectiveness of information transfer. It should be noted, however, that usability is a broader concept, a subset of which is accessibility, including issues such as interface handling problems experienced by people with disabilities [9]. The studies [10] described in the literature indicate that the quality of websites and the various services they provide can be determined in many ways, with usability being one of its main measures. According to these studies, usability, which most often refers to IT products, is the most important criterion as far as websites are concerned.

In the literature, usability is defined in a variety of ways. According to ISO 9241-210:2019 [11], usability is defined as "the extent to which a system, product or service can be used by specified users to achieve specified goals with effectiveness, efficiency and satisfaction in a specified context of use", while the standard ISO/IEC 25010:2011 [12], related to software engineering and product quality, describes usability as the ability of the software product to be understood, its operation learned, to be operated, and to be attractive to the user. In the literature, usability is defined as the device's "capacity to be used" [13] and depends on what the user wants to do [14].

According to J. Nielsen, usability "is a quality attribute that assesses how easy user interfaces are to use" [1], comprising 5 components:

- Learnability: How easy is it for users to accomplish basic tasks the first time they encounter the design?
- Efficiency: Once users have learned the design, how quickly can they perform tasks?
- Memorability: When users return to the design after a period of not using it, how easily can they re-establish proficiency?
- Errors: How many errors do users make, how severe are these errors, and how easily can they recover from the errors?
- Satisfaction: How pleasant is it to use the design? [1].

The above-specified components indicate that a website is useful if the user is able to use it effectively and efficiently, achieving certain goals [1].

In the literature, numerous methods of testing the usability of websites are de-scribed, among which the following can be distinguished: the heuristic method, individual in-depth interviews, group interviews, check-lists, the scoring method, the Keystroke-Level Model method, cognitive migration, survey questionnaires, observations, usability tests, eye-tracking, click-tracking, and A/B tests [13, 15–17].

2.2 The Heuristic Evaluation Applied for Studying Websites

The heuristic evaluation is an expert method considered one of the inspection methods of identifying usability problems. It consists in indicating the extent to which a given piece of software or a website complies with the developed rules and standards (called usability heuristics [13]) for the design of human-computer interactions. In other words, experts indicate what is correct or incorrect [18]. The heuristic analysis of a website is a universal and easily applicable method.

The method is used in tests of entire websites or their selected areas, both in general and contextual usability studies. The heuristic assessment, apart from determining the current state of website or service quality, should also indicate how to improve the product and what should be the direction of its development. It is a relatively inexpensive method as there is no need to involve users and the number of experts indicated is limited. It is considered that the optimal number of experts is between three and eight [19].

In this method, experts indicate what is correct and what is incorrect about the website being evaluated in terms of the heuristics applied [18]. An independent analysis performed by each expert supports the study's objectivity and effectiveness. Thanks to this method, it is possible to detect many small as well as major errors related to the website's performance. Also, it allows one to identify the elements of the website that may adversely affect its usability.

Heuristics were created as a result of research into the recognition and division of factors influencing the perception of usability of IT systems by their users. Heuristics are also guidelines for usability [13]. The following heuristics developed by J. Nielsen, also referred to as traditional, are most commonly used [1]:

(1)   Visibility of system status.
(2)   Correspondence between the system and the real world.
(3)   User control and freedom.
(4)   Consistency and standards.
(5)   Prevention of errors.
(6)   Recognition rather than recall.
(7)   Flexibility and efficiency of use.
(8)   Aesthetic and minimalist design.
(9)   Help users recognize, diagnose, and recover errors.
(10) Help and documentation.

In addition to the heuristics described above, the literature provides many other approaches to evaluating usefulness with this method, including the following:

• Cognitive Engineering Principles for Enhancing Human-Computer Performance [20],
• Weinschenk and Barker classification [21],
• The Eight Golden Rules of Interface Design [22],
• Usability Heuristics for Touchscreen-based Mobile Devices [23],
• First Principles of Interaction Design [24],
• 7 Usability Heuristics That All UI Designers Should Know [25].

Many of the above rules and guidelines are based on J. Nielsen's classic heuristics. The aim of many heuristics creators is to update and match them to the study of specific IT systems [26, 27]. New heuristics proposals also result from a change in the way of looking at the interface usability issue. For example, the aforementioned Gerhardt-Powals [20] takes a more holistic approach to evaluation, including principles such as: automate unwanted workload, group data in consistently meaningful ways, practice judicious redundancy. A more detailed and fragmented approach is proposed by Susan Weinschenk and Dean Barker [21] on their list of twenty guidelines. These include: user control, accommodation, simplicity or predictability. Ben Shneiderman's goal was to create flexible principles that can be adapted to interfaces in different programming environments. For example: strive for consistency, seek universal usability, permit easy reversal of actions [22]. A similar point of view is represented by Bruce Tognazzini's guidelines, such as: aesthetic design, anticipation, autonomy, discoverability [24]. Most interface usability experts follow similar principles or build on existing proposals.

2.3 The Public Information Bulletin as an Example of a Public Administration Website

Detailed guidelines are required to test accessibility, which is inherent in usability. The most important and widespread standard for this feature in the world is the WCAG (Web Content Accessibility Guidelines). Many countries are implementing additional recommendations and legal requirements to ensure the quality of public websites containing information and content of particular interest to the general public. Among the examples thereof are the US Section 508 of the Workforce Rehabilitation Act [28], the German Barrierefreie-Informationstechnik-Verordnung [29], or the Italian Stanca Act [30], adjusting the law to the W3C WCAG 2.0 accessibility requirements.

In Poland, the Public Information Bulletin (PIB) is an example of a website of public administration units. Apart from the main website of the PIB (https://bip.gov.pl), the bulletin consists of services provided by entities obliged to maintain them, such as public authorities, economic and professional self-government bodies, entities representing state organizational units, political parties, and many others. Their task is to inform the public about their activity, i.e. to make public information available. They should meet the minimum requirements for ICT systems specified in the Regulation of the Council of Ministers of April 12, 2012, on the National Interoperability Framework [31], minimum requirements for public registers and information exchange in electronic form, as well as minimum requirements for ICT systems. The main PIB website also provides many other descriptions of these websites' required level of quality. Additionally, detailed requirements and recommendations for PIB administrators can be found on the website of the Ministry of Digitisation [32]. The straight majority of the above quality requirements come down to the concept of usability. PIB websites should, therefore, be exemplary in terms of this requirement in the context of heuristics adopted both as guidelines for the development of websites, as well as those used for research and evaluation of their usefulness applying the heuristic method.

PIB websites are always marked with the appropriate logotype. Although a PIB website is linked to the authorities of a given city, it is a separate website and one differing from the website of the city's administration unit. Given that, administrators of the respective types of websites (i.e. PIB and city administration, such as https://www.wroclaw.pl and http://bip.um.wroc.pl), often cooperate by providing hyperlinks to each other's websites or by distributing content according to its function. In some cases, both websites are placed next to each other, i.e. on the same server, but still being two different and separate projects.

3 Research Methodology and Findings

3.1 Research Questions and Procedure

To effectively apply the heuristic method, it is necessary to adapt it to PIB services. Bearing this in mind, the following research question was asked:

Q1. What basic errors are found on the pages of the Public Information Bulletin in Poland when the heuristic evaluation is applied for the research purposes?
Q2. Which of these errors occur most frequently on the pages of the Public Information Bulletin?

The study consisted of two stages and was carried out according to the following procedure:
Stage no.1:

- Selecting sixty websites of the PIB for research purposes.
- Researching the websites of the PIB using J. Nielsen's heuristics.
- Identification of basic errors related to the usability of the PIB websites examined.
- Categorization of usability errors.
- Assignment of rank to each category established.
- Evaluation of the importance and ranking of the different categories of errors.

Stage no. 2:

- Selection of the twenty most populous Polish cities to be examined.
- Evaluation of the PIB websites of selected cities according to identified groups of errors.
- Analysis of the results obtained.

The results of the study are presented in the paragraphs below.

3.2 Identification of Basic Errors Related to the Usability of the Public Information Bulletin Websites Examined

The research began with an analysis of sixty websites of the Public Information Bulletin of large Polish cities. The research was conducted by specially trained 120 students aged 23-40, during classes on the subject of "the usability of the human-computer inter-face". The students worked in tandems two-person groups, each of which researched one website. The test results were then verified by an expert. The website evaluation procedure was based on Nielsen's heuristics. After determining the general state of the usefulness of websites of this type, the research was narrowed down to twenty largest cities in terms of population (the most up-to-date data from the Central Statistical Office, i.e. from 31.12.2015 were used) [33]. This time, the analysis was more in-depth due to the fact that it included accessibility aspects. A number of errors and violations were thus identified, which had a material impact on the usability assessment. At a later stage, those had to be classified. A detailed analysis allowed us to identify the areas of the most frequently occurring errors and problems. Fourteen categories of errors were formulated:

F01. Website ergonomics: non-intuitive and unusual location of the website's key elements (e.g. main menu, search fields, accessibility functions, etc.) and too large and unstructured accumulation of elements on the main page, including many unnecessary ones.

F02. Website consistency: the selective appearance of key elements that should appear on each page within the website (e.g. main menu, footer, search field, etc.).

F03. Content and its form: errors in the text (spelling, punctuation, etc.), incorrect encoding of diacritical marks, illegible and inconsistent formatting and arrangement of the text (typefaces, colours, boldening, indentations, spaces, etc.), too few or too many graphic elements (including photographs) affecting the quality of the visitor's website experience, non-standard or user-unfriendly content presentation, and frequent replacement of content with external attachments (e.g. as PDF files).

F04. Substantive content: outdated or incomplete information, inconsistency of the information presented within pages belonging to a single category (e.g. selective contact details for individual departments of the city council – telephone and fax numbers provided for some of them and only an e-mail address provided for others), use of a specialist (legal or technical vocabulary) or convoluted (multiply compound sentences, etc.) language.

F05. Navigation, menus, and grouping of web pages: too many or too few options in the main or auxiliary menu (the problem of a proper number of nests), non-intuitive arrangement and illegible presentation of options, lack of clear information about the possibility of rolling down submenus, recurring menu panels across one page, inconsistencies of individual instances of the website's main or auxiliary menu.

F06. Navigation between web pages: lack of or errors in breadcrumb navigation, poorly visible navigation panel, inconsistently performing links, lack of return to parent location button, lack of redirection to the homepage after pressing the logotype or title.

F07. Navigation – website search engine: performance errors, lack of results, unconventional format of results (e.g. official documents only), lack or a small number of advanced search options (filtering), lack of hints when entering text.

F08. Navigation – links: incorrectly described (alternative text) and outdated hyperlinks, references to non-existent locations, lack of description of error 404, lack of information about redirecting to an external website, lack of options for opening new pages in a new tab or in a new window.

F09. Accessibility – mobile devices: lack of website responsiveness, incorrectly executed mobile version of the website, problems with scaling individual elements (e.g. search fields).

F10. Accessibility – colour set: aesthetically unpleasant shades of colours and their saturation, too big or too small variety of colours, too big or too small contrasts.

F11. Accessibility – functions: illegible text, incorrect performance or lack of buttons related to accessibility (e.g. text scaling, changing contrast, etc.).

F12. Accessibility – website map: lack of or incorrectly designed, illegible website map.

F13. Help: hardly exhaustive or even non-existent help section, errors in the help section (problems which also concern the frequently asked questions), lack of hints and messages in problematic areas of the website.

F14. Other errors and limitations: the website loading time is too long or the loading process is completely stopped – often without any messages, access to all functionalities of the website is possible only after registration.

By means of expert analysis, each category of errors was rated in terms of its importance for the overall evaluated of the service's usefulness. The highest ranks were assigned to the categories that determine the possibility of using the website's function-alities, while the lowest ones reflect problems causing only users' moderate discomfort. The scale of the ranks is as follows:

1 – a problem of least significance;
2 – a minor problem;
3 – a problem of average significance;
4 – a major error;
5 – a critical error.

Each of the identified error areas was assigned one of five ranks. The results of this study are presented in Table 1.

The most serious problems (rank 5 and 4) found across the PIB websites under examination are navigation difficulties (F05–F08) and availability limitations (F09 and F11). Violations such as F05–F08 i.e. ones related to website navigation can make it completely impossible to find the information needed by the user. During testing, in many cases, the unintuitive menu layout, containing an enormous number of mixed and unnecessary options, combined with an unoperational search engine, made it impossible to find the searched content.

The second type of serious error concerns availability. An increasing number of people are using smartphones and tablets, more and more often abandoning desktop computers. The lack of possibility to use a mobile device or limitations in this respect may effectively discourage many Internet users. Also, the lack of accessibility-related functions (e.g. change of contrast) means a serious barrier for people with medical conditions, thus striking the basic principles and sense of PIB websites. The importance of colour choices (F10) has been rated as slightly lesser (average rank, i.e. 3) as it is solved by the contrast matching option mentioned above. Moreover, in none of the cases analysed did the colour scheme pose a considerable problem when reading the content. The same rank was assigned to F03 and F04. These are important aspects of a website, but rather than preventing its use they result in the user's impatience and irritation. The last area, F14, was also given an average rating, due to the diversity and occasionality of errors. The first two categories are less important for the perception of the website and are associated with bad user experience rather than serious impairment of usability, therefore they were assigned a lower rank of 2. The least important are areas F12 and F13, which should be only a supplement to a well-developed website.

The comparison of identified error categories with J. Nielsen's heuristics is described in more detail in [34].

Table 1. Ranks of error categories [34]

No.	Error categories	Rank
F01	Website ergonomics	2
F02	Consistency across the website	2
F03	Content and the form of content presentation	3
F04	Content and the substantive matter	3
F05	Navigation, menu, and page grouping	5
F06	Navigation between web pages	5
F07	Navigation – website search engine	4
F08	Navigation – links	5
F09	Accessibility – mobile devices	4
F10	Accessibility – colour set	3
F11	Accessibility – functions	5
F12	Accessibility – website map	1
F13	Help	1
F14	Other errors and hindrances	3

3.3 Examination of the Public Information Bulletin Websites of Selected Cities

The websites of the twenty most populous Polish cities were selected for detailed study and analysis based on data from the Central Statistical Office [33]. These are: Białystok, Bydgoszcz, Częstochowa, Gdańsk, Gdynia, Gliwice, Katowice, Kielce, Kraków, Lublin, Łódź, Poznań, Radom, Rzeszów, Sosnowiec, Szczecin, Toruń, Warszawa, Wrocław and Zabrze.

Table 2 shows the usability errors identified in the twenty PIB services examined. 14 defined groups were used.

When analysing the results obtained and answering the research question Q2, it can be stated that the most serious errors that occur most often are: F05–F08 (navigation, menu, control, search engine, and links) and F11 (accessibility functions). Individual usability violations covered by these areas occurred on at least half of the websites examined. The worst results of the study were as follows: the exceptionally illegible Szczecin bulletin, filled with hundreds of links, and the badly functioning main menu of Kielce's PIB website. In contrast, the PIB website of the city of Lublin turned out to be unrivalled. There, identification of any irregularities required a much deeper analysis than in the cases of the other cities. However, even this website is not completely free of usability errors.

During the general research on the usability and accessibility of websites of public administration units, many types of errors were identified. These problems differ in the frequency of occurrence on individual web pages, and how much impact they had on the overall perception by users.

Table 2. Identified usability errors of PIB websites in the twenty largest cities in Poland

PIB websites	No.	F01 Website ergonomics	F02 Consistency across the website	F03 Content and the form of content presentation	F04 Content and the substantive matter	F05 Navigation, menu, and page grouping	F06 Navigation between web pages	F07 Navigation – website search engine	F08 Navigation – links	F09 Accessibility – mobile devices	F10 Accessibility – colour set	F11 Accessibility – functions	F12 Accessibility – website map	F13 Help	F14 Other errors and hindrances	Number of errors linked to the website
bip.warszawa.pl	S01								X	X		X				3
bip.krakow.pl	S02	X		X		X		X							X	5
bip.uml.lodz.pl	S03	X		X		X		X		X	X	X				7
bip.um.wroc.pl	S04					X	X								X	3
bip.poznan.pl	S05	X	X		X			X								4
bip.gdansk.pl	S06	X				X	X	X					X	X		6
bip.um.szczecin.pl	S07	X		X	X	X		X	X	X	X	X		X		10
bip.um.bydgoszcz.pl	S08	X			X		X	X	X				X		X	7
bip.lublin.eu	S09						X						X			2
bip.katowice.eu	S10		X				X	X								3
bip.bialystok.pl	S11					X		X				X				3
gdynia.pl/bip	S12			X	X	X		X	X				X			6
bip.czestochowa.pl	S13			X	X	X		X				X		X	X	7
bip.radom.pl	S14	X		X	X	X		X	X				X			7
bip.um.sosnowiec.pl	S15			X	X	X	X			X						5
bip.torun.pl	S16	X		X		X		X		X		X	X		X	8
bip.kielce.eu	S17	X	X	X		X	X	X	X	X		X				9
bip.erzeszow.pl	S18					X	X	X	X	X		X	X	X		8
bip.gliwice.eu	S19	X		X	X	X	X					X		X		7
bip.um.zabrze.pl	S20			X	X	X	X	X		X			X			7
Number of websites with an error		10	2	9	9	14	11	14	10	8	2	10	6	8	4	

The interfaces analysed differ significantly in quality, but even those positively rated contain significant usability or accessibility errors. It should be remembered that we are dealing with websites that have legal requirements. These web pages should feature excellent workmanship and be fully user-friendly. There is no doubt, however, that they do not meet these criteria.

4 Conclusion and Future Works

The paper presents a proposal of 14 heuristics for testing the usability of public administration websites, which were used to evaluate the PIB websites of the twenty largest cities in Poland.

The heuristic method, applied for the purpose of the study, is one of the basic methods of testing the usability of the human-computer interface. This method is also an effective tool for testing the usability of a website, allowing one to assess its quality as well as find out what needs to be improved in order to increase the user's positive experience. Aside from its many advantages, this method also has drawbacks and limitations. It is aimed at examining a single website while failing at comparing multiple websites, as it lacks formalisation with respect to the aggregation of the data obtained as well as the comparison of results.

The paper presents a study which contains two stages. The first stage involved the examination of sixty PIB websites. On this basis, various errors were identified that affect the usability assessment of these sites. A detailed analysis of these faults allowed us to identify the areas of the most frequent errors and problems. For each of them, possible types of usability violations were identified, based on which 14 categories of errors were formulated (answer to research question Q1). The categories established are universal in nature and can, therefore, be applied to the analysis and evaluation of any public administration website in any country.

Identification of these groups of errors was the basis for the evaluation of selected websites of the Public Information Bulletin of the twenty largest Polish cities (the stage no. 2 of the presented research). Based on this study, it can be indicated that the most serious errors that occur most often pertain to navigation, menu, control, search engine, links, and accessibility functions.

At the end of point 2.2. of this article it is indicated that there are many types of heuristic methods. They differ mostly in the reasons why they were created and approaches to identifying problems, including their level of details. As a result of our research, a new, universal heuristic method was created, adapted to the analysis of public websites, based on practical errors of use. Work on the presented heuristic method also made it possible to identify the most common and serious problems of the websites of the Public Information Bulletin.

Further research aims to incorporate the developed heuristics into a new, wider method of testing the usability and accessibility of public services. The new method of website analysis will go beyond the heuristic approach and will enable a comprehensive assessment of the quality of this type of websites. It will be a combination of different, complementary research methods. This approach will eliminate many disadvantages and imperfections of each of them. We hope that research in this area will contribute to a significant improvement in the quality of the websites discussed in this article in the future and will positively affect the experience of their users.

References

1. Nielsen, J.: Usability 101: Introduction to Usability (2012). https://www.nngroup.com/articles/usability-101-introduction-to-usability. Accessed 1 Dec 2019
2. Introduction to Web Accessibility – Web Accessibility Initiative (WAI) – W3C. https://www.w3.org/WAI/fundamentals/accessibility-intro. Accessed 14 Dec 2019
3. Accessibility, Usability, and Inclusion – Web Accessibility Initiative (WAI) – W3C. https://www.w3.org/WAI/fundamentals/accessibility-usability-inclusion. Accessed 14 Dec 2019
4. Streich, S.: Accessibility is NOT just for people with disabilities (2019). https://vimm.com/website-accessibility. Accessed 1 May 2019
5. Constitution of the Republic of Poland of 2 April (1997). http://prawo.sejm.gov.pl/isap.nsf/DocDetails.xsp?id=WDU19970780483. Accessed 1 Dec 2019
6. Act on Access to Public Information (2001). http://prawo.sejm.gov.pl/isap.nsf/DocDetails.xsp?id=WDU20011121198&type=3. Accessed 1 Dec 2019
7. Searchmetrics, Website Definition (2019). https://www.searchmetrics.com/glossary/website. Accessed 1 Dec 2019
8. Gąsiorkiewicz, A.: Main factors for web traffic level in B2C E-commerce websites and their impact on conversion ratio. In: Łongiewska-Wijas, E. (ed.) E-gospodarka w Polsce Stan obecny i perspektywy rozwoju, vol. 597, pp. 637–645. Zeszyty Naukowe Uniwersytetu Szczecińskiego, Szczecin (2010)
9. Waddell, C., et al.: Constructing Accessible Web Sites. Apress Publishing House, New York (2003)
10. Khalid, H., Hedge, A., Ahram, T.: Advances in Ergonomics Modeling and Usability Evaluation. CRC Press, Boca Raton (2011)
11. ISO 9241-210:2019(en) Ergonomics of human-system interaction – Part 210: Human-centred design for interactive systems (2019). https://www.iso.org/obp/ui/#iso:std:iso:9241:-210:ed-2:v1:en. Accessed 1 Dec 2019
12. ISO/IEC 25010:2011(en) Systems and software engineering – Systems and software Quality Requirements and Evaluation (SQuaRE) – System and software quality models (2011). https://www.iso.org/obp/ui/#iso:std:iso-iec:25010:ed-1:v1:en. Accessed 1 Dec 2019
13. Quiñones, D., Rusu, C.: How to develop usability heuristics: a systematic literature review. Comput. Stand. Interfaces **53**, 89–122 (2017). https://doi.org/10.1016/j.csi.2017.03.009
14. Inostroza, R., Rusu, C., Roncagliolo, S., Rusu, V., Collazos, C.A.: Developing SMASH: a set of smartphone's usability heuristics. Comput. Stand. Interfaces **43**, 40–52 (2016)
15. Fernandez, A., Insfran, E., Abrahão, S.: Usability evaluation methods for the web: a systematic mapping study. Inf. Softw. Technol. **53**(8), 789–817 (2011). https://doi.org/10.1016/j.infsof.2011.02.007
16. Lazar, J., Feng, J.H., Hochheiser, H.: Research Methods in Human-Computer Interaction. Wiley, Hoboken (2010)
17. Paz, F., Pow-Sang, J.A.: A systematic mapping review of usability evaluation methods for software development process. Int. J. Softw. Eng. Appl. **10**(1), 165–178 (2016)
18. Scholtz, J.: Usability evaluation (2004). http://notification.etisalat.com.eg/etisalat/templates.backup.16082011/582/Usability%2520Evaluation_rev1%5B1%5D.pdf. Accessed 15 Sept 2018
19. Philips, M.: Elevate Your UX with a Heuristic Analysis – How to Run a Usability Evaluation (2017). https://www.linkedin.com/pulse/elevate-your-ux-heuristic-analysis-how-run-miklos-philips. Accessed 15 Sept 2018
20. Gerhardt-Powals, J.: Cognitive engineering principles for enhancing human-computer performance. Int. J. Hum. Comput. Interact. **8**(2), 189–211 (1996)

21. Weinschenk, S., Barker, D.T.: Designing Effective Speech Interfaces. Wiley, Hoboken (2000)
22. Shneiderman, B.: The Eight Golden Rules of Interface Design. Designing the User Interface, 6th edn. Pearson, London (2006). Section 3.3.4
23. Inostroza, R., Rusu, C., Roncagliolo, S., Jimenez, C., Rusu, V.: Usability heuristics for touchscreen-based mobile devices. IEEE Xplore (2012). https://doi.org/10.1109/ITNG.2012.134
24. Tognazzini, B.: First Principles of Interaction Design (Revised & Expanded). askTog (2014). https://asktog.com/atc/principles-of-interaction-design. Accessed 9 May 2019
25. Douglas, S.: 7 Usability Heuristics That All UI Designers Should Know. Usability Geek (2017). https://usabilitygeek.com/usability-heuristics-ui-designers-know. Accessed 19 Jan 2019
26. Jimenez, C., Lozada, P., Rosas, P.: Usability heuristics: a systematic review. In: 11th Colombian Computing Conference, Popayan, Colombia, 27–30 September 2016 (2016). https://doi.org/10.1109/ColumbianCC.2016.7750805
27. Dourado, M.A.D., Canedo E.D.: Usability heuristics for mobile applications – a systematic review. In: Proceedings of the 20th International Conference on Enterprise Information Systems (ICEIS' 2018), vol. 2, pp. 483–494 (2018). https://doi.org/10.5220/0006781404830494
28. Section 508 of the Rehabilitation Act. – 29 U.S.C. § 798. Section 508 – Electronic and Information Technology. https://www.fcc.gov/general/section-508-rehabilitation-act. Accessed 20 Feb 2019
29. Barrierefreie Informationstechnik-Verordnung – BITV 2.0. https://www.barrierefreies-webdesign.de/bitv/bitv-2.0.html. Accessed 20 Feb 2019
30. Accessibilità siti web. AgID promuove l'accessibilità dei siti web in relazione alla normativa vigente. https://www.agid.gov.it/it/design-servizi/accessibilita-siti-web. Accessed 20 Feb 2019
31. Regulation of the Council of Ministers of 12 April 2012, on the National Interoperability Framework. http://prawo.sejm.gov.pl/isap.nsf/DocDetails.xsp?id=WDU20120000526. Accessed 1 Dec 2019
32. Information for PIB editors. https://www.bip.gov.pl/articles/view/43. Accessed 1 Dec 2019
33. Central Statistical Office of 31 December 2015. https://stat.gov.pl/statystyka-regionalna/rankingi-statystyczne/miasta-najwieksze-pod-wzgledem-liczby-ludnosci. Accessed 20 Sept 2018
34. Krawiec, Ł., Dudycz, H.: Identification of heuristics for assessing the usability of websites of public administration units. In: Ganzha, M., Maciaszek, L., Paprzycki, M. (eds.) Proceedings of the 2019 Federated Conference on Computer Science and Information Systems, Leipzig, 1–4 September 2019, pp. 651–657 (2019). https://doi.org/10.15439/2019F307

Quantity Vs. Quality in Online Marketplaces: The Case of Kiva

Haim Mendelson[1] and Yuanyuan Shen[2]

[1] Stanford University, Stanford, CA 94305, USA
haim@stanford.edu
[2] Microsoft Corporation, Sunnyvale, CA 94089, USA
anashen@alumni.gsb.stanford.edu

Abstract. This paper studies Kiva, the world's largest online, peer-to-peer social lending marketplace. We consider two stages in the development of the Kiva marketplace: a growth stage when Kiva was focused on *quantity*, and a maturity stage when Kiva shifted to emphasize *quality* (broadly defined). Our starting point is the common hypothesis that marketplace success is driven by network effects which facilitate growth – a quantity focus. We argue, however, that as a marketplace becomes mainstream, it focus shifts to improving quality – creating additional sources of value for users by adding capabilities and improving the user experience. We test this proposition using data from Kiva. Our proposition is supported: while network effects are strong and significant during the early growth phase of the marketplace, they become weak or disappear as the marketplace becomes mainstream. We study the implications of our findings for the deployment, implementation and management of online marketplaces.

Keywords: Online marketplaces · Network effects · Peer-to-peer lending · Online services · Quality

1 Introduction

Advanced information technologies are changing the structure of economic activity, with many traditional processes being transformed through the use of electronic marketplaces. Activities such as buying, selling and lending are moving from the established but labor-intensive and inefficient brick-and-mortar format to online marketplaces that increase efficiency, transparency and effectiveness and have already become a major sector of the economy.

In this paper we study Kiva, the world's largest online, peer-to-peer lending marketplace that allows lenders in developed countries to lend to entrepreneurs in developing countries. By crowdfunding small loans posted on its website, Kiva enables microfinance institutions to draw upon ordinary web-users from the developed world as philanthropic lenders who access Kiva to underwrite the delivery of microcredit services to the credit-needy. We use data that record

© Springer Nature Switzerland AG 2020
E. Ziemba (Ed.): AITM 2019/ISM 2019, LNBIP 380, pp. 76–91, 2020.
https://doi.org/10.1007/978-3-030-43353-6_5

the marketplace behavior on Kiva's platform. Founded in 2006, Kiva has since successfully connected with millions of web-users and raised $1.4 billion in micro-credit for 3.4 million borrowers by 2019.

Marketplace development is known to hinge on network effects [1,2], which are introduced in more detail in Sect. 2. In a commerce marketplace such as eBay, for example, more sellers make the marketplace more attractive to buyers, and more buyers make it more attractive to sellers. As a result, marketplaces often focus on growing the number of participants on both sides of the market.

We argue that as marketplaces mature, they should – and do – shift their focus from quantity to quality. Early in the life cycle of a marketplace, it has to emphasize growth to survive and achieve a critical mass, and some try to win a "winner take all" competition which requires, among other factors, strong network effects. During the early growth period, network effects are all impor-tant. We argue, however, that as a marketplace matures, its focus has to shift to quality.

How does that happen? Yahoo! Japan Auctions is a classic case in point. Yahoo! Japan has been (and continues to be) Japan's most visited website, offering a suite of highly successful Internet services. In September 1999, Yahoo! Japan launched its auction service, fashioned after eBay. The site quickly became highly successful, and in less than two months had 30,000 daily auctions [3]. By June 2001, the number of auctions grew to 2.4 million and the site had 5.3 million monthly unique users; these numbers increased to 4.2 million and 7.3 million, respectively, by March 2002 [4]. But while the quantity of listings increased by 75%, their quality actually declined. In June 2001, 33% of listings converted to actual transactions on average. The average conversion rate declined to 27% by March 2002 [4].

Following many other marketplaces, Yahoo! Japan Auctions did not initially charge any fees for its services so as to fuel growth. This attracted to the mar-ketplace many low-quality listings that did not convert to transactions. In April 2002, Yahoo! Japan Auctions introduced a listing fee of 10 Yen per item and in May 2002, it started charging a transaction fee (generally 3% of the auction pro-ceeds with some variation depending on category) which had the effect of increas-ing listing quality. Yahoo! Japan Auctions also phased in multiple improvements to increase the quality of the user experience. Immediately following the institu-tion of the listing fee, the number of listings dropped to 2.1 million in May 2002 but the average conversion rate to transactions increased to 44% and stabilized in the 40%–50% range. Growth followed thereafter as the higher listing quality attracted more buyers and sellers to the site.

Thus, Yahoo! Japan Auctions started with a focus on growth to increase quantities and win the network effects game, but then shifted its emphasis to increasing quality – even at the expense of quantity. We argue that a similar effect governs the development of other marketplaces and we test this proposition using evidence from Kiva. Specifically, we hypothesize that Kiva's growth was characterized by network effects in the site's initial growth period, but these network effects became weaker or disappeared as Kiva matured.

The rest of the paper is organized as follows. Section 2 reviews the relevant literature on marketplaces, Kiva and network effects. Section 3 is a Kiva overview. Section 4 develops our hypotheses and describes our data and test methodology. Section 5 presents our results, and Sect. 6 studies their implications. We briefly conclude in Sect. 7.

2   Literature Review and Theoretical Background

A number of papers use Kiva as a research site. Liu et al. and Mckinnon et al. both study what motivates Kiva's lenders [5,6]. Liu et al. find that these motivations are related to the lenders' subsequent lending rates, e.g., lenders who lend to fulfill a religious duty lend more than others [5]. McKinnon et al. find that many lenders do not lend out of pure altruism and are also driven by the desire to enhance their self-esteem [6]. Other researchers study factors that influence the availability and speed of funding Kiva projects, including geographical or cultural proximity [7,8], borrower's gender [8,9] and loan category [9].

Beyond Kiva, online marketplaces have become increasingly important features of contemporary commerce, and the literature in this area has grown as well (see, for example, reviews in [1,10]). On the quality dimension, [11] and [12] present a usability study of leading marketplaces (operated as auction websites) based on the PEQUAL methodology discussed in more detail in Sect. 6. On the other hand, the extant literature views network effects (i.e., quantity) as a central driver of success or failure for online marketplaces. The importance of network effects in marketplaces such as eBay is well known (see, e.g. [2,13,14]) and their effect on online peer-to-peer lending is widely acknowledged (e.g. [15–17]). Our empirical tests focus on the existence, or non-existence, of network effects over the life cycle of the marketplace. We thus provide next an overview of network effects and their implications for online marketplaces.

Network effects, also referred to as network externalities, reflect a positive relationship between the installed base of users on a platform and its value to users [18–20]. They are *direct* when there is a direct positive relationship between the size of the installed base and the value to users within that installed base. The classic example is the telephone network: adding a new user to the network increases the number of potential calls users can make, which increases the utility users derive from the network [21]. *Indirect* network effects arise when *(i)* the network is based on two complementary components, say A and B; *(ii)* there is a positive relationship between the installed base of B and the value to users of A, and *(iii)* there is a corresponding positive relationship between the installed base of A and the value to users of B [20]. This results in a positive feedback loop between the installed bases of A and B: an increase in the installed base of A makes the network more attractive to the Bs, and as more Bs join the network, it becomes more attractive to the As. This means that more As attract yet more As indirectly through the Bs—hence the term *indirect*. In Sect. 4 we test the existence of this positive feedback loop during different periods in the life cycle of a marketplace.

Network effects have a major impact on the way technology-based solutions are deployed and managed as they affect choices of efficiency, effectiveness and speed: in the presence of network effects, a highly-efficient and effective solution that does not achieve critical mass may fail regardless of its technical or economic merit. Further, if the network effects are sustainable, a solution that manages to control a large user base may prevail even when it is inferior on a stand-alone basis [20]. Thus, network effects have a paramount impact on the deployment and management of platforms, and in particular—on online marketplaces.

In a peer-to-peer online lending marketplace, prospective borrowers post loan requests online either directly, on their own, or indirectly, through marketplace partners. Lenders browse the loan requests and decide which loans to bid on. Lenders who wish to fund a loan submit conditional or unconditional funding commitments to the marketplace. The marketplace then matches loan requests to funding commitments, funds some of the loans, and services them until they are repaid (or until they default). It is commonly assumed that such lending marketplaces are characterized by indirect network effects between lenders and borrowers, as more lenders increase the probability of a loan request being funded, and more borrowers make the market more attractive to lenders, who can better diversify their loans and are more likely to find a match they are willing to fund. The latter consideration is important on Kiva, where lenders seek to support entrepreneurs with particular characteristics, and with more entrepreneurs and loan requests on the site, a lender is more likely to find one she is willing to support.

Network effects were found in a variety of industries ranging from telecommunications to Information Technology (cf. [22–26]). Economides and Himmelberg find that the growth of the U.S. Fax market was strongly influenced by network effects [22]. Brynjolfsson and Kemerer study the microcomputer spreadsheet industry and find a 1% increase in the installed user base to be associated with a 0.75% increase in its price and attribute this phenomenon to network effects [23]. Hannan and McDowell find larger banks and those operating in more concentrated local banking markets to be more likely to adopt automatic teller machines because of the expected network effects of a large user base [24]. Lin and Bhattacherjee argue that network effects increase users' intention to employ interactive IT directly and enhance their perceived enjoyment indirectly. They also validate this argument by a survey of instant messaging usage by Taiwanese students [25]. Madden and Dalzell [26] study the growth of mobile telephony, finding network effects of different strengths across countries. They attribute these differences to the differences between high- and low-income countries and to non-linearities.

Some authors argue that direct network effects may be mitigated by other factors. However, they do not study two-sided marketplaces nor any lending services nor indirect network effects, and they do not argue for a life cycle effect. Asvanund et al. identify both positive and negative network effects in six popular music-sharing networks that are characterized by direct network effects [27]. Negative network externalities arise when more users impose cost to the networks, e.g. congestion. They argue that the optimal size of these networks is therefore bounded. Feldman et al. provide a theoretical argument, showing that free-riding and whitewashing (users who rejoin with new identities to avoid reputational penalties) can both lead to degraded performance in systems that are otherwise characterized by direct network effects [28].

While the theoretical literature views network effects as an inherent feature of online marketplaces, we could not identify an empirical study that directly confirmed or alternatively rejected their existence in online peer-to-peer lending marketplaces. One of the contributions of this paper is to narrow this gap by investigating whether network effects actually exist on Kiva, as the theoretical literature suggests. We further argue that marketplace behavior is more nuanced than suggested by the network effects literature: network effects (quantity) are important drivers of growth in the early development phase of the marketplace, but as the marketplace matures, quality becomes more important.

3   Kiva

Founded in October 2005, Kiva operates a website where entrepreneurs from developing countries post loans through field partners—microfinance institutions, social businesses, schools, and other non-profit organizations. Loans come from individual lenders from across the globe, primarily from developed countries. Between 2005 and 2019, Kiva funded $1.4 billion in loans extended to 3.4 million borrowers in 77 countries from 1.8 million lenders. These loans had an impressive repayment rate approaching 97%.

The Kiva website lists hundreds of borrowers who are looking for loans to grow their businesses, go to school, buy farm equipment, etc. Kiva lenders are social investors who receive no interest and make no profit on their loans. They are motivated by the social impact their loans make on the entrepreneurs they fund and the communities they live in. Loans serve the needs of poor, underserved, or financially excluded (e.g., unbanked or underbanked) populations and aim to achieve a social or environmental impact. Lenders browse the loan requests and decide who they will lend to and the amount to lend, and may contribute $25 or more to fund the loans they select. Figure 1 shows the distribution of loan categories on Kiva. As shown in the Figure, the majority of loans are made in the agriculture, food and retail categories.

Kiva relies on its Field Partners, local micro-finance institutions, to administer each loan. The Field Partners are responsible for screening borrowers, posting loan requests to Kiva (many borrowers do not have Internet access), disbursing loans and collecting repayments, and otherwise administering each loan. Even though lenders do not profit from the loan, the Field Partners may charge interest to the borrowers to fund their operations. Loan requests remain posted on Kiva for up to 30 days. If a loan is not fully funded within that period, it expires and all lenders' commitments are refunded. If the loan is fully funded, Kiva's Field Partner sends the money to the entrepreneur. When there is a default, it is usually the lender who bears the risk (this, however, changed over time, as

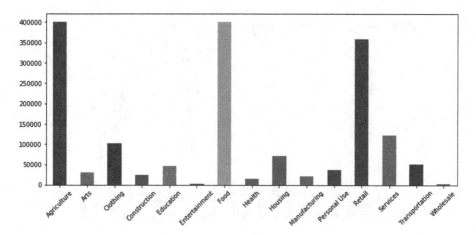

Fig. 1. Number of loans by loan category on Kiva since foundation through June 2016.

discussed below). As the borrower repays the loan, the Field Partner returns the principal through Kiva to the lenders who funded it. Loans are usually termed to be repaid on a monthly schedule. Thus, lenders usually receive portions of their loan back gradually, instead of all of it at the end of the loan term. Loan terms average 1.5 years. A loan draws about 23 contributing lenders on average.

We obtained our data from Kiva's data snapshot on `build.kiva.org`, augmented by querying Kiva's API. In addition to basic data on borrowers and prospective lenders, we have loan-specific information through June 2016. The sample period for our detailed estimations is January 2007 through June 2016 (we also have some earlier data for our monthly time series). As of the end of our sample period (June 2016), about 95% of loan requests were fully funded. In our sample, the majority (84.8%) of loan requests come from Asia, Africa and South America while most (89.4%) lenders come from developed countries in North America and Europe.

Figure 2 shows the evolution of Kiva's loan fulfillment rate – the percentage of loan requests that were funded – over time. Conceptually, this metric is analogous to the listing conversion rate on Yahoo! Japan Auctions.

As seen in Fig. 2, the loan fulfillment rate is close to 100% from Kiva's early years through 2011, and it then deteriorates and shows significant variation over time. In response, Kiva took a series of steps to improve the balance of loan supply and demand. Kiva gradually became a highly curated marketplace that proactively drives both supply and demand towards a desirable balance. Kiva directly controls the number and amount of loan requests by budgeting specific loan request targets to its Field Partners, controlling the rate at which Field Partners are allowed to post loan requests, recruiting new Field Partners to its platform and terminating Field Partners who generate substantial imbalances. Kiva aims to have on the site at least $2.5 million of outstanding loan requests to make the variety on the site attractive to lenders. When the amount is lower,

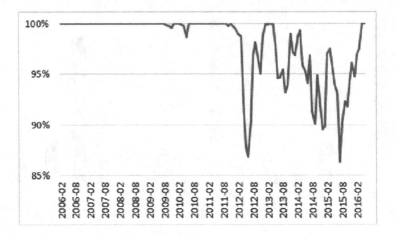

Fig. 2. Loan fulfillment rate (percentage of loan requests that were funded) on Kiva, February 2006-May 2016.

Kiva staff start messaging Field Partners and encouraging them to post more loans. In addition, a group of Kiva staff members meet twice a month to analyze the demand and supply and take corrective action when imbalances take place. Thus, while demand and supply are influenced by market forces, they are ultimately driven by Kiva itself to improve the experience of both borrowers and lenders. To improve the user experience, Kiva developed a variety of tools, filters and calculators that help lenders select loans to invest in and track their loans and took steps to increase transparency for both lenders and Field Partners. And, while early on, Field Partners were permitted or even encouraged to make payments on behalf of entrepreneurs who had defaulted, this practice was prohibited starting in 2012. Thus, lenders who were protected from the effects of default early on – a practice that attracted more lenders to Kiva – started bearing a default risk risk in 2012.

4   Research Methodology

4.1   The Network Effects Hypotheses

Our key research hypothesis is that online marketplaces such as Kiva exhibit network effects in their early growth stage, but these effects cease to exist as key drivers once the marketplace matures. We thus test the network effects hypothesis in two subperiods (in this case, the two halves of our sample period) and we expect to find they are supported in the first subperiod but not in the second subperiod. The traditional network effects literature would expect network effects to persist in both subperiods.

The network effects hypothesis can be formalized by considering the interaction between lenders and borrowers. As discussed above, the theory of network

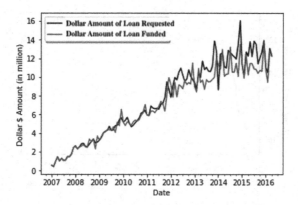

Fig. 3. Dollar amounts of loans requested and funded on Kiva, January 2007-June 2006.

effects implies a positive feedback loop between the number of lenders and the amount of open loans (measured by their number or aggregate dollar amount): with more lenders, the platform should attract more loan requests, and with more loan requests, the platform should attract more lenders. This results in two key hypotheses which, taken together, would imply the existence of network effects:

Hypothesis 1. *The dollar amount and number of open loans on Kiva should increase in the lagged number of active lenders.*

Hypothesis 2. *The number of active lenders on Kiva should increase in the lagged number and amount of open loan requests.*

Network effects and the associated feedback loop require *both* Hypotheses to hold. Hypotheses 1 and 2 not only enable us to test the existence of network effects in online lending marketplaces, but also help us to gain an understanding of the supply and demand on these platforms.

4.2 Data, Descriptive Summaries and Empirical Methodology

We construct weekly time series for Kiva's performance over our sample period (2007–2016). We identify two phases in the development of the Kiva platform: a *growth* phase covering the first half of our sample period, and a maturity phase during the second half of our sample period. During the growth phase, both the amount of loans requested and the amount funded grow quickly. Then, the growth in both supply and demand flatten out. Further, during the second subperiod, the gap between the number of loans requested and the number of loans funded becomes larger (see also Fig. 3).

Figure 4 shows the number of active lenders (i.e., those who have bid on at least one loan in the past six months) and Fig. 5 shows the number of open loan

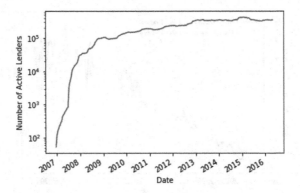

Fig. 4. Number of active lenders on Kiva.

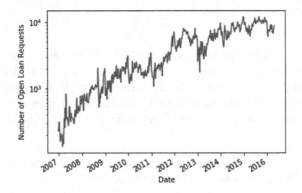

Fig. 5. Number of loan requests open on Kiva.

requests on Kiva each week over our sample period, both on a logarithmic scale. The figures show how growth has abated between the earlier growth period and the latter maturity period, when the number of active lenders flattens out and the growth in open loan requests deteriorates. Interestingly, the growth of the active lender base does not match the exponential growth of the registered lender base, implying that the lender retention rate dropped in the second subperiod.

These patterns show distinct differences between the earlier growth period and the latter maturity period which are not recognized by the extant network effects literature. We have argued that network effects – quantity – should be more prominent during the earlier growth period, when the growing installed base is a key driver of adoption. Once the platform stabilizes, we expect quality to overtake network effects as a driver of performance. As discussed in detail in Sect. 3, while peer-to-peer lending has been growing rapidly around the globe [29], Kiva experienced a declining loan fulfillment rates in 2011–12 and in response it started honing its business model, proactively managing demand and supply to reduce imbalances, assure a wide selection of loan requests, and improve user experience and transparency [30,31]. Quality differentiation becomes even more important due to the effects of competition. Indeed, Kiva was facing increased competition from new social microfunding sites (e.g., MyC4 in Europe, Wokai in China and MicroPlace in the U.S.), as well as from for-profit lending sites that catered to entrepreneurs (e.g, Zopa in Europe and CreditEase in China; these sites, which charge interest, compete with Kiva since many field partners charge interest to the entrepreneurs they serve).

To test for these different behaviors, we divide our sample period into two halves, *(i)* January 2007 to August 2011 and *(ii)* September 2011 to June 2016. Table 1 displays the correlation matrix among our key variables for the two sample subperiods.

Table 1. Correlations between the number of active lenders, the dollar amount and the number of loan requests for the two sample subperiods

Subperiod/Variable	Amount of loan requests	No. loan requests
Jan 2007–Aug 2011		
No. active lenders	0.87	0.87
Amount of Loan Requests	–	0.99
Sept 2011–June 2016		
No. Active Lenders	0.46	0.46
Amount of loan requests	–	0.95

In Table 1, we observe a strong correlation between the number of active lenders and the number and dollar amount of loan requests during the first subperiod. These correlations substantially decline in the second subperiod.

We test each of our hypotheses separately over each subperiod. For Week t, we denote by n_t the number of active lenders (defined as those who placed at least one bid over the past six months), by a_t the dollar amount of open loan requests, and by l_t the number of open loan requests. We estimate (heteroskedasticity-corrected) OLS regressions using the specification below to test Hypothesis 1 that the dollar amount of loan requests increases in the number of active lenders:

$$\log(a_t + 1) = \alpha_0 + \alpha_1 \log(n_{t-1} + 1) + \boldsymbol{\alpha_3}\boldsymbol{x}_{t-1} + \epsilon_t, \tag{1}$$

where the vector $\boldsymbol{x}_{t-1}$ comprises the default rate on Kiva loans as of the end of Week $t-1$, the effective yield on the ICE BofAML Emerging Markets Corporate Plus Index [32], dummy variables representing the year of t, and a trend variable.

An alternative test of Hypothesis 1 focuses on the relationship between the number of loan requests and the number of active lenders:

$$\log(l_t + 1) = \beta_0 + \beta_1 \log(n_{t-1} + 1) + \boldsymbol{\beta_3}\boldsymbol{x}_{t-1} + \zeta_t. \tag{2}$$

To test Hypothesis 2 that the number of active lenders increases in the dollar amount of loan requests, we estimate the regression:

$$\log(n_t + 1) = \gamma_0 + \gamma_1 \log(a_{t-1} + 1) + \boldsymbol{\gamma_2}\boldsymbol{x}_{t-1} + \omega_t. \tag{3}$$

Table 2. Results for Hypotheses 1 and 2

Regressors	Jan 2007–Aug 2011					
	Eq. (1)	Eq. (2)	Eq. (3)	Eq. (3a)	Eq.(4)	Eq. (4a)
Intercept	9.67***	1.52$^+$	8.03***	−10,432$^+$	8.21***	−7,040
	(0.89)	(0.79)	(0.71)	(6,118)	(3.87)	(3,046)
No. active lenders	0.36***	0.46***	–	–	–	–
	(0.08)	(0.08)	–	–	–	–
Amount loan requests	–	–	0.17**	866.83$^+$	–	–
	–	–	(0.05)	(470.40)	–	–
No. loan requests	–	–	–	–	0.32***	1,248**
	–	–	–	–	(0.06)	(482)
Default rate	−1.67	−2.23	−3.34	5,578	−3.88	4,542
	(6.32)	(6.03)	(2.30)	(41,893)	(2.49)	(42,179)
Interest rate	−0.02$^+$	−0.004	0.01	103.17	0.01	92.16
	(0.01)	(0.01)	(0.01)	(71.12)	(0.01)	(70.55)
Trend	0.01***	0.01	0.01***	−7.46	0.005***	−13.73
	(0.001)	(0.001)	(0.001)	(10.28)	(0.001)	(10.93)
Year dDummy	Yes	Yes	Yes	Yes	Yes	Yes
R^2	0.91	0.91	0.94	0.04	0.94	0.05

***: $p < 0.001$, **: $0.001 \leq p < 0.01$, *: $0.01 \leq p < 0.05$, $^+$ indicates $0.05 \leq p < 0.1$.

Likewise, we test whether the number of active lenders increases in the number of open loan requests by estimating the equation:

$$\log(n_t + 1) = \kappa_0 + \kappa_1 \log(l_{t-1} + 1) + \boldsymbol{\kappa_3}\boldsymbol{x}_{t-1} + \psi_t. \tag{4}$$

In Eq. (1) through (4), $\epsilon_t, \zeta_t, \omega_t, \eta_t$ are random noise. As a macroeconomic control, our regressions use the effective yield on the ICE BofAML Emerging Markets Corporate Plus Index [32], which is available on a daily basis and is expected to influence loan funding in emerging markets (we also used the GDP growth rate and unemployment rate, which turned out insignificant).

5 Research Findings

Tables 2 and 3 show the results of our OLS estimations using White's method to account for heteroskedasticity [33].

As hypothesized, we observe positive and strongly-significant coefficients for our network effect variables during Kiva's growth period: a 1% increase in the number of active lenders results in a 0.36% increase in the dollar amount and a 0.46% increase in the number of open loan requests. A 1% increase in the dollar amount of open loan requests leads to a 0.17% increase in the number of active lenders, and a 1% increase in the number of loan requests leads to a

0.32% increase in the number of active lenders. These results are both economically meaningful and strongly statistically significant, confirming our hypotheses. Given that *both* hypotheses hold, we have the feedback loop confirming the existence of network effects during the growth period.

Table 3. Results for Hypotheses 1 and 2 (cont'd)

Regressors	Sept 2011–June 2016					
	Eq. (1)	Eq. (2)	Eq. (3)	Eq. (3a)	Eq. (4)	Eq. (4a)
Intercept	11.93**	4.22	12.48***	−35,236*	12.55***	−18,462+
	(3.79)	(0.15)	(17,294)	(0.09)	(10,908)	
No. active lenders	0.13	0.22	–	–	–	–
	(0.31)	(0.30)	–	–	–	–
Amount loan requests	–	–	0.02	2,485*	–	–
	–	–	(0.01)	(1,171)	–	–
No. loan requests	–	–	–	–	0.02+	2,446+
	–	–	–	–	(0.01)	(1,299)
Default rate	102.65***	96.22***	6.50*	−26,047	6.08+	−12,015
	(18.71)	(16.57)	(3.11)	(263,670)	(3.11)	(268,525)
Interest rate	−0.02	−0.03	−0.06***	−260.01	−0.06***	−222.5
	(0.06)	(0.06)	(0.01)	(818.33)	(0.01)	(817)
Trend	0.001	0.002	−0.001*	−79.34***	−0.0005*	−82.83***
	(0.002)	(0.002)	(0.0003)	(24.46)	(0.0003)	(25.15)
Year dummy	Yes	Yes	Yes	Yes	Yes	Yes
R^2	0.55	0.56	0.80	0.07	0.80	0.07

***: $p < 0.001$, **: $0.001 \leq p < 0.01$, *: $0.01 \leq p < 0.05$, + indicates $0.05 \leq p < 0.1$.

For the second, maturity subperiod (September 2011 through June 2016), the network effect coefficients become small and, for the most part, insignificant (the exception is the coefficient of the number of open loan requests in Eq. (4), which is significant, but only at the 90% level). Based on Eqs. (1)–(3), *both* hypotheses are rejected. Because a rejection of either one of our hypotheses leads to the rejection of network effects, we conclude that there are no meaningful network effects during the second subperiod. These results are consistent with our argument for the differences between the two subperiods (Sect. 4.2).

Equations (3)–(4) use the number of active lenders to estimate the dependent variable, which leads to autocorrelated residuals. To address this issue, we reestimated Eqs. (3)–(4) by differencing the number of active lenders, using $(n_t - n_{t-1})$ as our dependent variable. The results are shown in columns (3a) and (4a) of Table 2. The main difference between the two specifications is that in Eq. (3a), the significance of the amount of loan requests declines in the first subperiod and increases in the second. Our conclusion remains intact: there are strong and significant network effects in the first subperiod whereas in the second subperiod, there are no network effects, as Hypothesis 1 fails to hold.

6 Discussion

From a management, culture and technology perspective, there are vast differences between managing for network effects (quantity) and managing for quality (broadly defined). Managing for network effects requires speed and an emphasis on customer acquisition. It calls for outsourcing development resources, fast iterative product development, minimum viable products that do the job and a satisfying approach to quality assurance and testing. In contrast, organizations that differentiate themselves on product capability and quality maintain tight control over their development resources, aim for zero defects, make sure every interaction engenders empathy and enhances trust, and meticulously engage in feature development.

Our findings suggest that while online marketplaces may need to grow early on with an emphasis on network effects (quantity), their long-term survival as they reach maturity requires a quality focus. The inflection point when a marketplace shifts its focus from a quantity orientation to a quality orientation is a point of high risk, as the business model, technology approaches and organizational characteristics that have made the marketplace successful in the first place need to undergo major changes. One approach organizations may take to facilitate these changes is to build the seeds of a quality orientation early on, and to increase the amount of resources dedicated to that part of the organization along with the growth of the marketplace. This may result in a smoother and more successful transition in addition to the obvious benefits of greater quality during the growth period.

We use the term "quality" broadly, as it encompasses both business model drivers such as the conversion rate for a marketplace like Yahoo! Japan Auctions or the loan fulfillment and default rates for Kiva and site usability drivers. Both drivers, as well as the integration between them, are important [34]. The business model drivers, however, vary depending on the specific markets and users served by the marketplace, whereas common frameworks for evaluating website usability have been developed across applications and markets. [11] have proposed the application of Multiple Criteria Decision Analysis methods in conjunction with the Preference Ranking Organization Method for Enrichment Evaluation (PROMETHEE II) to evaluate website quality. Their methodology, called PEQUAL, has been applied in particular to auction platforms [12] ([11,12] also provide an excellent review of the literature on website evaluation). The criteria used by [11,12] include usability, site design, information quality, trust and empathy.

7 Conclusion

This paper studies Kiva, the world's largest philanthropic lending marketplace. Testing the existence of a positive feedback loop between the number of active lenders and the amount (in dollar value or number) of open loans, we identify strong and positive network effects during Kiva's initial stage of growth.

However, the network effects essentially disappear in Kiva's maturity period. Our results suggest that network effects are particularly important during the initial growth phase of a marketplace platform. As growth abates and competition becomes fierce, the importance of network effects declines and the emphasis has to shift to quality, broadly defined. This difference between the early growth and stability periods is largely ignored in the literature.

The implications of these results for the way a marketplace such as Kiva is deployed and managed are important. Early on, network effects prevail, customer acquisition and speed are key success factors, and the primary objective is to grow and achieve critical mass. However, the marketplace cannot rest on its laurels following its initial growth. Rather, the network effects weaken or disappear, forcing the marketplace to engage in constant optimization and quality improvement, broadly defined. We suggest that business metrics that are marketplace-specific have to be integrated with website quality metrics such as the ones developed in [11,12] and that these metrics have to be followed closely and continuously optimized.

We have suggested a life cycle approach to the analysis of these issues. Additional research is needed, however, as our results are based on a single research site. Given the potential impact of our results, we believe it is worth studying how they apply in other marketplaces. Further, sophisticated econometric techniques applying additional data that may be available may be used to study the drivers of marketplace adoption. In light of our current results and their implications, we believe such extensions provide fruitful avenues for future research.

References

1. Evans, D.S., Schmalensee, R.: Matchmakers: The New Economics of Multisided Platforms. Harvard Business Review Press, Brighton (2016)
2. Rochet, J.C., Tirole, J.: Two-sided markets: a progress report. RAND J. Econ. **37**(3), 645–667 (2006). https://doi.org/10.1111/j.1756-2171.2006.tb00036.x
3. Altaba.com: Yahoo! auctions surpasses one million simultaneous daily auctions, November 1999. https://www.altaba.com/news-releases/news-release-details/yahoo-auctions-surpasses-one-million-simultaneous-daily-auctions. Accessed Nov 2019. Posted on 01 Nov 1999
4. Yahoo! Japan: Yahoo! japan 2001-2002 financial reports, March 2002. https://www.z-holdings.co.jp/en/ir/. Accessed Nov 2019
5. Liu, Y., Chen, R., Chen, Y., Mei, Q., Salib, S.: I loan because...: understanding motivations for pro-social lending. In: Proceedings of the Fifth ACM International Conference on Web Search and Data Mining, pp. 503–512. ACM (2012). https://doi.org/10.1145/2124295.2124356
6. McKinnon, S.L., Dickinson, E., Carr, J.N., Chávez, K.R.: Kiva.org, person-to-person lending, and the conditions of intercultural contact. Howard J. Commun. **24**(4), 327–347 (2013). https://doi.org/10.1080/10646175.2013.805983
7. Burtch, G., Ghose, A., Wattal, S.: Cultural differences and geography as determinants of online pro-social lending. MIS Q. **38**(3), 773–794 (2013). https://doi.org/10.2139/ssrn.2271298

8. Heller, L.R., Badding, K.D.: For compassion or money? The factors influencing the funding of micro loans. J. Socio Econ. **41**(6), 831–835 (2012). https://doi.org/10.1016/j.socec.2012.08.005

9. Desai, R.M., Kharas, H.: Democratizing foreign aid: online philanthropy and international development assistance. NYU J. Int. Law Politics **42**, 1111 (2009)

10. Levin, J.D.: The economics of internet markets. Technical report, National Bureau of Economic Research (2011). https://doi.org/10.3386/w16852

11. Wątróbski, J., Ziemba, P., Jankowski, J., Wolski, W.: Pequal-e-commerce websites quality evaluation methodology. In: 2016 Federated Conference on Computer Science and Information Systems (FedCSIS), pp. 1317–1327. IEEE (2016). https://doi.org/10.15439/2016F469

12. Wątróbski, J., Ziemba, P., Jankowski, J., Wolski, W.: Using PEQUAL methodology in auction platforms evaluation process. In: Ziemba, E. (ed.) AITM/ISM 2016. LNBIP, vol. 277, pp. 222–241. Springer, Cham (2017). https://doi.org/10.1007/978-3-319-53076-5_12

13. Evans, D.S., Schmalensee, R.: The industrial organization of markets with two-sided platforms. Technical report, National Bureau of Economic Research (2005). https://doi.org/10.3386/w11603

14. Rochet, J.C., Tirole, J.: Platform competition in two-sided markets. J. Eur. Econ. Assoc. **1**(4), 990–1029 (2003). https://doi.org/10.1162/154247603322493212

15. Lovejoy, K., Waters, R.D., Saxton, G.D.: Engaging stakeholders through Twitter: how nonprofit organizations are getting more out of 140 characters or less. Public Relat. Rev. **38**(2), 313–318 (2012). https://doi.org/10.1016/j.pubrev.2012.01.005

16. Saloner, G., Spence, A.M.: Creating and Capturing Value: Perspectives and Cases on Electronic Commerce. Wiley, New York (2002). https://doi.org/10.1093/oso/9780198816225.001.0001

17. Saxton, G.D., Guo, S.C., Brown, W.A.: New dimensions of nonprofit responsiveness: the application and promise of internet-based technologies. Public Perform. Manage. Rev. **31**(2), 144–173 (2007). https://doi.org/10.2753/pmr1530-9576310201

18. Hagiu, A., Wright, J.: Multi-sided platforms. Int. J. Ind. Organ. **43**, 162–174 (2015). https://doi.org/10.1016/j.ijindorg.2015.03.003

19. Katz, M.L., Shapiro, C.: Systems competition and network effects. J. Econ. Perspect. **8**(2), 93–115 (1994). https://doi.org/10.1257/jep.8.2.93

20. Mendelson, H.: Platform Business Models: Text and Case Studies. Electronic Business Case Collection, Kindle Edition (2017). https://www.amazon.com/Platform-Business-Models-Electronic-Collection-ebook/dp/B078H3CDW9

21. Rohlfs, J.: A theory of interdependent demand for a communications service. Bell J. Econ. Manage. Sci. 16–37 (1974). https://doi.org/10.2307/3003090

22. Economides, N., Himmelberg, C.P.: Critical mass and network size with application to the us fax market. NYU Stern School of Business EC-95-11 (1995). https://doi.org/10.2139/ssrn.6858

23. Brynjolfsson, E., Kemerer, C.F.: Network externalities in microcomputer software: an econometric analysis of the spreadsheet market. Manage. Sci. **42**(12), 1627–1647 (1996). https://doi.org/10.1287/mnsc.42.12.1627

24. Hannan, T.H., McDowell, J.M.: The determinants of technology adoption: the case of the banking firm. RAND J. Econ. 328–335 (1984). https://doi.org/10.2307/2555441

25. Lin, C.P., Bhattacherjee, A.: Elucidating individual intention to use interactive information technologies: the role of network externalities. Int. J. Electron. Commer. **13**(1), 85–108 (2008). https://doi.org/10.2753/JEC1086-4415130103

26. Madden, G., Grant, C.N., Dalzell, B.: A dynamic model of mobile telephony subscription incorporating a network effect. Telecommun. Policy, 133–144 (2004). https://doi.org/10.1016/j.telpol.2003.12.002
27. Asvanund, A., Clay, K., Krishnan, R., Smith, M.D.: An empirical analysis of network externalities in peer-to-peer music-sharing networks. Inf. Syst. Res. **15**(2), 155–174 (2004). https://doi.org/10.1287/isre.1040.0020
28. Feldman, M., Papadimitriou, C., Chuang, J., Stoica, I.: Free-riding and whitewashing in peer-to-peer systems. IEEE J. Sel. Areas Commun. **24**(5), 1010–1019 (2006). https://doi.org/10.1109/JSAC.2006.872882
29. Lloyd, B., Surana, M.: Online marketplaces for loans are growing rapidly. Should banks be worried? (2019). https://www.hardingloevner.com/fundamental-thinking/online-marketplaces-for-loans-are-growing-rapidly-should-banks-be-worried/. Accessed 05 July 2019
30. Kiva Blog: Expiring loans (2012). https://pages.kiva.org/blog/qa-expiring-loans-credit-limits-and-the-evolution-of-kiva
31. Kiva Blog: Supply and demand (2014). http://blog.kiva.org/supply-and-demand#findingtrouble
32. ICE Benchmark Administration Limited (IBA): ICE BofAML emerging markets corporate plus index effective yield [BAMLEMCBPIEY], Retrieved from FRED, Federal Reserve Bank of St. Louis (2019). https://fred.stlouisfed.org/series/BAMLEMCBPIEY
33. White, H.: A heteroskedasticity-consistent covariance matrix estimator and a direct test for heteroskedasticity. Econometrica **48**(4), 817–838 (1980). https://doi.org/10.2307/1912934
34. Pinker, E.J., Seidmann, A., Vakrat, Y.: Managing online auctions: current business and research issues. Manage. Sci. **49**(11), 1457–1484 (2003). https://doi.org/10.1287/mnsc.49.11.1457.20584

Methods and Models for Designing Information Technology

Modelling and Optimization of Wind Farms' Processes Using BPM

Vincenza Carchiolo[1]([✉]) [iD], Giovanni Catalano[3], Michele Malgeri[2] [iD],
Carlo Pellegrino[2], Giulio Platania[2], and Natalia Trapani[2] [iD]

[1] Dipartimento di Matematica ed Informatica, Universitá di Catania, Catania, Italy
vincenza.carchiolo@unict.it
[2] Dipartimento Ingegneria Elettrica Elettronica Informatica,
Universitá di Catania, Catania, Italy
{michele.malgeri,natalia.trapani}@unict.it
[3] Development and Support Center BaxEnergy - Acireale, Acireale, Italy
giovanni.catalano@baxenergy.it

Abstract. Business Process Management (BPM) is an accepted discipline and its importance for industrial automation is recognized by all players today. The complexity of modern management process will lead to chaos without a well-designed and effective BPM. Today, several tools exist, both commercial and open-source, but the selection of the appropriate tool for each organization could be a hard work. The first result of these research is a state-of-the-art of Intelligent Business Process Management Suites and a compared analysis of their features in order to choose the most suitable for processes' management in a renewable energy power plant. The second research finding is the expliting of BPMN approach to simplify the processes of a Wind Farm company. Process flow optimization had a positive impact both on processes' efficacy and efficiency and then on the business value proposition. A relevant result of the study was also the definition of some typical maintenance related processes and of maintenance management metrics based on specific KPIs.

Keywords: Supply chain · BPMS · Asset management ·
Maintenance · Renewable energy

1 Introduction

The complexity and variety of business models in modern companies require to face different challenges: e.g. spanning over different sites, strong time constraints, continue interchange with other companies and service. This make difficult to ensure a good quality together with a long durability of the final products either it is a physical product or a service [1]. Moreover, maintenance management has changed in the last decades thanks to ICT development. In last decades Computerized Maintenance Management System (CMMS) has contributed to

E. Ziemba (Ed.): AITM 2019/ISM 2019, LNBIP 380, pp. 95–115, 2020.
https://doi.org/10.1007/978-3-030-43353-6_6

enhance the control of maintenance activities [2] and maintenance is considered a relevant business function, able to interact with all other strategic functions. Maintenance modern challenges also require an evolution from CMMS to more complex but more efficient Asset Management Systems.

The correct definition of the business processes is the first step toward developing an efficient Asset Management System and to achieve an effective processes' automation   [3]. Thus, the adoption of a Business Process Modelling (BPM) framework that covers all phases from business process engineering to their analytic performance measurement is recognized, both in theory and in practice, as the best approach when a company have to manage different methods, processes and realms inside the same production flow.

BPMN 2.0 allow a logical description of business processes and shows how they operate focusing both on process implementation and process simulation [4,5]. BPM frameworks widely use *Business Process Diagrams* to describe processes; they look like flowcharts enriched by new elements that describe interactions, deadline, communications and several other concrete process elements. The diagrams capture a lot of information about the workflow and they allow to identify critical tasks during design or simulation allowing the supervisors and the managers to improve the process. Process engineering through Business Process Modelling and Notation (BPMN) allows to exactly know [6] in which phase the process currently is, to whom next phase is assigned, if an action is required (push/pull logic) to proceed, which phase can be considered a bottleneck and the values of the parameters useful to calculate Key Performance Indicators (KPI).

In literature, the use of the BPM approach for maintenance management is not so common [7,8]. However, most authors [9,10] suggest that an Asset Management System Software can help organizations to achieve operational excellence, through a more effective cost control, a more efficient asset planning, a reducing in capital expenses, an optimization of operational costs, thus extending asset life cycle and obtaining a higher Return On Asset.

This works discusses the design and development of a new BPM tool by the company BaxEnergy©, aimed at optimizing the maintenance of *renewable energy power plants*, to be offered as a service to their customers, which are renewable-energy production companies. Renewable-energy Power Plants face different challenges [11–13]:

- production units are usually spread over a large territories and they are quite difficult to reach, they are often characterized by high levels of automation and they are not locally supervised installations i.e. there is no personnel units on site;
- replacement parts are sometimes very big and expensive;
- maintenance management effectiveness, to a large extent, depends on knowledge of the managers and maintenance operators and on the effectiveness of internal and external collaborative environments;
- maintenance effectiveness is deeply studied according to Timeliness, Completeness and Accuracy quality requirements.

In such conditions, timely interventions and predictive maintenance are the only way to minimize downtime, optimize operations and obtain good operational performances (specifically high availability, reduced costs, long equipment lifetime, high labour safety, limited impact on environment, and best spare parts management).

The paper presents a comparison of commercially available BPM Suite at the moment of selection, the reasons that lead to the final choice of one of them and a case study to show how BPM was used for process engineering or re-engineering of operational and maintenance processes in a renewable energy production company.

Section 2 introduces BPMNs common features and Sect. 3 overviews several platform that was available at the moment of the study and compare them according to the criteria previously introduced. Finally, Sect. 4 discussed a case study developed using the selected platform.

2   BPMS Common Features

The principal users of BPMS are Software Developers, who works to add on-demand features and compatibility to APIs, and Business Process developers, who model Business Processes. Today, the vision is that even *"citizens"*, not Business process developers only, can develop Business Process so some companies developed the feature of *Citizen Developer Application Composition* [9] to be independent from IT staff and to speed up the process of modelling. BPMN 2.0 is the current standard that adds the following characteristics: *human-readability*, that is a standard visible notation for modelling processes; *accessibility*, that means that must be understandable to all actors; *machine-readability*, that implies the use of the XML notation for simulating and executing processes [6].

A BPMN system provides support during all the life cycle of a business process, from designing to management and optimization. It provides tools *to model* the system helping the developer to specify the behaviour of the system including the best practices and the production standard then it is possible to simulate in order to validate the model. Moreover, he/she can define some figures to measure the goal achievement – Key Goal Indicators (KGIs) – and the performance – Key Performance Indicators (KPIs). After development phase, BPMN supports the execution of the model in real environment, the monitoring of the process. Finally, it provides developers with a lot of information, gathered during both simulation and monitoring, useful to improve the whole process. Basically, BPMN is a graphically representation of the process that uses a set of standard symbol that can be easily understood by both developers and users [4], the most important are: *swim lane, pool, box, event, task.*

Swim Lane and Pool. The *swim lanes* enable to visually distinguish job sharing and responsibilities, they allow people to organize activities into separate visual categories in order to illustrate different functional capabilities or responsibilities; these contain one or more *pools* and at least one *lane* for pool.

We can assume that BPMN Pools describe whole organizations while BPMN Lanes describe who is executing a specific set of tasks.

The *pool* performs the coordination, in literature also called *orchestration*, of the process contained inside it. The pools are represented by rectangles with a label, usually horizontally positioned. There are two type of pools: *white box* where all process details are exposed and *black box* which hides its content, the latter is more used in *choreography* because it put the focus on the communication between pools.

Event. The *events*, represented by a circle, model something that happens every moment during the life cycle of the process (at the beginning, within, or at the end). The process can reacts to an event, that is the event triggers an action, or it *throws a result*. Each event belongs to a standard type, e.g. time-based, message-based, rule-based, signal-based, exception-based, etc.

Task. A fundamental element of BPMNs is certainly the *task*. It allows us to describe the action performed by the actors during process evolution. The most important types of task supported by the BPMN 2.0 are listed below:

- *normal task*: it is a single action that occurs in a business process, i.e. mailing a letter. Normal tasks are used to depict each of the activities. It is also called an "abstract" task, because its type is not specified;
- sub-processes: they are a subset of regular task types that favour simplicity. In a typical work environment, BPMN diagrams are used to communicate processes to stakeholders and developers alike. Stakeholders generally don't likes complexity as developers do, then sub-processes allow to collapse and expand tasks to quickly convey information to both groups. In BPMN exist different useful sub processes:
    - *Ad hoc*: this allows to group sub-processes whose exclusive purpose is to complete a piece of a process. For example, an ad hoc sub-process might deal with one vendor who has a unique payment system;
    - *loop*: it iterates something. The loop task signals your intention to repeatedly do something before a final action. To explain the conditions of the loop task, you might also add an annotation saying that you will continue to do an activity until another figure decide to stop it;
    - *multiple instance*: this happens multiple times. They can evolve either in parallel or sequentially. For instance, when more people want to work on an activity and give feedback, a multiple instance task is better than loop task. This task type permits to give reports on an activity to multiple people at the same time;
    - *compensation loop*: it makes compensation a recurring event;
- call activity: it is a global process that is used whenever a certain process needs to be implemented. Whenever the call activity notation is used, control of the process is pushed to the global predefined process;
- transactions: this activity is a specialized sub-process symbol that represents payment processes. All transaction activities are contained by a double line. Transactions must verify that all participants have completed their parts of the transaction before the sub-process can be completed.

Gateway. Another fundamental element needs to model dynamic behaviours is the *gateway*. It allows the designer to choose where the flow of a diagram must follow a path or another by evaluating a condition. Two types are defined in the standard: *XOR* or *Exclusive*. Gateway is the task that drives the evolution of a process by evaluating a condition and selecting the next task, *OR* or *Parallel* Gateway split the evolution into two parallel branches that must be joined with the same element when the evolution of the process does not support parallel activities.

3 Survey of BPMNs Platforms

According to the Gartner Magic Quadrant (Fig. 1), the most complete system is PegaSystems followed by Appian and IBM, however the peculiarities of green power management leads to different evaluation criteria.

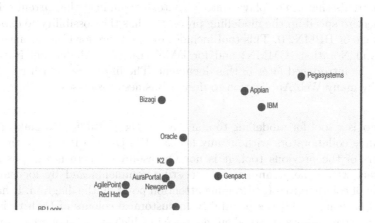

Fig. 1. Gartner's model of processes maturity [9]

The evaluation criteria used throughout this work are based on Critical Capabilities such as Interaction Management, Monitoring and Business Alignment, Rules and Decision Management, Analytic and they are evaluated on the base of some Use Cases. Great importance is given to Continuous Process Improvement (referred as CPI) and to Citizen Developer Application Composition (that is the ability to leave aside from IT development staff) [4].

3.1 BPMN Platforms

The adoption of BPMN is done by deploying or purchasing the service in the cloud of an Intelligent Business Process Management Suite, *iBPMs*. These are platforms, often hosted on a cloud, that supports the full cycle of process and decision discovery, analysis, design, implementation, execution, monitoring, and optimization. Such BPM suites support highly intelligent applications which integrate more-advanced decision automation technologies (e.g. predictive analytic, artificial intelligence) and decision support for knowledge workers to automate business processes that require an adaptive behaviour [4]. It means that actually *iBPMs* is not a simple modelling software or a validation engine for BPMN, but it both bounds and integrates other functionalities that keeps track of statistics and, sometimes, let even the user to define performance indicators.

BPMN.IO is a tool for modelling process diagrams [14]. It can be embedded into new application, because it is Opensource and there is the possibility to fork the project on GitHub. However, it is just a tool for modelling and visualizing BPMN diagrams into Web Browsers and it have neither the possibility to collaborate in team to modify the same diagram nor the possibility to collaborate by sharing comments or by focusing a point of the process. About available Functionality-based criteria, BPMN.IO has a Drag&Drop feature and some shortcuts that are displayed into a Context Menu near the current selected component to speed up the modelling process. It has the possibility to export as SVG image or BPMN2.0. This tool includes even editors for Case Management Model and Notation (CMMN) and for DMN (Decision Model and Notation) that will be introduced later in this document. The library on which it is based is used by many Web Application to design Business Processes.

Cawemo is a tool for modelling too, and it has the possibility to make a team up to three collaborators without any license [15]. Despite it is from the same producers of the previous tool, it is not Opensource. There is the possibility to interact with other teammates by posting comments and by focusing the attention of collaborators by dropping attention point on the diagram. It has the Drag&Drop feature and the possibility to customize colours of both tasks and events. Every user has a personal online space in which can load or create his own models or share it with other users: in this way the work can be better organized. Finally, it can share a diagram by public link to invite even collaborators that are not registered to Cawemo and it can export as PDF, PNG or BPMN2.0.

Camunda is an Opensource execution engines for BPMN workflows and DMN decisions paired with essential applications for process automation projects [16]. It has a community and developers can find solution even on StackOverflow. It is available license-free the Community Edition that provides all the necessary Software Modules. The Enterprise License unlocks all the features of Cockpit and the Optimize module. The Community edition provides tools to monitor workflows and analyze technical problems while Enterprise Edition allows to create reports and to configure alerts when performance goals are missed. The Camunda Engine does support diagram written in BPMN2.0 notation. It runs inside Tomcat and can be used with a Web Browser. It provides three main functionality: To start processes and to communicate with Camunda engine, a

REST API is provided, so it is only necessary to have a REST Client to run processes and to pass JSON object to the Software: thanks to REST API, this software allows the developer to integrate Camunda with its own tools or to develop other services that can integrate with that.

- *Admin* to manage Roles for various activities and to list the users saved in this session, to list groups of users and to control the execution metrics and so on.
- *Cockpit* that shows the number of running processes, the number of process definition available, the decision tables, the human tasks and several details about deployment of process instances.
- *Tasklist* that manages task creation, monitoring and assignment to user.

The developer can even builds automated workers for Service/Script Tasks using NodeJS or Java EE with a publisher-subscriber/Long Polling pattern.

Camunda's Modeler is a stand-alone application based on BPMN.IO library and includes other tools from the same producer to make the design workflow more flexible by the use of DMN and CMMN. It can export diagrams into various image format and into BPMN2.0. There is an integrated editor for forms. It does not support the online team working during the development of diagrams. Camunda supports templates only for Service Tasks and Process versioning by only changing a line of code when starting an instance or by changing properties of a process model before launching it.

The UI of the Web Application is easy to use: it allows to start and kill processes and to assign users to each task. Each time the admin starts a process, the web application sends a REST call to the Engine that will deploy it; once started the process can be monitored by navigating the UI and the user can check status of process variables.

Simulation of processes is not directly supported by Camunda, but the community provides various tools to simulate and to check KPIs in Process design.

Bizagi is not opensource and it provides three software modules that can be integrated with Cloud services: Modeler, Studio and Engine [17]. The first two are free to use. It has a dedicated Community for Bizagi Modeler and Studio. In the modeler there are a rich variety of exporting formats for the BPMN Diagrams and it is compliant to the BPMN2.0 Standard. Two kind of API, SOAP Web Service and Data services, allows to retrieve information from Bizagi and all of his background data. There are available several Business2Business connectors to use Bizagi with other online tools and an Integration Layer that allow to call Web Services from a process instance. Bizagi Modeler can be integrated with Cloud Services to collaborate online, but this feature is not available with the free license. Bizagi has a library for process templates and it allows the creation of documents (e.g. Word, Excel, Pdf) that are filled with information coming from the business process. The Modeler has the ability to holds previous version of a process diagram to support Process Versioning. The UI is simple to use, it has the Drag&Drop feature for designing process diagrams and in the Wizard of Bizagi Studio there is an editor for customizing.

Bizagi Engine is the module that allows to deploy the process diagram. It is possible to simulate and test diagrams using Bizagi Studio and the Bizagi Engine Software, however, to enable versioning. Once a model has been saved and published there is the possibility to validate and to debug the model: this allows to monitor in real time a process instance while it is in run and is the equivalent of the simulation without statistical results. As Bizagi, Appian provides a feature that allows to fill documents template with process data while the process instance is running. There are some process diagrams ready to use as templates.

Appian has a patented GUI called SAIL, that stands for Self-Assembling Interface Layer, that allow a user to customize the information that will be shown in a dashboard for a particular process [18]. Therefore, Appian has a mobile UI that allow field operators to execute tasks and receive notification while on site. Appian Cloud architecture offers key reliability features, including data redundancy, high availability, and disaster recovery. Plus, Appian Cloud gives organizations the ability to create a secure Virtual Private Network (VPN) with strong algorithms for data encryption and isolation. The admin must create records for each user giving a temporary password that will be changed at the first login: each user can be assigned to a group to give some privileges.

Activiti is an opensource BPMS. Its latest version is now on container image and it is possible to deploy on a cloud [19]. It has a Web Modeler but it lacks the possibility to simulate process instances. The admin can create new users and assign them to groups. Activiti supports process and model versioning, but it does not allow to validate, test or debug a model. It cannot collaborate online during the development of a diagram even if there is the possibility to share modelled diagrams with other users. The Visual Editor of Activiti has the possibility to export/import in BPMN2.0 the modelled process.

IBM Business Process Management on Cloud is one of the most competitive on the market, basing on the analysis reported in [9], It is not license free or Open Source [20].

There are several modules available:

- *Process center* that allows to manage, model and modify process diagrams, services and GUI.
- *Process Portal* that allows to execute tasks and starts process instances.
- *IU REST* where REST API can be used to retrieve information from server and to get a list of all the services that can run.
- *Process admin Console* that allows admin to monitor the instances of processes.

The modeler is online, and it has the Drag&Drop feature. For the creation of GUI there are many options to customize the appearance on different screen sizes. The modeller can decide to expose some variables and can decide to who these variables can be exposed by accessing the Admin Console. Once the process has been modelled, it can be run and debugged before making it available to be instantiated. Process and model versioning is supported with a mechanism called "Snapshots". Forms and User friendly User Interfaces are generated by Coach that is composed by "coach views" that are user interface widgets.

JBPM is a tool supported by RedHat, based on jBoss now called Wildfly, that is an application server [21]. It is open source and can be deployed on the cloud thanks to the container images for Docker. There are two possibility to model processes: Eclipse Neon, that will be installed along with jBPM unless otherwise specified, and an online modeller. Since the modeler is integrated in Eclipse Neon, it has the Drag&Drop feature, and, more important, the IDE itself is Open Source, so it is easy to add new plugins. Unfortunately, the possibility to collaborate online with the Eclipse editor is not available. jBPM workbench supports the entire Life cycle of a business process: from designing online or offline to the deploying for use as a blueprint for process instances. There are four functionalities: Design, Deploy, Manage and Track. The versioning system works with commits, this makes it very simple to use. There is a tool for validation that will help to track errors in BPM notation and a tool for simulation. Also this Suite expose a REST API to start processes and retrieve information from the System.

KissFlow is not an OpenSource Suite, it has a sort of Wizard that drives users along the Workflow to define tasks in a process [22]. As the creators of the platform state, this platform was designed for workflows, repetitive actions that involve more persons, not for task management. This platform is very user-friendly, forms, workflows and all tasks can be easily modified. Unfortunately, is not possible to simulate processes and there is no integration between WS or other scripts. Most of the elements are predefined and cannot be changed and there is no possibility to customize it. Finally, it is not BPMN2.0 compatible.

QuickFlow is a BPMS that allows to track and manage the four stages of standard life-cycle of a BPM project [23]. It is integrated with SalesForce and it is not stand-alone. It is not an open source project. It uses standard BPMN2.0 notation and it relies on the data model from Salesforce to change the state of objects involved in a process. QuickFlow tools are web-based. The Support to the editing of Forms is well done and is one of the two way to interact with Humans. Even if Forms are not so modern like in other tested BPMS, they are functional and pretty fast to create. The implementation of Service Tasks can be done by predefined methods. The user must only map process variables to data variables of "Datas" created before the creation of a process. Then the integration with services given by SalesForce is available.

3.2   Evaluation Criteria

There is no doubt that some interesting features for a Software developer are meaningless by the point of view of a Business Process developer, and are even more meaningless for a standard employee, therefore the evaluation Criteria are grouped into two classes.

The first group deals with the feature useful to software developers, the most important are as follows:

- *OpenSource*, software suite refers to open source model, that means that products are released under an open source license, this feature allows to inspect the source and to add any additional features;
- *Community*, the community supporting the software suite should be as large as possible to share problems and their solutions. A large community implies Documentation and Tutorial are easy to find and this is useful both for software and model developers;
- *BPMN 2.0 supported*, this is a must for any new software, since today BPMN 2.0 standard is largely supported;
- *Additional modules and connectors*, they permits to extend the functionality of the Software and to write new custom connectors;
- *API provided*, this can be useful to easily add functionalities to the BPMS.
- *Innovation*, of course, it is important that software solution supports all recent technologies and methodologies but it must be also "mature" (according, for instance, with Gartner Magic Quadrant [9]). Some examples of innovative features are mobile device deployment without the need to develop a dedicated application, low-code Platforms, integration with Artificial Intelligence for performance metrics and so on;

Second group of features, that we call *Functionality-based evaluation criteria*, belongs to Business Process Developers that focus on the processes themselves and, usually, have no specific experience in software development. They need to model, describe and test production processes aiming at optimizing them according to some metrics (e.g. cost, duration, response time) often conflicting. The most important are listed below:

- *Web Modeler/Collaboration enabled*, it enables collaboration between developers;
- *Template Library*, the presence of a library of reusable models is a valuable add-on to any Suite;
- *Model and Process Versioning*, since processes run for long times, the ability to control the current version of Models and the ability to roll back to a previous version are very useful;
- *Powerful graphic interface*, the interface should support advanced interface functions as, for instance, Drag&Drop of models/processes, Form Editing that allows final users to create and edit data, to customize the colours of element in a diagram to make it more readable;

- *Process deployment*, the system should allows to make an instance of the modelled process to check errors and to locate performance indicators or failures;
- *Testing and Simulation*, the presence of an engine for simulating the process and/or validate the model is an essential feature;
- *Customizable Properties*, that means the ability to change the properties of the trial modelling tool.
- *Business rule engine and activity Monitoring*, possibility to integrate business rules for the process and to monitor the execution of a process;
- *Integration with Cloud*: since some BPMS are integrated with cloud service, it is important to support the integration between BPMS and Cloud.
- *Role Based Security*, that allows to manage of the security rules for each role.

Table 1. Evaluation criteria (development and functionality)

	OpenSource	Community	Innovation	API
(a) Criteria related to development				
BPMN.IO	Y	–	Y	–
Cawemo	–	–	Y	–
Camunda	Y	Y	Y	Y
Bizagi	–	Y	Y	Y
Appian	–	Y	Y	Y
Activiti	Y	Y	Y	Y
IBM	–	Y	Y	Y
jBPM	Y	Y	Y	Y
KissFlow	–	Y	Y	Y
QuickFlow	–	–	–	–

	Web functions	Versioning	Testing & Simulation	Monitoring
(b) Criteria related to functionality				
BPMN.IO	P (Partial)	–	–	–
Cawemo	P	–	–	–
Camunda	Y	Y	P	Y
Bizagi	Y	Y	Y	Y
Appian	Y	Y	Y	Y
Activiti	Y	Y	–	Y
IBM	Y	Y	Y	Y
jBPM	Y	Y	Y	Y
KissFlow	Y	–	–	–
QuickFlow	Y	–	–	(SalesForce)

Table 1 summarizes some of the characteristics of the tools at the time of analysis. Since the use of an open source platform covering all the process, from development to monitoring, exposing a flexible ReST API to integrate easier with existing software are the most important requisites the selected platform was Camunda. The lack of the capability to simulate processes is overcome thanks to the a great support of Javascript libraries that can be integrated with no effort.

4   Case Study

4.1   Description of the Project

The case study was developed in an Austrian company that focuses on wind power projects: some projects let the company produce electrical power by itself in wind turbine farms, others are developed in cooperation with investors or partners. They deal with operations and maintenance processes of wind turbine farms. Wind farms are clusters of wind turbines that produce large amounts of electricity. A wind farm usually has many turbines scattered over a large area: a large wind farm may have several individual wind turbines and may cover an area of hundreds of square miles.

Wind turbines surely present lots of challenges in relation to maintenance and requires large investments. The challenge increase when wind turbines are installed in remote locations. Harsh climate conditions are often present during routine or planned inspections. Therefore, monitoring and diagnostics plays an important role in competitive operation of wind farms (Power Engineering, 2018). Another characteristic of wind turbine is that inspections are required several times a year and repairs often need to go up about 100 m in the air: such elements require that wind turbine maintenance force should be specifically trained. Moreover, owners and maintenance service providers are conscious that preventive maintenance is worthy more than corrective maintenance actions, both from business continuity and from costs point of view. That is why considerable efforts are being made to forecast failures, minimize downtime and optimize maintenance processes. As it was previously discussed, BPM allows modelling and, through the analysis of bottlenecks, optimization of processes in order to better meet the strategic goal of a company.

4.2   Process Re-engineering

The company has 92 relevant processes, classified into two maintenance processes' categories: *Core processes*, in which are considered technical activities, and *Support processes*, related to organizational and financial activities. Within them a subset of 39 processes were selected as they are the most frequently activated and because of their relevance also for other companies in the same business sector. Using the same criteria other ten maintenance related core-processes were implemented in order to guarantee better maintenance performance. An asset and operation management tool for wind farms becomes essential for organizing work, keeping track of data and information and sharing them with actors involved. For example, in the process *Budgeting* a supervisor (financing/-controlling) of the process needs to receive some additional information before going on with next task. In this case, the supervisor has to do two actions (Fig. 2): (1) Perform a *send task* to ask for additional data, or (2) to receive data from the *financial controller* of the process.

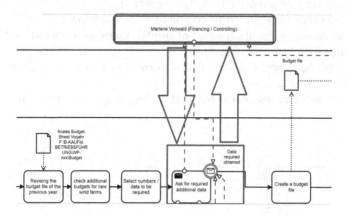

Fig. 2. Collaboration between actors of a process

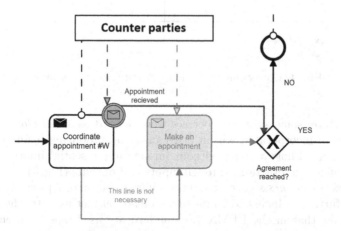

Fig. 3. Process simplification: red elements are deleted and purple are added (color figure online)

Considering the BPMN 2.0 standard it was found that some elements of the company's processes are used incorrectly or that some flows are too much complex. A first revision of the modelled processes allowed to increase the general comprehension of process workflows, by the company. In particular, it consisted in the elimination of not-added value tasks through the reduction of bureaucracy and elimination of duplicated tasks, the use of a simpler language to identify tasks, and the implementation of an Asset Management System, in order to obtain activities standardization, task automation (when it was possible), tracing and tracking of maintenance actions, more efficient maintenance scheduling plans and, thus, generating reduction in time for executing a task and also in asset downtime. Moreover, to follow the correct logic of BPMN 2.0:

- The use of *send* and *receive* task was corrected;
- Some *End event* were added to complete some workflows;
- Some *Intermediate* events instead of useless tasks were introduced in order to simplify some process (Fig. 3);
- Some *script tasks* were modified into *normal tasks* (because scripts will be added in a future phase);
- The use of *gateway* was corrected and useless ones were eliminated (Fig. 4):

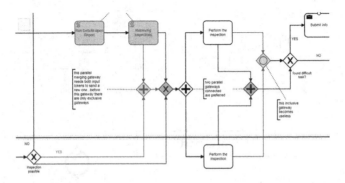

Fig. 4. Correction of the flow sequence using gateways

Furthermore, some specific processes were deleted as *stand-alone processes* and they were incorporated within other ones, by producing a unique layout representing the whole activity without missing any essential information and better visualizing interactions through inputs and outputs (Fig. 5).

This *process synthesis* generated a total incorporation of 7 process into other ones, thus further reducing to 26 processes out of 39. Let us note, the presence of *swim lanes* that in the BPMN 2.0 standard are used mostly to enable the collaboration between core and supporting elements of the processes, and that was used in the case study to create an interaction between pools and collapsed pools inside the processes.

The company used the interaction between actors also to support the BPM system in communications with the ticket system, e.g. if a user wants to create a ticket while performing a part of a process, it can send a message to the ticket system for opening a ticket. Thanks to the BPM system, that will be implemented in the asset management system, this use of send/receive tasks is no more necessary (Fig. 6a) but it requires just a simple task in the asset management system (Fig. 6b). In this way, there is a reduction of about 70

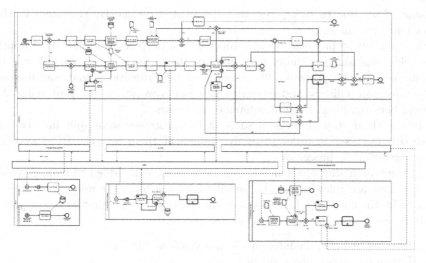

Fig. 5. Audit synthesis

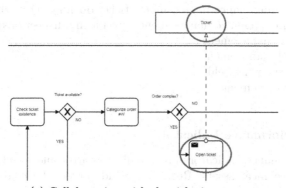

(a) Collaboration with the ticketing system

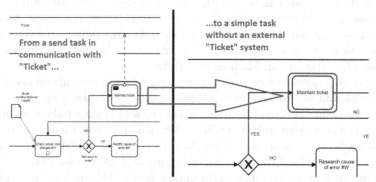

(b) From ticket system to a simple task

Fig. 6. Ticket system

message flows due to ticket system implemented on the BPM system in the asset management system.

These relevant processes were subjected to a deep revision in order to optimize elements and workflows and simplify them. Such a revision allowed to eliminate from the processes 26 phases and 106 transitions that was useless, obtaining more efficacy and efficiency in process workflow and improving the general performances of the maintenance processes.

In the third step of revision some of the processes were split into two or more sub-processes in order to easily implement them into the BPM system, thus generating 31 processes.

In the fourth step some maintenance processes were added to manage some aspects that are relevant for the specific business but that never were implemented by the company. In particular, the following topics that were not previously covered, were introduced in specific processes:

1. Planning ordinary maintenance's intervention (Fig. 7a);
2. Human resources management
3. Warehouse management with spare parts and consumables;
4. Personnel qualification management to meet normative requirements;
5. Corrective maintenance management (ticket opening) (Fig. 7b);
6. Predictive maintenance management (specifically inspections) (Fig. 7c);
7. Asset status management
8. Service level management
9. Maintenance on the field
10. Logistics management

4.3   Key Performance Indicators

The Key Performance Indicators are useful to control and eventually improve utilization of technical assets. Regarding wind power, the competitiveness is increasing together with the reduction the cost of electricity.

The section in which KPIs have the biggest role is surely the wind turbine maintenance and the most influencing factors are certainly economical, technical and organizational. Maintenance performance indicators reflect achievement and progresses in meeting a goal; clearly, the greater is the installed capacity the higher are Operational and Maintenance costs.

In measuring maintenance performances, the focus in not only on good maintenance work, but also on capability of maintenance activities in removing risk of failures from plant. This requires a mix of lagging and leading indicators in order to obtain a clear understanding of what is happening to performance of physical assets through maintenance activities. To better understand what it means it is of worthy to understand the meaning of lagging and leading indicators.

Leading indicators measure performance before the maintenance process results starts to follow a particular trend and monitor if maintenance activities are producing good results in a long-term period. An example *Preventive Maintenance (PM) Completion Rate*: a low completion rate for PM would generate

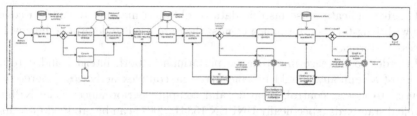

(a) Planning ordinary maintenance's intervention

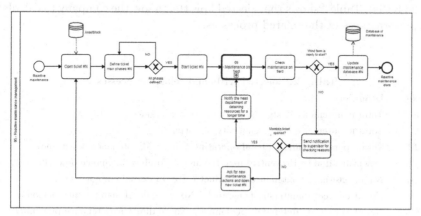

(b) Corrective Maintenance Management Process

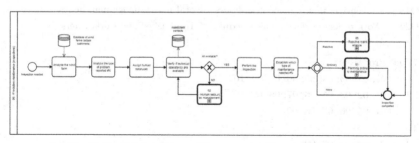

(c) Predictive Maintenance Management Process (inspection)

Fig. 7. Example of new processes

an increasing in asset maintenance work while a high completion rate means that asset preventive maintenance request is correctly being completed and, probably, future corrective maintenance requests will be reduced. Another example is the *Outage Schedule Compliance* an important metric to track future maintenance work because it allows to measure deferred asset maintenance, resulting in an increased risks and likelihood that asset performance will decrease at a future time, leading to lower capacity, increased downtime, and greater expenses.

Lagging indicators use historic data to obtain a measure to confirm coherence with long-term performance trends; they are used to determine how well a process performs.

In order to increase maintenance performance, both internal and external factors of a company should be considered as complex activities. Therefore is essential to assess, control, measure and compare performances. The KPIs in technical standards (specifically UNI EN 15341: 2007) can be grouped into three categories: *economical* (E, 21 KPIs), *technical* (T, 21 KPIs) and *organizational* (O, 26 KPIs). Table 2 shows the selected kpis that allow the company to calculate the performances of the related processes.

Table 2. Selected KPIs and related processes

Name	Definition
E1	Total maintenance costs / Asset, replacement value
E3	Total maintenance cost / Quantity of output
T1	Total operating time / (Total operating time + Maintenance downtime)
T8	Downtime due to Preventive maintenance / Total Maintenance downtime
O1	No. of internal maintenance personnel / Total internal employees
O2	No. of indirect maintenan. personnel / No. of internal maintenance personnel
O3	No. of indirect maintenance personnel / No. of direct maintenance personnel
O16	Corrective maintenance man-hours / Total maintenance man-hours
O18	Preventive maintenance man-hours / Total maintenance man-hours
O22	Work orders performed as scheduled / Total scheduled work orders

Type	Processes
E1	01; 02; 03; 04; 05; 06; 07; 09; 10
E3	01; 02; 03; 05; 06; 07; 08; 09; 10
T1	01; 05; 06; 07; 08; 09
T8	06; 09
O1	01; 02; 05; 06; 09
O2	01; 02; 05; 06; 09
O3	01; 02; 05; 06; 09
O16	01; 05; 06; 09
O18	01; 05; 06; 09
O22	01; 02; 05; 09

5   Conclusions

This paper discusses all the development stages applied to a specific case: it presents the criteria adopted by the company to select the BPMN tool, then, it presents the analysis of the company's original processes, finally, it shows the implementation discussing some of the most important processes. The comparison of different tools lead us to define a set of criteria to compare the platforms taking into account both the literature and the specific needs typical of the company's characteristics.

This study gives a contribute to the state-of-the-art analysis of iBPMs in the specific area of the companies working in Green Energy production business. This paper aims at highlighting the effectiveness of iBPM in the context of Wind Farm productions holding peculiar features as very large and distributed production area, difficulty to reach the production units, very high cost of the spare parts, and also human and technological factors as weather conditions, personnel availability and events such as logistics, administrative or technical. All factors and features can change in an unpredictable way the process performances. Although in literature it is possible to find BPMN applications and examples, no discussion about the use of BPMN 2.0 into asset management tools of Wind Production Farms for efficiently control exists, at least not to our knowledge. The study provides a practical examples of BPMN use to efficiently monitor and share information among all actors involved in the context of Energy production. More specifically, the paper deeply discusses the matter of maintenance management of wind turbines.

The introduction of BPMN 2.0 into asset management tools, according to the presented case study, increased the knowledge management and allowed them to implement a system of KPIs that can be extended to physical assets' management of industrial plants. Moreover, the Energy production management, mainly from Wind, today stands at the heart of industrial and public attention and this paper aim at providing a contribute to make more efficient the process regardless from specific country or regional peculiarities. The developed BPM system allows us the definition and execution of management processes within renewable energy power plant, simplifying relations among company functions, introducing standard activities for each process, assigning tasks to users, eliminating non added value phases thus providing an overall reduction of downtime of wind turbines, procurement optimisation due to higher efficiency in warehousing, human resources management, maintenance cost reduction.

Further research regards the definition of specific metrics mainly to obtain real time monitoring and the analysis of the data coming from reports. In order to further reduce the maintenance costs, the use of Artificial Intelligent (AI) methodologies to analyze the massive amount of data will allows to perform predictive analysis to better anticipate, for instance, failures, production's peaks, weather forecast.

References

1. The Institute of Asset Management: IAM asset management maturity guide v1.1. Technical report, The Institute of Asset Management, June 2016. http://www.theiam.org/

2. Trapani, N., Macchi, M., Fumagalli, L.: Risk driven engineering of prognostics and health management systems in manufacturing. IFAC-PapersOnLine **48**(3), 995–1000 (2015). http://www.sciencedirect.com/science/article/pii/S2405896315004528. 15th IFAC Symposium on Information Control Problems in Manufacturing. https://doi.org/10.1016/j.ifacol.2015.06.213

3. Reliabilityweb.com: Research report on asset management practices, investments and challenges 2014–2019. Technical report (2015). https://reliabilityweb.com/articles/entry/asset_management_practices_investments_and_challenges_2014-2019/. Accessed 10 May 2019

4. Allweyer, T.: BPMN 2.0: Introduction to the Standard for Business Process Modeling. Books on Demand (2016). https://books.google.it/books?id=sowaDAAAQBAJ

5. Gabryelczyk, R.: Exploring BPM adoption factors: insights into literature and experts knowledge. In: Ziemba, E. (ed.) AITM/ISM -2018. LNBIP, vol. 346, pp. 155–175. Springer, Cham (2019). https://doi.org/10.1007/978-3-030-15154-6_9

6. Ciaramella, A., Cimino, M.G., Lazzerini, B., Marcelloni, F.: Using BPMN and tracing for rapid business process prototyping environments, pp. 206–212 (2009). https://doi.org/10.5220/0002005002060212

7. Jasiulewicz-Kaczmarek, M., Waszkowski, R., Piechowski, M., Wyczółkowski, R.: Implementing BPMN in maintenance process modeling. In: Świątek, J., Borzemski, L., Wilimowska, Z. (eds.) ISAT 2017. AISC, vol. 656, pp. 300–309. Springer, Cham (2018). https://doi.org/10.1007/978-3-319-67229-8_27

8. Carchiolo, V., Catalano, G., Malgeri, M., Pellegrino, C., Platania, G., Trapani, N.: BPM tools for asset management in renewable energy power plants. In: Proceedings of the 2019 Federated Conference on Computer Science and Information Systems, FedCSIS 2019, pp. 645–649 (2019). https://doi.org/10.15439/2019F110

9. Gartner: Magic quadrant for intelligent business process management suites. Technical report. Gartner (2019). https://www.gartner.com/en/documents/3899484. Accessed 10 May 2019

10. IBM Corporation: Understanding the impact and value of enterprise asset management. Technical report (2016). https://www.ibm.com/downloads/cas/XJRD7M1Z. Accessed 10 May 2019

11. Accenture: The future of onshore wind operations and maintenance. Technical report. Accenture (2017). https://www.accenture.com/us-en/insight-future-onshore-wind-operations-maintenance. Accessed 10 May 2019

12. Shafiee, M., Sørensen, J.D.: Maintenance optimization and inspection planning of wind energy assets: models, methods and strategies. Reliab. Eng. Syst. Saf. **192**, 105993 (2019). https://doi.org/10.1016/j.ress.2017.10.025

13. Wang, J., Zhao, X., Guo, X.: Optimizing wind turbine's maintenance policies under performance-based contract. Renewable Energy **135**, 626–634 (2019). https://doi.org/10.1016/j.renene.2018.12.006

14. BPMN.io. https://bpmn.io/. Accessed 04 Dec 2019

15. Business process modeling. https://cawemo.com/. Accessed 04 Dec 2019

16. Workflow and decision automation platform. https://camunda.com/. Accessed 04 Dec 2019

17. Bizagi - digital process automation and BPM. https://bizagi.com/. Accessed 04 Dec 2019

18. Appian: low-code enterprise application development. https://www.appian.com/. Accessed 04 Dec 2019

19. Open sourcebusiness automation. https://www.activiti.org/. Accessed 04 Dec 2019

20. Han, Y.B., Sun, J.Y., Wang, G.L., Li, H.F.: A cloud-based BPM architecture with user-end distribution of non-compute-intensive activities and sensitive data. J. Comput. Sci. Technol. **25**(6), 1157–1167 (2010). https://doi.org/10.1007/s11390-010-9396-z
21. jBPM - open source business automation toolkit. https://www.jbpm.org. Accessed 04 Dec 2019
22. Kissflow - digital workplace. https://kissflow.com/. Accessed 04 Dec 2019
23. Quickflow - business agility in the cloud. http://www.quickflows.com/html/solutions.html. Accessed 04 Dec 2019

Multi-criteria Approach to Planning of Information Spreading Processes Focused on Their Initialization with the Use of Sequential Seeding

Artur Karczmarczyk[1], Jarosław Wątróbski[2](✉), and Jarosław Jankowski[1]

[1] Faculty of Computer Science and Information Technology, West Pomeranian University of Technology in Szczecin, Żołnierska 49, 71-210 Szczecin, Poland
{artur.karczmarczyk,jaroslaw.jankowski}@zut.edu.pl
[2] University of Szczecin, Mickewicza 64, 71-101 Szczecin, Poland
jaroslaw.watrobski@usz.edu.pl

Abstract. Information spreading within social networks and techniques related to viral marketing has begun to attract more interest of online marketers. While much of the prior research focuses on increasing the coverage of the viral marketing campaign, in real-life applications also other campaign goals and limitations need to be considered, such as limited time or budget, or assumed dynamics of the process. This paper presents a multi-criteria approach to planning of information spreading processes, with focus on the campaign initialization with the use of sequential seeding. A framework and example set of criteria was proposed for evaluation of viral marketing campaign strategies. The initial results showed that an increase of the count of seeding iterations and the interval between them increases the achieved coverage at the cost of increased process duration, yet without the need to increase seeding fraction or to provide incentives for increased propagation probability.

Keywords: Social networks · Complex networks · Viral marketing campaign planning · Viral marketing campaign evaluation · MCDA · TOPSIS · Sequential seeding

1 Introduction

Social media platforms have evolved from early stage technical systems to widely used online platforms with integrated mechanics of their users' interactions close to the real world [1–3]. Marketers have turned their focus on social networks due to the fact that the trust users give to their fellow users result in better information propagation than traditional marketing communication methods. This, in turn, results in possibility to obtain high information coverage in the network with relatively slow advertising budgets, which apart from theoretical studies, was presented for real viral campaigns [4–6].

ⓒ Springer Nature Switzerland AG 2020
E. Ziemba (Ed.): AITM 2019/ISM 2019, LNBIP 380, pp. 116–134, 2020.
https://doi.org/10.1007/978-3-030-43353-6_7

The up-to-date research focuses on increasing coverage [7], information spreading processes dynamics [8,9] and coverage prediction [10]. The information spreading processes are studied on complex networks of static and dynamic nature [11–13]. Moreover, there is research on modifying the structure of the network to increase the coverage [14–16].

Researchers can base their studies on real network models, which can be obtained from numerous network repositories. However, the availability of real network models is limited, sometimes outdated, or the information about the network nodes is limited. Therefore, oftentimes theoretic models are used to produce synthetic networks for research. These networks are parametrised, which allows to focus the research efforts on particular characteristics of the network. The theoretical models used most often are Barabasi-Albert [17], Watts-Strogatz [18] and Erdos-Renyi [19]. Moreover, a prior research exists based on samples and partially observed networks [20,21].

Viral marketing campaigns, from practical point of view, are often based on various strategies to achieve the assumed campaign goals. Although the majority of research in this field focuses on maximising the number of nodes infected in the network (i.e. increasing coverage), the actual goals and means of the marketer might vary [22]. Whilst full network coverage with the information would be an ideal outcome of the campaign, the limited campaign budget and time might render such outcome unfeasible. Different marketing campaign strategy would be selected for obtaining immense count of potential clients in short period of time, and different when the marketer aims at slow yet steady development of the customer base [23]. For these reasons, tools for planning and evaluating viral marketing campaigns are needed [24]. Approaches based on multi-criteria decision analysis (MCDA) methods proved to be useful for assessing which strategy, based on what parameters' values, would best accomplish the goals of particular campaigns [25,26].

The authors' prior research studied the possibility to reduce the computational complexity of viral marketing campaign planning with the use of theoretical models and network samples. Moreover, it was demonstrated in [27] that re-initialising the campaign multiple times for yet-uninfected initial nodes (seeds) allows to increase the final coverage compared to the traditional approach at the cost of increasing duration of the process, compared to the traditional one-off approaches. Whilst such innovative approach would not be satisfactory for campaign goals focused on achieving high coverage within shortest possible time span, it can bring promising effects for campaign goals focused on maximizing coverage or extending the duration of the company's appearance in the social media. Therefore, in this paper, the authors have extended the parameters' set from [28] with the criteria of count of seeding iterations and the interval between them.

This paper consists of five main sections. After this introduction, a literature review is presented in Sect. 2, followed by the methodological framework in Sect. 3. Section 4 presents the empirical study of the proposed framework and discusses the obtained results. Eventually, the conclusions and possible future works are presented in Sect. 5.

2   Literature Review

Social media platforms collect information on user behaviour and social relations in order to better address marketing campaigns. Social networks can be used as a tool using social influence mechanisms [29, 30] to spread information among acquaintances and, in next hops, their acquaintances and so on. Social networks have been used in parliament elections in Poland [31] or presidential elections in USA [32]. Due to its complex nature, the research on information propagation in complex networks is based on interdisciplinary efforts from fields such as sociology, computer studies, physics and management, based on various theoretical and practical foundations and goals [33].

In order to profoundly study the processes of information diffusion in complex networks, often theoretic models and sample real networks are used and implemented in agent-based environments. The methodological background is often based on models such as SIR and SIS, invented in order to study epidemics [34]. The diffusion process is often verified from the microscopic level with the use of linear threshold [30] and independent cascades [35, 36] models.

The majority of research on information propagation in complex networks is founded on the selection of the initial clients in the form of seeds. These clients are provided with product samples or other marketing materials with a hope that they will pass the information about the product to their acquaintances in the network [7]. This problem is NP-hard, but some greedy solutions exist, which provide relatively good results, but at high computational cost [35]. More practical solutions are based on heuristic approaches, where the seeds are selected based on centrality measures such as degree, betweenness, page rank, eigenvector or closeness [37].

Moreover, the knowledge about information propagation in given network can be collected and reused in that network for improving the characteristics of the information propagation process. The literature review resulted in finding some adaptive approaches [38], spreading the seeds over time in order to better use the natural information diffusion process [39], voting mechanics [40] or k-shell based approach [41].

On the other hand, there are approaches which instead of focusing on the initial seeds, try to increase the incentives provided to the network users in order to motivate the subsequent users on the information propagation process to pass the information further in the network (increasing the propagation probability) [42].

The authors' prior study showed that viral marketing campaigns can be planned with the use of significantly smaller theoretical models. Although the used synthetic networks were much smaller and less computationally complex, the correlation coefficient of the results on the synthetic network and the real network exceeded the value of 0.9. The literature review shows that the viral campaign strategy evaluation criteria utilised in [28] can be further extended with sequential seeding [43]. More than a single seeding iteration can occur. Moreover, the seeding iterations can either follow each other without breaks, or be dispersed over the campaign with a specified interval. This, in turn, states an interesting research question, if extending the decision model for selection of viral marketing campaign strategies with these new parameters would allow for better adjustment of the campaign to the marketers' needs.

3   Research Methodology

Viral marketing campaigns can be based on various strategy. During the campaign planning stage, decisions need to be made regarding the fraction of the nodes that need to be initially infected (seeds), how these nodes should be selected, what incentives should be provided to the network members to increase the information propagation probability, to name just a few. The values of the aforementioned parameters are adjusted based on the overall goals of the planned campaign. Certainly, different campaign efficiency metrics would be expected when maximal coverage is desired, than when the campaign ordering party is most focused on making the campaign last as long as possible.

Mappings of real networks, as well as theoretical models having structure similar to the real networks, allow researchers to use tools such as the independent cascades model in order to evaluate various campaign strategies prior to the actual campaign execution and to choose the one which best accommodates the campaign goals. Nonetheless, evaluations based on the real network models are complex computationally. Accordingly, it is often worth to conduct the study and simulations on significantly smaller (e.g. 10%, 30%, 50% of the real network's size) theoretical models. Despite their reduced size, the theoretical models maintain the characteristics of the real network. In the proposed approach (see Fig. 1), multiple theoretical networks are generated based on various configurations of the models' parameters, followed by the selection of the model most similar to the real network with the use of the Kullback-Leibler divergence (KLD) metric.

In the proposed approach, simulations are then computed for various campaign strategies, based on multiple parameters. In this research, the authors suggest a set of 5 input parameters for the simulations:

Par1 – seeding fraction
    The fraction of the total nodes that are selected to be originally provided
    with the information to further spread.
Par2 – propagation probability
    The assumed probability of passing information from one infected node to
    other non-infected nodes. The level of the propagation probability can be
    adjusted by providing incentives to the users to pass the information.
Par3 – seeding iterations' count
    In the original research [28], a single seeding was performed only to bootstrap
    the information propagation process. Based on the initial successes obtained
    in [28], the authors have decided to extend the original model with sequential
    seeding procedures. This parameter specifies how many times, in total, the
    information will be input to the network (including both the initial seeding
    and subsequent ones).

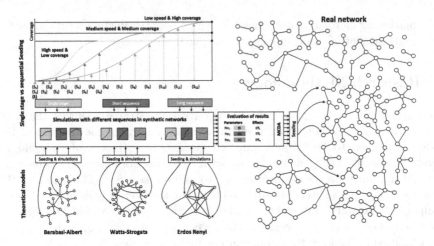

Fig. 1. Conceptual framework of the proposed approach

Par4 – seeding iteration's interval
  The initial seeding is always performed in the first iteration. If there are more than a single seeding iteration (see Par3), Par4 specifies what is the interval between each reseeding procedures in the network.
Par5 – measure used to rank nodes
  The nodes selected for the initial seeding of information are not selected randomly. First they are ordered by a chosen metric and then the top ones are selected. Each possible metric is characterized by a specific computational cost.

Afterwards, the simulations are being computed and the results are saved. Consequently, two performance parameters are obtained:

Eff6 – iteration of last infection
  This represents the moment in simulation when the last infection happened, i.e. when the information propagation process died out. The value of this parameter is at least $1 + (Par3 - 1) \times Par4$.
Eff7 – total coverage
  This is the total coverage achieved by the simulations for a strategy based on the Par1–Par5 parameters, i.e. the ratio of infected nodes to the total nodes.

Last, but not least, after the simulations are concluded and efficiency parameters for all campaign strategies are collected, all gathered information is used to build a decision matrix for the strategies' evaluation.

The procedure of evaluation of the viral campaign strategies requires to consider multiple criteria Par1–Eff7, some of which are conflicting with each other. Depending on the campaign goals, the importance (weight) assigned by the deciding party to each of the criteria might be different. Both weights and the actual values of the parameters Par1–Eff7 can be expressed on a quantitative scale. Moreover, because the evaluation is based on a complete set of simulations, the problem of uncertainty of data is eliminated here. Eventually, the ultimate goal of the evaluation is to rank all the possible strategies and choose the best one. Due to the said reasons, the authors, using the generalised framework for MCDA methods' selection [44,45], have decided to use the TOPSIS method for evaluating the viral marketing campaign strategies in the proposed approach.

4   Empirical Study

The proposed framework can be used to evaluate viral marketing campaign strategies on real networks, as well as to plan campaigns on considerably smaller synthetic networks. During the empirical study, first such real network campaign strategy evaluation was performed, followed by planning a strategy for social network viral marketing campaign based on two separate goals. Eventually, the effect of Par4 and Par5 parameters on the strategies was studied.

4.1   Evaluation of Viral Marketing Campaign Strategies on a Real Network

The evaluation of real network viral marketing campaign strategies was based on the Gnutella network [46], precisely its snapshot from 2002. The network contains 8846 nodes and 31839 edges. Its metrics are presented in Table 1.

In order to ascertain repeatability of the study regardless of the chosen parameters, ten information propagation scenarios were prepared for the network. For each edge between each two nodes a random value was drawn in such scenarios, which subsequently, during the simulations, was used to decide whether or not the infection passed from one node to the other.

A total of 91000 simulations was performed, based on the parameters' values presented in Table 2.

Table 1. The metrics of the real network [46]

Metric	Symbol	Value
Total degree	D	7.1985
Closeness	C	$1.587441e{-}07$
Page rank	PR	0.0001130454
Eigen vector	EV	0.01602488
Clustering coefficient	CC	0.0001130838
Betweenness	B	19104.87

Table 2. Simulation parameters

Criterion	Values
Par1	0.01, 0.02, 0.03, 0.04, 0.05
Par2	0.1, 0.2, 0.3, 0.4, 0.5
Par3	1, 2, 3, 4, 5, 6, 7, 8, 9, 10
Par4	1, 2, 3, 4, 5, 6, 7, 8, 9, 10
Par5	degree (1), closeness (2), EV centrality (3), betweenness (4)

Next, the Eff6 and Eff7 parameter values were computed and the decision matrix for the TOPSIS method was built, containing 9100 strategy alternatives (A1 – A9100). For the evaluation, each of the 7 criteria were given an equal importance weight. The assumed goal of the campaign was to cover as much of the network as possible within fastest possible time and with minimum possible costs. Therefore, the impact of Par1–Eff6 criteria on the strategy score was negative and the Eff7 impact was positive. The top 20 strategies are presented along with their scores in Table 3. The analysis of the table shows that most of the winning strategies were based on a very low value of Par1 (0.01–0.02), low values of Par2 ($\leq$0.3). Regarding Par5, only degree and closeness measures can be found on the top 20 strategies' list, however degree is the measure used in the top-scored alternatives. Because one of the goals of the campaign was to minimize the campaign duration, Par3 and Par4 tend to have low values ($\leq$3). The leading strategy A367 obtained the coverage value of 0.5174 within 14.4 iterations, whereas the runner-up alternative A731 resulted in higher coverage and shorter duration, however the propagation probability was higher, which potentially could lead to higher costs.

4.2   Selection of Synthetic Networks

The proposed MCDA approach allows to successfully evaluate multiple viral marketing campaign strategies conducted over a real network, as it was presented above. Nevertheless, simulations over real networks, characterised by multitude of nodes and edges, require significant computational power. Moreover, the full real network mapping might not always be available. However, it is possible to perform simulations on considerably smaller yet accurate synthetic networks before executing the campaign on the real network.

In the subsequent part of the empirical research, the authors used synthetic networks of 50% size of the real network to perform the simulations and plan a potential campaign on the real network. The results were then compared to the ranking obtained for the real network.

Table 3. Top 20 strategies for the real network

Rank	Alternative	Score	Par1	Par2	Par3	Par4	Par5	Eff6	Eff7
1	A367	0.8454657	0.01	0.2	1	1	1	14.4	0.517386389
2	A731	0.844435	0.01	0.3	1	1	1	9.5	0.683404929
3	A371	0.8391214	0.01	0.2	2	1	1	14.7	0.517386389
4	A735	0.8386404	0.01	0.3	2	1	1	9.8	0.683404929
5	A739	0.8326058	0.01	0.3	2	2	1	9.8	0.683404929
6	A375	0.8323418	0.01	0.2	2	2	1	14.9	0.517397694
7	A2187	0.8320079	0.02	0.2	1	1	1	13.2	0.518923807
8	A2551	0.8298695	0.02	0.3	1	1	1	8.6	0.683563192
9	A775	0.8268715	0.01	0.3	3	1	1	10	0.683404929
10	A411	0.8261902	0.01	0.2	3	1	1	15.1	0.517386389
11	A2191	0.8253991	0.02	0.2	2	1	1	13.7	0.518923807
12	A2555	0.8238216	0.02	0.3	2	1	1	9.2	0.683563192
13	A366	0.8237788	0.01	0.2	1	1	2	14.2	0.517635089
14	A730	0.8233488	0.01	0.3	1	1	2	9.4	0.683495365
15	A779	0.8209285	0.01	0.3	3	2	1	10	0.683563192
16	A415	0.8200903	0.01	0.2	3	2	1	15.1	0.517895094
17	A743	0.8200089	0.01	0.3	2	3	1	9.8	0.683529279
18	A379	0.8193105	0.01	0.2	2	3	1	14.9	0.51786118
19	A2195	0.8189998	0.02	0.2	2	2	1	13.8	0.519262944
20	A734	0.8176981	0.01	0.3	2	1	2	9.7	0.683495365

A set of 15 synthetic networks was generated based on 3 theoretic models with 5 sets of parameters each:

1. BA – number of edges m to add in each step equal to $1, 2, ..., 5$;
2. WS – the neighborhood within which the vertices of the lattice will be connected equal to $1, 2, ..., 5$;
3. ER – number of edges equal to the number of nodes multiplied by $1, 2, ..., 5$.

Kullback-Leibler divergence (KLD) measure was used in order to avoid arbitrary selection of the theoretic model network. Based on the KLD measure of the degree distribution of each of the generated networks with the real network, the network BA-4423-5 was selected, i.e. Barabasi-Albert model with 50% nodes of the real network and $m = 5$. The network characteristics and ints KLD measure value are presented in Table 4.

Table 4. Kullback-Leibler divergence measure for the selected synthetic network

Edges to add	Num of nodes	Num of edges	Perc. of edges	KLD
5	4423	22100	0.694117278%	0.000521317

4.3   Planning of the Viral Marketing Campaign Strategies

Two opposite campaign goals were studied during this part of the empirical study: maximization of coverage within smallest possible time, and maximization of coverage and process duration.

Maximization of Coverage and Minimization of Duration. For the evaluation, each of the 7 criteria were given an equal importance weight. The assumed impact on the strategy score of Par1–Eff6 criteria was negative and the Eff7 impact was positive. The top 20 strategies are presented along with their scores in Table 5.

Similarly to the evaluation of strategies for the real-network, also in case of the synthetic network the top strategies were based on a very low value of the Par1 parameter (0.01–0.02), low values of the Par2 parameter (0.2–0.3). The winning strategies were based on the degree and closeness centrality measures. The coverage for the first 9 strategies is almost equal, i.e. 0.7026 and the duration oscillates around 11 s. The strategy A1936, ranked 9, is based on splitting the seeding process into two steps, in the first and fourth iteration of the process. This results in an equal coverage to the winning strategy, and the duration averagely extended by 0.1 s.

It is important to note, that the above-mentioned ranking was generated for equal weights of all criteria. In order how the weights of individual criteria affect the final rankings, a sensitivity analysis was performed. However, for the reasons of readability, the sensitivity analysis was limited to the top 20 strategies. The results of the analysis are presented on Fig. 2 for the evaluation scores and Fig. 3 for the evaluation ranks.

The analysis of Fig. 2 allows to see how the scores of each strategy are affected by the increase of weight of each criteria. For example, it can be observed that the leading alternative A1914 is supported by criteria Par1, Par3, Par4, Par5 and Eff6, i.e. its score raises along with the raise of the importance of each of these criteria. On the other hand, if more importance was given to the Par2 or Eff7 criteria, the score of strategy A1914 would decrease. The CCi sensitivity chart allows also to see how much each criterion supports or conflicts each alternative.

Table 5. Top 20 strategies for the synthetic network for maximum coverage and minimum duration

Rank	Strategy	Score	Par1	Par2	Par3	Par4	Par5	Eff6	Eff7
1	A1914	0.8776064	0.01	0.2	1	1	1	11.2	0.702645263
2	A1918	0.871181	0.01	0.2	2	1	1	11.3	0.702645263
3	A1922	0.8643984	0.01	0.2	2	2	1	11.3	0.702645263
4	A1940	0.8596561	0.02	0.2	1	1	1	10.7	0.702645263
5	A1929	0.8567826	0.01	0.2	3	1	1	11.4	0.702645263
6	A1943	0.8531567	0.02	0.2	2	1	1	11	0.702645263
7	A1913	0.8513274	0.01	0.2	1	1	2	11.3	0.702645263
8	A1973	0.8507025	0.01	0.2	3	2	1	11.3	0.703640063
9	A1926	0.8489333	0.01	0.2	2	3	1	11.4	0.702645263
10	A3825	0.8464421	0.01	0.3	1	1	1	8.3	0.888175447
11	A1946	0.8462135	0.02	0.2	2	2	1	11.2	0.702645263
12	A1917	0.8456965	0.01	0.2	2	1	2	11.3	0.702645263
13	A3829	0.8408425	0.01	0.3	2	1	1	8.6	0.888175447
14	A1949	0.8395764	0.02	0.2	3	1	1	11.3	0.702645263
15	A1921	0.8394273	0.01	0.2	2	2	2	11.3	0.702645263
16	A2071	0.8384225	0.01	0.2	3	3	1	10.8	0.709586254
17	A1933	0.8363776	0.01	0.2	4	1	1	11.8	0.702645263
18	A1939	0.8357937	0.02	0.2	1	1	2	10.7	0.702645263
19	A3833	0.8350406	0.01	0.3	2	2	1	8.6	0.888175447
20	A2020	0.8347077	0.02	0.2	3	2	1	10.8	0.70594619

For example, Fig. 2C shows that the increase of weight of Par3 decreases the score of both strategies A1933 and A2020. If the weights of all criteria are equal, the strategy A1933 is ranked 17 and A2020 is ranked 20. However, the raise of importance of criterion Par3 affects the strategy A1933 more than A2020, and in case of a 10% increase of the importance of Par3, the rank of strategy A1933 drop below the rank of strategy A2020.

On the other hand, Fig. 3 allows to easily track how the ranks of the strategies change along with changes of weights of individual criteria. It can be clearly observed that the rank of the leading strategy A1914 is very stable and only considerable changes of Eff7 criterion weight can result in change of its rank from 1 to 9 (see Fig. 3G). Furthermore, Fig. 3A and E show that in case of considerable changes of weights of criteria Par1 and Par5, the strategies from the bottom of the top-20 list would be replaced by strategies previously outside of the top-20 list.

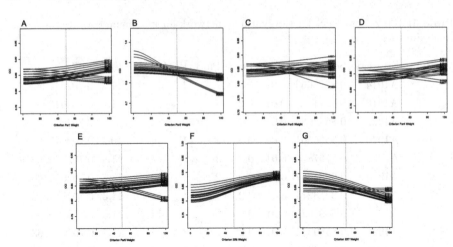

Fig. 2. Sensitivity analysis for the CCi values fot the top 20 strategies for the synthetic network scenario maximizing coverage and minimizing duration

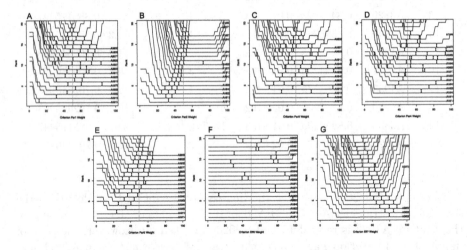

Fig. 3. Sensitivity analysis for the ranks of the top 20 strategies for the synthetic network scenario maximizing coverage and minimizing duration

Maximization of Coverage and Duration. For this scenario, the assumed impact of Par1–Par3 criteria was negative and the Par4–Eff7 impact was positive. Similarly as in the previous experiment, each of the 7 criteria were given an equal importance weight. The top 20 strategies are presented along with their scores in Table 6.

When Table 6 is analysed, it can be observed that the average values of the Par1, Par2, Par5 and Eff7 criteria are very similar for the top 20 alternatives in both scenarios. However, a considerable difference in average values can be observed for Par3, Par4 and Eff6 (see Table 7). While in case of the first scenario,

Table 6. Top 20 strategies for the synthetic network for maximum coverage and maximum duration

Rank	Strategy	Score	Par1	Par2	Par3	Par4	Par5	Eff6	Eff7
1	A2450	0.8872772	0.01	0.2	10	10	1	92.4	0.72233778
2	A2956	0.8714643	0.02	0.2	10	10	1	93.3	0.741419851
3	A2441	0.8604204	0.01	0.2	10	10	2	92.9	0.722156907
4	A2449	0.8566093	0.01	0.2	10	9	1	83.4	0.722292562
5	A2489	0.8533866	0.01	0.2	9	10	1	82.3	0.723965634
6	A4346	0.8468385	0.01	0.3	10	10	1	91.9	0.900474791
7	A2942	0.8455437	0.02	0.2	10	10	2	92.7	0.741058105
8	A2953	0.8443063	0.02	0.2	10	9	1	84.3	0.741397242
9	A2937	0.841499	0.02	0.2	9	10	1	83.3	0.740854624
10	A2437	0.8341213	0.01	0.2	10	9	2	83.9	0.722111689
11	A2487	0.8323953	0.01	0.2	9	10	2	83.1	0.723943025
12	A4822	0.8322019	0.02	0.3	10	10	1	92	0.913361972
13	A3307	0.8297117	0.03	0.2	10	10	1	92.5	0.754171377
14	A4330	0.8263723	0.01	0.3	10	10	2	92	0.900180873
15	A4345	0.8210995	0.01	0.3	10	9	1	82.9	0.900474791
16	A2940	0.8192291	0.02	0.2	10	9	2	83.7	0.740922451
17	A390	0.8187792	0.01	0.1	10	10	1	94.3	0.300836536
18	A4382	0.818645	0.01	0.3	9	10	1	81.9	0.901560027
19	A2931	0.8169775	0.02	0.2	9	10	2	82.8	0.740741578
20	A922	0.8135993	0.02	0.1	10	10	1	95.4	0.332240561

the average duration of the campaign (Eff6) was little lower than 11 iterations, in case of the second scenario the average duration was over 88 iterations. However, at the same time, the average coverage (Eff7) for the top 20 strategies for both scenarios was almost the same. In case of the second scenario, the strategies tended to be based on multiple seeding stages (Par3, averagely 9.75 compared to 2.1 in the first scenario) with long intervals between them (Par4, averagely 9.75, compared to 1.5 in the first scenario).

When the individual winning strategies are analysed in Table 6, it can be observed that the top strategy A2450 was based on 0.01 seeding fraction, 0.2 propagation probability, 10 seeding iterations with 10 iterations interval and degree used as the nodes' selection measure. This resulted in averagely 92.4 iterations and 0.7223 coverage. The second-best strategy A2956 achieved slightly longer duration and better coverage (93.3 and 0.7414 respectively), but it was based on 0.02 seeding fraction, which potentially could lead to higher costs, which would not be compensated by the aforementioned slight increase of coverage and duration of the information spreading process.

Table 7. Comparison of average values of Par1–Eff7 criteria values for the 20 top-ranked alternatives based on synthetic network scenario (A) maximising coverage and minimising duration; and (B) maximising coverage and duration

	Par1	Par2	Par3	Par4	Par5	Eff6	Eff7
(A) Max-Min	0.0130	0.2150	2.1000	1.5000	1.2000	10.7800	0.7310
(B) Max-Max	0.0150	0.2150	9.7500	9.7500	1.3500	88.0500	0.7343
|A − B|	0.0020	0.0000	7.6500	8.2500	0.1500	77.2700	0.0033

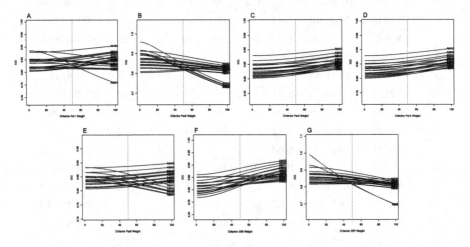

Fig. 4. Sensitivity analysis for the CCi values fot the top 20 strategies for the synthetic network scenario maximizing coverage and duration

Subsequently, a sensitivity analysis was performed. The obtained results are presented on Figs. 4 and 5, however for readability, only the top 20 alternatives are presented on the figures. The analysis of Figs. 4 and 5 allows to observe high stability of the ranks of the leading alternatives. However, the further a strategy is from the top of the ranking in terms of score, the less stable its rank is. This is most clearly visible on Fig. 5B and G.

4.4   Study of Sequential Seeding on Information Propagation Process

The empirical study was concluded by examination of the effect the two new criteria Par3 and Par4, i.e. seeding iterations and interval between them, have on the final coverage and information spreading process duration. Data from simulations performed on the real network [46] was further aggregated and presented on figures Figs. 6, 7 and 8.

The chart on Fig. 6 shows that along with increase of the count of seeding iterations, both the average coverage and process duration increased. The average duration growth can be approximated with a linear function $y = 4.9113x + 2.513$

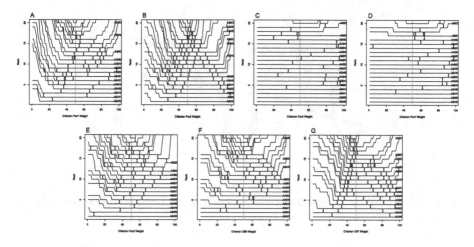

Fig. 5. Sensitivity analysis for the ranks of the top 20 strategies for the synthetic network scenario maximizing coverage and duration

with $R^2 = 0.9934$, whereas the average coverage growth can be approximated with logarithmic function $y = 0.0144 ln(x) + 0.5982$ with $R^2 = 0.9831$. Similar increase of average coverage and average information spreading process duration can be observed when the interval between seeding iterations is increased (see Fig. 7). The duration growth can be approximated with a linear function $y = 4.756x + 5.4968$ with $R^2 = 0.9987$, while the average coverage growth can be approximated with logarithmic function $y = 0.0109 ln(x) + 0.6062$ with $R^2 = 0.9568$.

Eventually, the simulation results were aggregated and grouped by seeding iterations' count and interval and ordered by both of these factors ascending. The results are presented on Fig. 8. The labels on the X axis of the chart are built of two components C:I, where C denotes the count of seeding iterations and I denotes the interval between them. The visual analysis of this chart allows to observe that the increase of the duration of the process is almost linear to the interval between seeding iterations. This means, that the longer the interval, the proportionally longer the process will last. In case of the average coverage, it can be observed that immediate increase can be achieved if the interval between seeding iterations is increased to 1–6. However, when the interval is increased over 6, the further increase of coverage is only slight. This observation suggests that in case of viral marketing campaign strategies oriented on coverage maximization and process duration minimization it might be more beneficial to increase the seeding iterations' interval only to some extent.

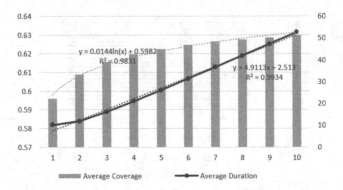

Fig. 6. Effect of seeding iterations' count on coverage and information spreading process duration

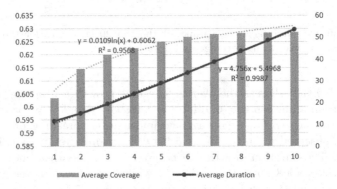

Fig. 7. Effect of seeding iterations' interval on coverage and information spreading process duration

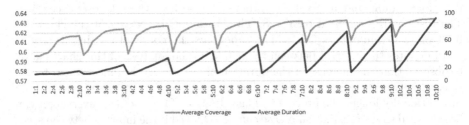

Fig. 8. Effect of seeding iterations' count and interval on coverage and information spreading process duration

5   Conclusions

Social media networks have become very popular and 45% of the population are active social media users. As a result, viral marketing campaigns in social networks began to bring better results than traditional online advertising. Marketers are now investing more effort into seeding information into social networks and providing incentives to increase the willingness of the users to propagate information further in the network. These increased efforts created a demand for providing manners for campaign planning and evaluation. In recent research the authors proposed a multi-criteria approach for such planning and evaluation.

In this paper, the authors have proposed extension of the multi-criteria approach for viral marketing campaign strategy planning and evaluation, in which strategies utilising sequential seeding are taken into account. This resulted in an evaluation framework containing five parametric criteria and two effectiveness criteria.

The authors' contributions in this paper include:

- multi-criteria framework to planning information spreading processes focused on their initialization with the use of sequential seeding;
- simulation engine for providing data for evaluation of viral marketing campaign strategies performed on real and synthetic networks;
- an example set of criteria to choose a satisfactory viral marketing campaign strategy according to the marketer's goals, taking into account its costs, dynamics, coverage, duration;
- the effect of increasing the count of seeding iterations and of increasing the interval between seeding iterations on the coverage and information propagation process duration was studied.

In practical terms, the empirical study has shown that an increase of the count of seeding iterations in the campaign can increase the achieved network coverage at the cost of the campaign duration increase. Moreover, it was observed that delaying the subsequent seeding iterations by several non-seeding iterations increases the network coverage even more. However, for the studied real network, best coverage increase was observed for 1–6 interval between seeding iterations, and if the interval was increased even further, the effects were less outstanding.

This research has identified some possible areas of improvement and future works. A detailed study of how the sequential seeding affects the process duration and coverage for various sets of other strategy parameters' values could be performed. Moreover, in this research, the seeds in subsequent seeding iterations were chosen based on the original nodes ranking. Possibly, better results could be achieved if the centrality measures for nodes' selection were recalculated in each subsequent seeding iteration. Last, but not least, the introduction of sequential seeding into the viral marketing campaigns calls for studying temporal aspects of the network status and its effect on information diffusion processes.

Acknowledgments. This work was supported by the National Science Centre, Poland, grant no. 2016/21/B/HS4/01562 (AK, JJ) and within the framework of the program of the Minister of Science and Higher Education under the name "Regional Excellence Initiative" in the years 2019–2022, project number 001/RID/2018/19, the amount of financing PLN 10,684,000.00 (JW).

References

1. Greenwood, S., Perrin, A., Duggan, M.: Social media update 2016. Pew Res. Cent. **11**(2) (2016)
2. Couldry, N.: Media, Society, World: Social Theory and Digital Media Practice. Polity Press, Cambridge (2012)
3. Chmielarz, W., Szumski, O.: Digital distribution of video games - an empirical study of game distribution platforms from the perspective of polish students (future managers). In: Ziemba, E. (ed.) AITM/ISM 2018. LNBIP, vol. 346, pp. 136–154. Springer, Cham (2019). https://doi.org/10.1007/978-3-030-15154-6_8
4. Leskovec, J., Adamic, L.A., Huberman, B.A.: The dynamics of viral marketing. ACM Trans. Web **1**(1), 5–44 (2007). https://doi.org/10.1145/1232722.1232727
5. Camarero, C., José, R.S.: Social and attitudinal determinants of viral marketing dynamics. Comput. Hum. Behav. **27**(6), 2292–2300 (2011). https://doi.org/10.1016/j.chb.2011.07.008
6. Jankowski, J., Bródka, P., Hamari, J.: A picture is worth a thousand words: an empirical study on the influence of content visibility on diffusion processes within a virtual world. Behav. Inf. Technol. **35**(11), 926–945 (2016). https://doi.org/10.1080/0144929X.2016.1212932
7. Hinz, O., Skiera, B., Barrot, C., Becker, J.U.: Seeding strategies for viral marketing: an empirical comparison. J. Mark. **75**(6), 55–71 (2011). https://doi.org/10.1509/jm.10.0088
8. Tang, J., Musolesi, M., Mascolo, C., Latora, V., Nicosia, V.: Analysing information flows and key mediators through temporal centrality metrics. In: Proceedings of the 3rd Workshop on Social Network Systems, p. 3. ACM (2010). https://doi.org/10.1145/1852658.1852661
9. Iribarren, J.L., Moro, E.: Branching dynamics of viral information spreading. Phys. Rev. E **84**, 046116 (2011). https://doi.org/10.1103/PhysRevE.84.046116
10. Jankowski, J., Michalski, R., Kazienko, P.: The multidimensional study of viral campaigns as branching processes. In: Aberer, K., Flache, A., Jager, W., Liu, L., Tang, J., Guéret, C. (eds.) SocInfo 2012. LNCS, vol. 7710, pp. 462–474. Springer, Heidelberg (2012). https://doi.org/10.1007/978-3-642-35386-4_34
11. Liu, C., Zhang, Z.K.: Information spreading on dynamic social networks. Commun. Nonlinear Sci. Numer. Simul. **19**(4), 896–904 (2014). https://doi.org/10.1016/j.cnsns.2013.08.028
12. Kempe, D., Kleinberg, J., Kumar, A.: Connectivity and inference problems for temporal networks. J. Comput. Syst. Sci. **64**(4), 820–842 (2002). https://doi.org/10.1006/jcss.2002.1829
13. Jankowski, J., Michalski, R., Kazienko, P.: Compensatory seeding in networks with varying avaliability of nodes. In: 2013 IEEE/ACM International Conference on Advances in Social Networks Analysis and Mining (ASONAM 2013), pp. 1242–1249. IEEE (2013). https://doi.org/10.1145/2492517.2500256
14. Ganesh, A., Massoulie, L., Towsley, D.: The effect of network topology on the spread of epidemics. In: Proceedings IEEE 24th Annual Joint Conference of the IEEE Computer and Communications Societies, vol. 2, pp. 1455–1466, March 2005. https://doi.org/10.1109/INFCOM.2005.1498374
15. Delre, S.A., Jager, W., Bijmolt, T.H.A., Janssen, M.A.: Will it spread or not? The effects of social influences and network topology on innovation diffusion. J. Prod. Innov. Manage. **27**(2), 267–282 (2010). https://doi.org/10.1111/j.1540-5885.2010.00714.x

16. Pazura, P., Jankowski, J., Bortko, K., Bartkow, P.: Increasing the diffusional characteristics of networks through optimal topology changes within sub-graphs (2019). https://doi.org/10.1145/3341161.3344823

17. Barabási, A.L., Albert, R.: Emergence of scaling in random networks. Science **286**(5439), 509–512 (1999). https://doi.org/10.1126/science.286.5439.509

18. Watts, D.J., Strogatz, S.H.: Collective dynamics of 'small-world' networks. Nature **393**(6684), 440 (1998). https://doi.org/10.1038/30918

19. Erdös, P., Rényi, A.: On random graphs I. Publicationes Mathematicae Debrecen **6**, 290 (1959)

20. Onnela, J.P., Christakis, N.A.: Spreading paths in partially observed social networks. Phys. Rev. E **85**, 036106 (2012). https://doi.org/10.1103/PhysRevE.85.036106

21. Génois, M., Vestergaard, C.L., Cattuto, C., Barrat, A.: Compensating for population sampling in simulations of epidemic spread on temporal contact networks. Nat. Commun. **6**, 8860 (2015). https://doi.org/10.1038/ncomms9860

22. Jankowski, J., Hamari, J., Wątróbski, J.: A gradual approach for maximising user conversion without compromising experience with high visual intensity website elements. Internet Res. **29**(1), 194–217 (2019). https://doi.org/10.1108/IntR-09-2016-0271

23. Sałabun, W., Palczewski, K., Wątróbski, J.: Multicriteria approach to sustainable transport evaluation under incomplete knowledge: electric bikes case study. Sustainability **11**(12), 3314 (2019). https://doi.org/10.3390/su11123314

24. Karczmarczyk, A., Wątróbski, J., Jankowski, J., Ziemba, E.: Comparative study of ICT and SIS measurement in polish households using a MCDA-based approach. Procedia Comput. Sci. **159**, 2616–2628 (2019). https://doi.org/10.1016/j.procs.2019.09.254

25. Karczmarczyk, A., Jankowski, J., Wątróbski, J.: Multi-criteria decision support for planning and evaluation of performance of viral marketing campaigns in social networks. PLoS ONE **13**(12), e0209372 (2018). https://doi.org/10.1371/journal.pone.0209372

26. Karczmarczyk, A., Jankowski, J., Watrobski, J.: Parametrization of spreading processes within complex networks with the use of knowledge acquired from network samples. Procedia Comput. Sci. **159**, 2279–2293 (2019). https://doi.org/10.1016/j.procs.2019.09.403

27. Jankowski, J., Zioło, M., Karczmarczyk, A., Wątróbski, J.: Towards sustainability in viral marketing with user engaging supporting campaigns. Sustainability **10**(1), 15 (2018). https://doi.org/10.3390/su10010015

28. Karczmarczyk, A., Jankowsk, J., Wątróbski, J.: Multi-criteria approach to viral marketing campaign planning in social networks, based on real networks, network samples and synthetic networks. In: 2019 Federated Conference on Computer Science and Information Systems (FedCSIS), pp. 663–673. IEEE (2019). https://doi.org/10.15439/2019F199

29. Chen, W., Wang, Y., Yang, S.: Efficient influence maximization in social networks. In: Proceedings of the 15th ACM SIGKDD International Conference on Knowledge Discovery and Data Mining, KDD 2009, pp. 199–208. Association for Computing Machinery, New York (2009). https://doi.org/10.1145/1557019.1557047

30. Chen, W., Yuan, Y., Zhang, L.: Scalable influence maximization in social networks under the linear threshold model. In: 2010 IEEE International Conference on Data Mining, pp. 88–97, December 2010. https://doi.org/10.1109/ICDM.2010.118

31. Marcinkiewicz, K., Stegmaier, M.: The parliamentary election in Poland, october 2015. Elect. Stud. **41**, 221–224 (2016). https://doi.org/10.1016/j.electstud.2016.01.004

32. Enli, G.: Twitter as arena for the authentic outsider: exploring the social media campaigns of trump and clinton in the 2016 US presidential election. Eur. J. Commun. **32**(1), 50–61 (2017). https://doi.org/10.1177/0267323116682802

33. Salehi, M., Sharma, R., Marzolla, M., Magnani, M., Siyari, P., Montesi, D.: Spreading processes in multilayer networks. IEEE Trans. Netw. Sci. Eng. **2**(2), 65–83 (2015). https://doi.org/10.1109/TNSE.2015.2425961

34. Kandhway, K., Kuri, J.: How to run a campaign: optimal control of SIS and SIR information epidemics. Appl. Math. Comput. **231**, 79–92 (2014). https://doi.org/10.1016/j.amc.2013.12.164. http://www.sciencedirect.com/science/article/pii/S0096300314000022

35. Kempe, D., Kleinberg, J., Tardos, É.: Maximizing the spread of influence through a social network. In: Proceedings of the Ninth ACM SIGKDD International Conference on Knowledge Discovery and Data Mining, pp. 137–146. ACM (2003). https://doi.org/10.1145/956750.956769

36. Wang, C., Chen, W., Wang, Y.: Scalable influence maximization for independent cascade model in large-scale social networks. Data Min. Knowl. Disc. **25**(3), 545–576 (2012). https://doi.org/10.1007/s10618-012-0262-1

37. Kiss, C., Bichler, M.: Identification of influencers — measuring influence in customer networks. Decis. Support Syst. **46**(1), 233–253 (2008). https://doi.org/10.1016/j.dss.2008.06.007

38. Seeman, L., Singer, Y.: Adaptive seeding in social networks. In: 2013 IEEE 54th Annual Symposium on Foundations of Computer Science, pp. 459–468. IEEE (2013). https://doi.org/10.1109/FOCS.2013.56

39. Kitsak, M., et al.: Identification of influential spreaders in complex networks. Nat. Phys. **6**(11), 888 (2010). https://doi.org/10.1038/nphys1746

40. Zhang, J.X., Chen, D.B., Dong, Q., Zhao, Z.D.: Identifying a set of influential spreaders in complex networks. Sci. Rep. **6**, 27823 (2016). https://doi.org/10.1038/srep27823

41. Lin, J.H., Guo, Q., Dong, W.Z., Tang, L.Y., Liu, J.G.: Identifying the node spreading influence with largest k-core values. Phys. Lett. A **378**(45), 3279–3284 (2014). https://doi.org/10.1016/j.physleta.2014.09.054

42. Ho, J.Y., Dempsey, M.: Viral marketing: motivations to forward online content. J. Bus. Res. **63**(9), 1000–1006 (2010). https://doi.org/10.1016/j.jbusres.2008.08.010

43. Jankowski, J., Bródka, P., Kazienko, P., Szymanski, B.K., Michalski, R., Kajdanowicz, T.: Balancing speed and coverage by sequential seeding in complex networks. Sci. Rep. **7**(1), 891 (2017). https://doi.org/10.1038/s41598-017-00937-8

44. Wątróbski, J., Jankowski, J., Ziemba, P., Karczmarczyk, A., Zioło, M.: Generalised framework for multi-criteria method selection. Omega **86**, 107–124 (2019). https://doi.org/10.1016/j.omega.2018.07.004

45. Wątróbski, J., Jankowski, J., Ziemba, P., Karczmarczyk, A., Zioło, M.: Generalised framework for multi-criteria method selection: rule set database and exemplary decision support system implementation blueprints. Data Brief **22**, 639 (2019). https://doi.org/10.1016/j.dib.2018.12.015

46. Ripeanu, M., Foster, I., Iamnitchi, A.: Mapping the Gnutella network: properties of large-scale peer-to-peer systems and implications for system design. arXiv:cs/0209028, September 2002

Predictive Models for Maintenance Optimization: An Analytical Literature Survey of Industrial Maintenance Strategies

Oana Merkt[✉] [iD]

Hohenheim University, Schloss Hohenheim 1, 70599 Stuttgart, Germany
Oana.Merkt@uni-hohenheim.de

Abstract. As machine learning (ML) techniques and sensor technology continue to gain importance, the data-driven perspective has become a relevant approach for improving the quality of maintenance for machines and processes in industrial environments. Our study provides an analytical literature review of existing industrial maintenance strategies showing first that, among all extant approaches to maintenance, each varying in terms of efficiency and complexity, predictive maintenance best fits the needs of a highly competitive industry setup. Predictive maintenance is an approach that allows maintenance actions to be based on changes in the monitored parameters of the assets by using a variety of techniques to study both live and historical information to learn prognostic data and make accurate predictions. Moreover, we argue that, in any industrial setup, the quality of maintenance improves when the applied data-driven techniques and methods (i) have economic justifications and (ii) take into consideration the conformity with the industry standards. Next, we consider ML to be a prediction methodology, and we show that multimodal ML methods enhance industrial maintenance with a critical component of intelligence: prediction. Based on the surveyed literature, we introduce taxonomies that cover relevant predictive models and their corresponding data-driven maintenance techniques. Moreover, we investigate the potential of multimodality for maintenance optimization, particularly the model-agnostic data fusion methods. We show the progress made in the literature toward the formalization of multimodal data fusion for industrial maintenance.

Keywords: Maintenance strategies · Predictive maintenance · Multimodal machine learning · Predictive models · Data fusion · CRISP_DM · Industrial Data Space

1 Introduction

A proper quality of maintenance is crucial in assuring both the desired quality of planning for the service/production/distribution chain and the desired quality of the commodities in any industry area. In the context of our research work, we investigate the optimization

This work was partly supported by a grant from the German Federal Ministry for Economic Affairs and Energy (BMWi) for the Platona-M project under the grant number 01MT19005D.

E. Ziemba (Ed.): AITM 2019/ISM 2019, LNBIP 380, pp. 135–154, 2020.
https://doi.org/10.1007/978-3-030-43353-6_8

of maintenance quality. Among all the existing approaches to maintenance, varying in terms of efficiency and complexity, predictive maintenance seems to fit the needs of a highly competitive industry setup, as argued by [1]. Predictive maintenance evolved from condition-based maintenance, where decisions are based on evaluation of the machine status through inspections and measurements.

Predictive maintenance allows maintenance actions to be based on changes in the parameters of industrial assets, that are continuously monitored by sensors. Due to recent advances in sensor technology, data communication, and computing, the ability to collect significant volumes of heterogeneous, raw sensor data produced by industrial assets under observation is exponentially increasing. Therefore, historical information about normal and abnormal patterns and the related corrective actions employed during the lifetime of an industrial asset is becoming available. Consequently, the capability of forecasting failures based on aggregated live and historical data—i.e., the predictive maintenance approach—is currently a relevant research topic with applicability in all industrial fields and the research object of our analytical literature review. To deal with such high-dimensional problems, predictive maintenance approaches must continuously optimize themselves using a variety of techniques and prediction models that study both live and historical information. This information is further used for learning prognostics data and making accurate diagnostics and predictions, as presented by references [2–4]. Although the authors argue that the implementation of effective prognosis for maintenance has a variety of benefits, including increased system safety, improved operational reliability, reduced service times/repair failure times, and life cycle costs, the existing literature does not inform us about the optimal methodologies to be used in practice for the implementation of a particular maintenance scenario. Past works on predictive maintenance show that maintenance actions are performed by employing various prediction models and modeling techniques by applying different perspectives; i.e., (i) knowledge-based perspective with prediction models comprising expert systems and fuzzy logic; (ii) data-based perspective with ANNs, stochastic and statistical models, respectively; and (iii) hybrid prediction models encompassing a mixture of distinct methods for reaching the same end goal: a higher maintenance quality.

Among statistical prediction models, machine learning (ML) methods are considered the most suitable to deal with high dimensional and unstructured data, as argued by [5, 6]. Moreover, multimodality is increasingly used by ML methods for combining data from multiple, diverse modalities and sources to retrieve new insights from the combined knowledge. There are a lot of previous works on multimodality, as the topic dates back to the 90s. Maintenance scenarios that implement multimodal ML methods for predictive maintenance optimization purposes are defined by [2, 3, 6, 7].

However, to date, no standard or good practice recommendations for the fusion and integration of multimodal data have emerged. Our research reviews the model-agnostic data fusion techniques to find solutions for their optimal usage. We argue that understanding the capabilities and challenges of existing multimodal data fusion methods and techniques has the potential to deliver better data analysis tools across all domains, including in the maintenance quality and management field of research.

Furthermore, we envision the problem of maintenance's quality as a complex topic with many complementary aspects: technical, economic, and the conformity with the mainstream industrial standards. The first aspect follows the classical optimization concerns relative to maintenance costs by considering aspects related to maintenance investment costs and resulting benefits. Traditional approaches consider maintenance only as a cost. However, maintenance activities have direct implications on production and quality and, therefore, should be treated as an investment, as argued by [8]. Moreover, choosing the appropriate timing for performing maintenance activities has economic justifications as explained by [9] in the description of the damage model. The damage model recommends the use of maintenance actions only when clear evidence of the machine or equipment status exists. It shows that, based on long-term historical data, it is possible to adapt the predictive maintenance interval to the industrial item life cycle by forecasting the item's wear and its impact on the production chain. Reference [9] explains that the probability that an item will fail is high at the beginning of its operational life in its burn-in period. During the burn-in period, the failure probability of an item decreases continuously. During the item's working period, the failure probability is low and remains constant; therefore, predicting the item's failure during the working period is challenging. The probability of failure increases with the number of working hours, so that, in the wear period, the probability for an item to fail is again high. Therefore, as a good practice, [9] recommends performing maintenance actions during the wear period of an item's life cycle.

The second aspect that we believe influences the quality of maintenance is conformity to industrial standards during the development life cycle of a maintenance product. Our review of the literature shows that ad-hoc maintenance model development and implementations that do not comply with existing mainstream standards are problematic. This situation leads to the absence of good practice recommendations or general solutions in the development of maintenance products. We briefly review two existing industrial standards for model development: Industrial Data Space [10] and Cross-Industry Standard Process for Data Mining (CRISP-DM) [11]. The CRISP-DM standard represents a guideline to follow in the process of prototyping a learning model for maintenance purposes. We shortly list the guideline steps: business understanding, data understanding, data preparation, data fusion, model prototyping, model evaluation, and deployment. On its turn, Industrial Data Space represents the solution to the actual problems raised by the huge volume of heterogeneous data that needs to be handled in a standardized way in the industrial setup. Among the expected benefits of any standard, we mention knowledge sharing and (re)use, which help build complex operational models.

The technical aspect of maintenance quality is related to the set of decisions concerning the appropriate techniques and methods that should be used for the development of an operational and highly qualitative maintenance model. Our literature survey focuses on analyzing the technical aspect, but further works are planned to consider its connections with the economic aspect. To our knowledge, none of the reviewed research works consider the conformity with industrial standards for model development and data management and security. One of the main issues with actual maintenance techniques and methods is precisely the absence of this holistic view in considering the problem of the maintenance quality, as directly influenced by all of the above three mentioned aspects; i.e., technical (data-driven oriented), economic (maintenance as a long-term investment), and conformity with industrial standards.

The rest of the paper is structured as follows: Sect. 2 describes the theoretical background of our paper, i.e., the maintenance taxonomy according to the terminology defined by both [12, 13] maintenance standards, and the multimodal ML methods, as in [14, 15]. The description of the review process and the selection of the literature are presented in Sect. 3. The findings and results of the investigated approaches are highlighted in Sect. 4. Section 5 discusses the identified problems and further research challenges for the reviewed topics. Finally, Sect. 6 concludes our review by outlining our approach and planned future works.

2 Theoretical Background

2.1 Classification of Maintenance Approaches

The European recognized maintenance standards: DIN EN 13306 - Maintenance Terminology [12] and DIN EN 31051 - Fundamentals of Maintenance [13], are defining maintenance-related terminology and concepts. According to the DIN EN 31051 standard, the maintenance concept is defined as: the combination of all technical and administrative actions as well as actions of management in the lifetime of a unit, in order to be in the fully functional state or to recover in this one so that this unit can fulfill his requirements. The main maintenance activities (i.e., service, inspection, repair, and improvement) are defined by the DIN EN 31051 standard. Their definitions, together with other relevant maintenance concepts defined by the DIN EN 31051 maintenance standard, are listed in Table 1. On the other hand, the DIN EN 13306 maintenance standard defines the existing maintenance strategies, i.e. corrective maintenance, preventive maintenance, condition-based maintenance, and predictive maintenance. They are discussed in the following subsections. Moreover, the definition of a further maintenance strategy, namely prescriptive maintenance—which is not yet standardized but is already used in practice—is discussed in the following subsection.

Corrective Maintenance. According to the DIN EN 13306 standard, corrective maintenance is defined as: the maintenance carried out after fault recognition that is intended to put an item into a state in which it can perform a required function. A system that employs corrective maintenance should be aware of all its predefined sets of failures and damages. However, in the industrial operational context, new faults and their corresponding patterns may appear over time because of the item's usage during working hours.

One main advantage of applying corrective maintenance techniques is that the wear limit of an item, i.e., the service time, is fully used. This implies that the effort for item inspection and for repairing or replacing the deteriorated item is significantly reduced compared with the case of preventive maintenance.

The main disadvantage is that corrective maintenance interventions are performed only after the occurrence of failures: it is the simplest approach to applying maintenance, and therefore it is still frequently adopted. However, it is the least effective, and the costs of interventions are substantial. The main challenge in applying corrective maintenance is that the item can fail at a time not previously known or decided and, consequently, can produce damages and additional costs of interventions that can be higher than the yield of the full usage of its wear margin.

Table 1. Fundamentals of maintenance - DIN EN 31051

Item	Defines a component, device, subsystem, functional unit, equipment or a system which can be described and considered as an entity.
Wear	Represents the reduction of wear margin due to chemical or physical processes.
Wear limit	Is the defined minimum value of the wear margin.
Wear margin	Defines the possible reserve function capacity under defined circumstances which a unit possesses.
Service	Includes all activities delaying the degradation of the wear margin. The activities include cleaning, conservation, greasing, oiling, complementing, changing and readjusting.
Inspection	Refers to all activities used to determine and evaluate the actual condition of facilities, machines, assemblies, or components. Inspection refers to collecting data, and related activities that can be measured, verified and monitored.
Repair	Covers activities for retrieving the nominal condition, such as renewing, patching and adjusting.
Improvement	Defines the combination of all technical and administrative activities as well as activities of management to increase the reliability, maintainability, or safety of an item without changing its initial function.

Preventive Maintenance. The DIN EN 13306 standard defines preventive maintenance as: the maintenance carried out at predetermined intervals or according to prescribed criteria and intended to reduce the probability of failure or the degradation of the functioning of an item. Consequently, preventive maintenance defines a set of actions carried out before failure, which is intended to prevent failures or the degradation of a machine.

One main challenge of preventive maintenance approaches in an operational context is that industrial scenarios for data analysis do not provide tracking of the past, abnormal behavior, or maintenance operations that were performed to correct or prevent a faulty behavior. The general assumption is that after several operational hours, the wear margin of an item is worn out. The employed approach is to change the item or overhaul part of it before the wear margin is used. Consequently, this approach leads to inefficient use of resources, as unnecessary corrective actions are often performed.

Condition-Based Maintenance. The DIN EN 13306 standard defines condition-based maintenance as preventive maintenance, which includes a combination of condition monitoring and/or inspection and/or testing, analysis, and ensuring maintenance actions. Condition-based maintenance (CbM) aims to anticipate a maintenance operation, based on the evidence of degradation and deviations from a supposed asset's normal behavior. The equipment is monitored with multiple sensors that are supposed to acquire relevant data about the equipment's operation life. Additionally, contextual parameters like vibration, temperature, humidity, etc., may also provide important information. Key Process Indicators (KPIs) or health indicators are usually computed and analyzed to discover trends that lead to abnormal contexts and failure events. Consequently, CbM enables existing failures to be detected, diagnosed, and corrected before breakdowns or other serious consequences occur.

The challenge is how to use this asset health information for optimizing the accuracy of predicting the remaining asset lifetime, optimizing maintenance schedules, and maximizing the industrial efficiency.

Predictive Maintenance. According to the DIN EN 13306 standard, predictive maintenance (PdM) is defined as: the condition-based maintenance carried out following a forecast derived from repeated analysis or known characteristics and evaluation of the significant parameters of the degradation of the item. PdM is a subclass of CbM. Consequently, PdM is performed based on an estimate of the asset's health status, e.g., detection of Remaining Useful Life (RUL), saving costs, and improving the overall process efficiency. PdM uses a variety of approaches and ML methods to study both real-time data and historical data and to learn prognostic models that are expected to make accurate predictions about the status of a machine or equipment. The main challenge of predictive models is that they rely on the assumption that there are certain contexts in the equipment lifetime where the failure rate is increasing. In the industrial operational context, there are patterns in which the failure probability does not increase but remains constant during the equipment's lifetime. Therefore, the equipment can fail at any time; this is the case with electrical and electronic components.

Prescriptive Maintenance. Terminologically, neither the DIN EN 13306 nor the DIN EN 31051 maintenance standards mentions it, but its functionality can be consequently deduced and is seen as: a recommendation of one or more courses of action based on the outcomes of models for corrective and predictive maintenance. Existing prescriptive maintenance models are based on ad-hoc model development where ML methods and data fusion techniques are jointly used with fuzzy reasoning, simulation techniques, and evolutionary algorithms. The main challenge of prescriptive maintenance is the difficulty with building prescriptive, operative models in practice.

Tables 3, 4 and 5 introduced in Sect. 4 are constructed based on the reviewed literature on corrective, preventive, and predictive maintenance strategies. The tables present the surveyed literature, a structured review of the maintenance type and goals correlated with a specific statistical or data-driven operational method, and the corresponding results.

2.2 Multimodal ML Methods

Understanding the specific application context, or the business requirements is the first step for any learning model developed and deployed in an industrial environment. The main business requirements in the form of business goals must be identified, as they strongly influence all processes of model development. The basic steps of the model development life cycle for maintenance purposes are formalized by the CRISP-DM standard and explained in [11] i.e. (1) Business understanding, (2) Data acquisition and understanding, (3) Data preparation, (4) Data fusion, (5) Model development, (6) Model evaluation, and (7) Deployment.

Table 2. Multimodal ML methods

Representation	Learning to represent heterogeneous information in a unitary way, easy to be understood and processed by a learning model.
Translation	Mapping the information from one modality to another in a most accurate way.
Alignment	Identifying the inherent relations between sub-components. It also implies dealing with similarity measurements.
Fusion	Joining/combining in a meaningful way the information from different modalities.
Co-learning	Transferring knowledge among modalities: the modality with limited resources can benefit from another with more information.

In the context of the CRISP-DM data-driven development life cycle, our focus is the model development and the understanding of multimodal ML methods, in particular the model-agnostic multimodal data fusion.

Multimodality is defined by [14] as referring to the way something happens or is experienced: we read textual information, we see objects, we hear sounds, we feel textures and smell odors. All these perceptions represent modalities. A research problem, application, or data set is multimodal when it includes multiple such modalities.

To understand and to make sense of the world around us, A.I. techniques multimodal ML, must be able to interpret multimodal information and further to reason about it and make decisions. Multimodal ML is a multi-disciplinary field of research that builds models, that process and relate information from multiple modalities, as defined in [14]. The main idea is that data from different sensors provide different representations of the same phenomena. In MML literature, this is known as multimodal, multi-view, multi-representation, or multi-source learning, as described in [15]. The main multimodal ML methods were identified and defined in [14] i.e., representation, translation, alignment, fusion, and co-learning. Their definitions, according to references [14, 15], are listed in Table 2.

3 Research Methodology

3.1 Selection of Literature

A systematic search was employed to find journals and proceeding between 2016 and 2019 using the English language and the keywords: maintenance AND machine learning. We iteratively continued the search using the following keywords: predictive maintenance, multimodal machine learning, multimodal methods, multimodality, maintenance AND big data, maintenance AND Industry 4.0. A useful and predictive condition-based maintenance literature review using bibliometric indicators [16] helped us determine the most influential journals, articles, authors, and institutions in predictive condition-based maintenance, with the only drawback that the research reviews articles published up until December 2017, with the most cited papers dating back to the interval 2006–2009. We finally obtained a shorter literature list, which was further reduced by eliminating the duplicates when similar topics and approaches were found. Science Direct, Scopus, and Google Scholars were used, due to their wide collection of proceedings and journals. The conference and journal publications selected for our review belong to the non-empirical conceptual and mathematical fields of research. Consequently, they describe issues and perspectives related to maintenance strategies and their modeling techniques applied in an industrial setup. The overview of the reviewed maintenance literature is presented in Sect. 4, in Tables 3, 4 and 5.

3.2 Description of the Criteria Used for Analysis

Our survey focuses on: (i) the decision process in choosing a specific maintenance approach, i.e., maintenance goals, benefits, challenges, and obtained results; and (ii) the implementation of the maintenance approach, i.e., the employed prediction models and their corresponding modeling techniques. The selected literature was carefully examined to extract useful information based on the following criteria:

- Prediction models: reveal a taxonomy of the most active prediction model types employed in a maintenance process, i.e., physical models, knowledge-based models, database models, and hybrid models.
- Modelling techniques: represent the implementation pipeline (data analysis + algorithms) used. It is a relevant criterion which further helps us select the set of the most used ML algorithms to be critically reviewed.
- Obtained results/performance metrics: extract the information concerning how the model was evaluated and give us a hint about how optimal the data analysis and learning algorithms were applied.
- Maintenance goals: provide us with a taxonomy of topics showing the final decisions of the algorithm's pipeline. Paired with the modeling techniques criterion, it gives useful information about the successful algorithm pipeline used for a certain maintenance goal.

The literature review we conduct is formalized by [17, 18] and starts with clarifying relevant maintenance terminology and definitions based on the accepted, European maintenance standards [12, 13]. Thereby, the surveyed works we consider are grouped by maintenance approach, and further on, they are grouped by prediction models and the modeling techniques used in the implementation of the maintenance strategies.

4 Research Findings

This section presents the reviewed results displayed in Tables 3, 4 and 5.

The surveyed works we consider are grouped by maintenance type, and further on, they are grouped by prediction modeling types and relevant modeling techniques used in the implementations.

4.1 Corrective Maintenance

Our survey shows that the fault recognition and diagnostic is generally seen as a process of pattern recognition, i.e., the process of mapping the information, i.e., the features obtained in the measurement space to the machine faults in the fault space, as described in [19–22].

Table 3. Review of corrective maintenance models and corresponding implementation techniques: simplified table view. Full table view available in [23]

Prediction models	Modeling techniques	Obtained results	Maintenance goals	References
Knowledge-based models	Expert Systems + fault tree analysis	Real time supervision and monitoring + detection of foreseen faults	Real time monitoring: maintenance inspection on request	(Alexandru, A.; 1998) [24]
	Fuzzy similarity, fuzzy c-means algorithm	Drawback: new faults cannot be classified into new groups without repeatedly applying the spectral analysis	Classification models for fault diagnosis using unsupervised clustering	(Baraldi, P. et al.; 2014) [22]
Data-based models	Stochastic model: HMMs	HMMs are fully probabilistic models incorporating quasi-stationarity as a feature + they build robust and flexible classification models	Machine health status diagnostics +defect type classification	(Bunks, C., et al.;2004) [19]
	Artificial Neural Networks ANNs	Minimizes the frequency of revision inspections + in time online warning for unexpected new failures	Machine health status diagnostics in useful time	(Deuszkiewick, P., et al.;2003) [20]
	Statistical model: SVM +k-fold cross validation	Accuracy: 90% even when the standard deviation of noise is 3 times larger than normal: a better generalization than ANNs	Identification of 3 most possible faults types	(Hao, Y., et al.;2005) [21]

Diagnosis is a necessary part of any maintenance system, as using prognostics only cannot provide, in practice, a sure prediction that covers all failures and faults. In case of an unsuccessful prognosis, a diagnosis is a complementary tool for providing maintenance decision support. The methods employed in order to deal with fault classification and diagnostics are diverse: from expert systems [24] to hidden Markov models (HMM)s as presented in [19], artificial neural networks (ANN)s as described in [20], a support vector machine (SVM) as in [21], and fuzzy algorithms enhanced with spectral clustering and Haar wavelet transform as described in [22].

4.2 Preventive Maintenance

The reviewed literature shows that a relevant class of preventive maintenance techniques are the prognostics through pattern recognition, classification, and machine health status identification.

Table 4. Review of preventive maintenance models and corresponding implementation techniques: simplified table view. Full table view available in [23]

Prediction models	Modeling techniques	Obtained results	Maintenance goals	References
Knowledge-based models	Fuzzy Classifier + Decision Tree	Feature extraction and classification explained. The performance of the fuzzy inference has 95% accuracy	Pattern recognition + fault recognition and classification	(Krishnakumari, A., et al.;2017) [25]
Data-based models	Statistical model: Bayesian Inference	Feature-based fusion + concepts of global/local fusion (explained) + Bayesian inference explained	Machine health status assessment and condition monitoring	(Jaramillo, V. H., et al.;2017) [26]
	Statistical model: SVM + Fourier transformation + discrete Wavelet decomposition	Accuracy: 90%- feature-based fusion with multiple sensors provides complementary information to machining conditions	Multiple machine condition monitoring and recognition	(Liu, C., et al.; 2016) [27]
	k-NN based outlier remover + clustering approach of vibration events and joints + Fourier transformation	Real-time health score learned from historical data and used to check new events based on cluster centroids and joints representatives	Damage detection of abnormal or damaged patterns	(Diez, A., et al.; 2016) [28]
	ANNs and Deep Learning	Deep learning with statistical feature representation shows better performance metrics. Statistical features: time, frequency and time-frequency domains have different representation capabilities for fault patterns	Fault diagnostic and fault patterns identification	(Li, C., et al.; 2017) [29]
Hybrid models	Outlier Detection	High degree outliers are effective indicators of incipient failures	Fault detection	(Manco, G., et al.;2017) [3]

Prognostics analyze data by automatically finding new insights in terms of behavioral patterns. The information extracted from the monitored data can help detect patterns that characterize the machine working conditions or anticipate and estimate critical events like fault detection as in [3] and Remaining Useful Life (RUL) estimation as in [5].

Prognostics are considered superior to diagnostics in the sense that they prevent faults and are employed for prediction problems with items like spare parts and human resources, saving unplanned maintenance costs. The reference [30] proposes a data mining maintenance approach for predicting material requirements in the automotive industry by measuring the similarity of customer order groups. Identifying behavioral patterns in data means classifying similar data in some data-groups that share the same characteristics, i.e., operational conditions, as described by references [25–29].

Within these classified groups, there are data-points that are far from the identified pattern (i.e., the outliers), or they may correspond to a distinctive property (i.e., the mean point or the group distribution). Such patterns may help to identify faults or any other type of abnormal behavior. Large groups of data are interpreted as normal behavior, while small groups of data or events that are far from the pattern usually represent anomalies.

4.3 Predictive Maintenance

The survey shows that the predictive maintenance process has the goal of providing an accurate estimate of the RUL, but also, it should assess the provided estimate, as argued in [31–33]. Time series analysis is used to anticipate anomalies and malfunctions in equipment and process maintenance procedures. Traditional approaches are moving at an average rate over a time window, ARMA/ARMAX, Kalman filter, and cumulative sum, as described in [6].

Recursive neuronal networks (RNNs) show relevant characteristics for time series forecasting, as their loops allow information to persist, as presented in [5]. Multi-sensor fusion ranges from multi-signal combinations, as argued in [5, 6], to a more complex integration of the conditional assessment, RUL estimations, and decision-making, as presented in [2] and [7].

Operational predictive approaches are based on a schema that implies frequent and sometimes unnecessary maintenance of the equipment and of the entire production process that leads to high maintenance time and costs. They use complex AI-based algorithms, and data fusion strategies—in an ad-hoc manner, usually after trial and error approaches—which imply the usage of consecutive fusion algorithms, as described by reference [27]. The uncertainty in prediction is always a challenge, and, to this time, the fuzzy logic is used to represent uncertainties in prediction, as argued by [4]. As a case of condition-based maintenance, reference [34] shows that techniques for condition monitoring and diagnostics are gaining acceptance in the industry sectors, as they also prove to be effective in the predictive maintenance and quality control areas. The authors apply a feature-based fusion technique implemented with the cascade correlation neuronal network to multiple sensor data collected from rotating imbalance vibration of a test rig. The results show that the multi-sensory data fusion outperforms the single sensor diagnostic. The reference [35] focuses on the capability of providing real-time maintenance by extracting knowledge from the monitored assets (with vibration sensors) on the production line. Using intelligent, data-driven monitoring algorithms (ADMM), data

Table 5. Review of predictive maintenance models and corresponding implementation techniques: simplified table view. Full table view available in [23]

Prediction models	Modeling techniques	Obtained results	Maintenance goals	References
Knowledge-based models	Rule-based fuzzy logic + condition-based fusion diagnosis	Greater accuracy for multiple classifier fusion (vibration/current features)	General Maintenance	(Niu, G., et al.;2017) [4]
Data-based models	ADMM (altering direction method of multipliers) algorithm + Decision Fusion	Minimize operational costs + efficient energy consumption	Real-time analysis and processing of machine faults + health status monitoring	(Xenakis, A., et al.; 2019) [35]
	RNN-based health indicator for RUL prediction	High RUL prediction accuracy of generator bearings	RUL Prediction	(Guo, L., et al.; 2017) [5]
	kNN + discrete Bayesian filter	3-fold cross validation is successfully validating the approach. Average MAPE is computed and generates low errors for both applications	RUL Prediction	(Mosallam, A., et al.;2016) [31]
	Statistics + Deep Learning	Health Condition Profile with RUL and PoF (Probability of Failure) computed in a predetermined window of time	RUL and PoF Prediction	(Cristaldi, I., et al.; 2016) [33]
	PCA + kNN	Data from different sensors provide more information (as using only one sensor)	Condition-based monitoring and diagnosis	(Safizadeh, M., et al.; 2014) [10]
Hybrid models	k-means, association rules (GSP, Apriori), ANNs, Random Forest, Decision Tree, kNN	Accuracy: 90%, Random Forest with low precision (38%) which implies false alarms Recall(74%-ANNs)	Fault Prediction	(Acorsi, R., et al.;2016) [6]
	Simulation + multi-sensor fusion	Digital twin concept and many levels of Fusion for hard/soft data	Health Status estimation and maintenance	(Liu, Z., et al.;2018) [2]

fusion strategies, and the proposed three-level (IoT, Fog with gateway nodes for sensors aggregation, and Decision) layered system model, the authors argue on the efficiency of cloud-oriented maintenance.

The uncertainty in prediction is always a challenge, and to this time, fuzzy logic is used to represent uncertainties in prediction, as argued by [4, 30, 36–38], which showed that the problem of scheduling under the constraint of the deadline for all production jobs could also be solved using predictive maintenance algorithms. The efficiency of the algorithms for predicting machine failures is further evaluated by using simulation tests. The results, i.e., the optimized job schedules, show a nearly 50% drop in the number of operations compared with the initial nominal schedule.

4.4 Multimodal ML Methods: Data Fusion

A relevant research challenge for the multimodal data fusion perspective is to identify patterns and common governance rules that can be used to apply the appropriate multimodal data fusion technique in an application-specific context or for a data set.

Reference [38] argues that data fusion is a multidisciplinary research area with ideas raised from many diverse research fields such as signal processing, information theory, statistical estimation and inference, and artificial intelligence.

Data fusion appeared in the literature as mathematical models for data manipulation. The diversity of the research fields is indeed reflected in the reviews of maintenance techniques in Tables 3, 4 and 5.

Multimodal data fusion represents the integration of information from multiple modalities, with the goal of (i) making a prediction, and (ii) retrieving new insights from the joined knowledge, as defined by [14].

There are many approaches to data fusion, as the topic dates back to the 90s. The model-agnostic technique of data fusion is discussed in [14, 39] and later described by [15], which also lays the ground for the formal multimodal data fusion theory. Multimodal data fusion has a direct economic impact on the implementation of maintenance techniques, that are based on the aggregation of data from heterogeneous sources into actionable decisions for maintenance purposes. Multimodal data fusion represents the core concept in MML, as argued in references [14, 15, 38, 39]. The model-agnostic data fusion types that are used in the operational environment are listed in Table 6.

Table 6. Model-agnostic fusion types

Early Fusion	Features from all the modalities are concatenated as one long input and trained by a single learner.
Hybrid Fusion	There is a single learning model that is trained with a preprocessed input from modalities in the fused layer. It is implemented by neural networks and multikernel support vector machine algorithms.
Late Fusion	Each modality is trained with a different learning model that independently decides. All decisions generated by learning models are later combined based on a fusing schema.

Reference [15] lays the grounds for the multimodal data fusion theory by giving a solution to the research problem of determining the appropriate type of data fusion for a specific application context or a data set. In the authors' view, the main challenge in multimodal data fusion research revolves around the dependency-problem, i.e., the arguments for choosing a specific type of data fusion. The assumption is that the optimal fusion type to be employed in an operational environment depends on the level of dependency we expect to see between the inputs in the modalities: (i) feature-based fusion assumes a dependency at the lowest level of features (or raw input unprocessed data), (ii) intermediate-fusion assumes a dependency at a more abstract, semantic level; and (iii) decision-based fusion assumes no dependency at all in the input, but only later at the level of decisions.

5 Discussion of Findings

Our literature review reveals that past works on industrial maintenance approaches show that maintenance actions are performed by employing various prediction models and modeling techniques.

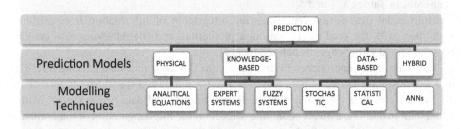

Fig. 1. Taxonomy of prediction models

However, the existent literature does not inform us to which extent the new A.I. technology, based on ML methods and techniques, is influencing and changing the maintenance strategies in the industrial environment.

We show in Fig. 1 that predictive maintenance models can be classified into four distinctive categories: physical models, knowledge-based models, data-driven models, and hybrid models.

Physical models use the laws of physics to describe the behavior of a failure, as presented in reference [2]. Knowledge-based models assess similarities among observed situations and a set of previously defined failures. These models can be sub-divided in expert system models that are able to answer complex queries as presented by reference [24] and fuzzy models as in reference [4]. Both model types employ a deductive, top-down approach that builds mathematical models and rule-based models, respectively, based on the domain experts' knowledge of the analyzed system. The higher complexity of real systems represents the main challenge for these models.

Data-driven models are based on acquired data. These types of models can further be distinguished among stochastic models, statistical models and artificial neural networks (ANNs). Data-based models employ an inductive, bottom-up approach that empirically builds a learning model from historical or live data. Stochastic models provide event-based information with hidden Markov models and Kalman filters belonging to this category. Statistical models predict a future state by comparing the monitored results with a machine-health state without faults. Hybrid models use combinations of two or more modeling techniques as in [40–42].

Among data-driven models, the ML models represent a category of relevant prediction models for maintenance optimization. Some consider them to be statistical models. However, the ML methods are focusing on increasing the accuracy of their predictions, while the classical statistical community is more concerned with the understanding of their models and of the model's parameters, i.e., model calibration and inference.

As displayed in Fig. 2, ML techniques for maintenance can be divided into two main categories depending on their type of employed ML approach: (i) a supervised approach, where information on the occurrence of failures is present in the dataset and (ii) an unsupervised approach, where the asset/process information is available but no maintenance-related data exists.

Classification is one of the most used ML methods that occurs in a wide range of maintenance scenarios. Classification models predict categorical (discrete and unordered) class labels. Maintenance classification techniques are applied when there is a need to distinguish between the faulty and non-faulty conditions of the system being monitored.

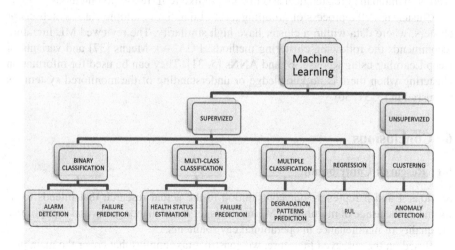

Fig. 2. ML approaches and techniques for prediction models

Binary classification methods are used to predict the probability that an industrial asset fails within an established time period in the future. The testing datasets must contain positive and negative examples that indicate the failure and normal operating conditions, respectively. Consequently, the target variables are usually categorical in nature. The learning model identifies each new example as likely to fail or likely to work over the next period.

The business requirements, the analyzed available data, and the domain experts make estimations for the (i) minimum lead time required to replace components, deploy resources, and perform maintenance actions to avoid a problem that is likely to occur in the future or (ii) a minimum count of events that can be triggered before a critical problem occurs. Multi-class classification methods are used for making predictions in the following possible scenarios: (i) defining a plan maintenance schedule, i.e., estimation of the time intervals when an asset has the bigger probability of failing; (ii) monitoring the health status of an asset, i.e., estimation of the probability that an asset will fail due to a specific cause-/root problem; and (iii) prediction that an asset will fail due to a specific type of failure. In this case, a set of prescriptive maintenance actions can be considered for each of the previously identified set of failures. Multiple classifiers represent a type of ML method for classification, which can be used in the process of knowledge discovery to discern patterns of data degradation for an asset or a process. The benefits of multiple classifiers reside in allowing the planning of the maintenance schedules using a statistical cost minimization approach, as discussed in [1].

Regressions are typically used to compute the RUL of an item, as presented in [36]. RUL is defined as the amount of time that an asset is operational before the next failure occurs. The operational historical data is needed because the RUL calculation is not possible without knowing how long the asset has survived before a failure. While classification methods are used to distinguish between faulty and healthy behaviors based on the historical data, they do not intuitively map to health factors that can be further used in maintenance-related decision making, unlike RUL regression methods.

Clustering is the process of grouping a set of data into multiple classes, subsets or clusters, where data within a cluster have high similarity. The reviewed ML literature recommends the following clustering methods: PCA + k-Means [37] and variants of Deep Learning using RNNs [36] and ANNs [5, 31]. They can be used for information clustering when there is no knowledge or understanding of the monitored system, as discussed in [5, 31, 36].

6 Conclusions

6.1 Research Contribution

Sections 4 and 5 represent our contribution to the actual research that intends to (i) formalize the usage of multimodal ML methods for maintenance goals, and (ii) optimize the quality of maintenance in operational environments.

Based on the surveyed literature, we construct taxonomies that cover the main predictive models and their modeling techniques relative to maintenance goals. We show that among all data-driven prediction models, the ML approaches are the most suitable to deal with big volumes of heterogeneous data. They are accepted in the field because prediction is considered easier than model inference, i.e., the ML models are performing tests to check how well a learning model that is trained on a data set, can accurately predict new data. This allows the ML methods to work with larger volumes of complex, heterogeneous, and unstructured data easily.

6.2 Implications for Research and Practice

Our review shows that ML and multimodality are receiving attention from both academia and practice as technical ways for implementing maintenance goals. However, the research is still in its early phase, as there are basic issues that are biasing the usage of multimodal ML methods in operational environments. As argued in reference [43], (i) there are no established, standard methods by which to identify feature dependencies in multiple sensors and modalities; (ii) the technology exists, but there are no standard methods by which to extract unbiased feature from raw data, and therefore, deep learning methods are preferred; (iii) multimodal data fusion best practices, i.e., data sets, fusion algorithms, success stories, training, and evaluation of results, should be recorded and shared; (iv) the absence of a clearly defined generic framework to standardize the usage of a data fusion pipeline, i.e., it is clear that in an operational environment, more than one data fusion technique should be applied; (v) there are no standard techniques for dealing with temporal and spatial (aka contextual) data alignment and synchronization; and (vi) there is a lack of research studies by which to analyze the performance of ML algorithms in a cloud environment.

Thus, we argue that the quality of maintenance in an industrial setup can be improved only when, in the development of a generalized architecture for predictive maintenance purposes, the following aspects are considered: (i) the technological aspect that recognizes the potential of multimodal ML methods for maintenance purposes; (ii) the business aspect that envisions a structured development of the implementation works, starting with the business model's conceptualization and assuring its conformity with industry standards, such as Industrial Data Space and CRISP_DM; and (iii) the economic aspect that follows the classical optimization concerns relative to maintenance costs.

The approach we envision for the optimization of predictive, industrial maintenance investigates the ML technical perspective and, consequently, focuses on a variety of (multimodal) ML methods that study both live and historical information to learn prognostics data and perform accurate diagnostics and predictions.

6.3 Limitations and Future Works

For our research work, we are not considering the empirical research perspective, i.e., we are not discussing the maintenance strategies and their operationalization based on information obtained from interviews or from analyzing relevant case studies.

Future works are planned to analyze the usage of multimodal ML methods combined with semantic technologies in a cloud-oriented environment. The goal is to overcome the problem of sensor integration for efficient data analysis. We recognize that the actual trend for maintenance engineering is cloud maintenance. Within this context, the envisioned digital platform is seen as a management system of smart services, i.e., prediction-as-a-service and maintenance-as-a-service, with expected benefits in terms of technology, performance, and costs.

References

1. Susto, G.A., Mcloone, S., Pampuri, S., Benghi, A., Schirru, A.: Machine learning for predictive maintenance: a multiple classifier approach. IEEE Trans. Ind. Informat. **11**(3), 812–820 (2015). https://doi.org/10.1109/TII.2014.2349359
2. Liu, Z., Norbert, M., Nezih, M.: The role of Data Fusion in predictive maintenance using Digital Twin. AIP Conf. Proc. **1949**(1), 020023 (2018). https://doi.org/10.1063/1.5031520

3. Manco, G., et al.: Fault detection and explanation through big data analysis on sensor streams. Expert Syst. Appl. **87**, 141–156 (2018). https://doi.org/10.1016/j.eswa.2017.05.079
4. Niu, G., Li, H.: IETM centered intelligent maintenance system integrating fuzzy semantic inference and data fusion. Microelectron. Reliab. **75**, 197–204 (2017). https://doi.org/10.1016/j.microrel.2017.03.015
5. Guo, L., Li, N., Jia, F., Lei, Y., Lin, J.: A recurrent neural network-based health indicator for remaining useful life prediction of bearings. Neurocomputing **240**, 98–109 (2017). https://doi.org/10.1016/j.neucom.2017.02.045
6. Acorsi, R., Manzini, R., Pascarella, P., Patella, M., Sassi, S.: Data Mining and Machine Learning for Condition-based Maintenance. In: (eds.) Proceedings of the 2017 International Conference on Flexible Automation and Intelligent Manufacturing FAIM, 27–30 June 2017, Modena, Italy, pp. 1153-1161 (2017). https://doi.org/10.1016/j.promfg.2017.07.239
7. Safizadeh, M., Latifi, S.: Using multisensory data fusion for vibration fault diagnosis of rolling element bearings by accelerometer and load cell. Inf. Fusion **18**(1), 1–8 (2014). https://doi.org/10.1016/j.inffus.2013.10.002
8. Schmidt, B., Sandberg, U., Wang, U.: Next generation condition based Predictive Maintenance. Methods **13306**, 4–11 (2014)
9. Schenk, M.: Instandhaltung technischer Systeme. Springer, Heidelberg (2009). https://doi.org/10.1007/978-3-642-03949-2
10. Otto, B., et al.: Industrial Data Space – Digital sovereignty over data, In: Fraunhofer Gesellschaft zur Förderung der angewandten Forschung (2016)
11. Diez-Olivan, A., del Ser, J., Galar, D., Sierra, B.: Data fusion and machine learning for industrial prognosis: Trends and perspectives towards Industry 40. Information Fusion **50**, 92–111 (2019). https://doi.org/10.1016/j.inffus.2018.10.005
12. DIN EN-13306. DIN Standards – Maintenance terminology, Beuth Publishing DIN (2018). https://dx.doi.org/10.31030/2641990
13. DIN EN-31051. DIN Standards – Fundamentals of maintenance, Beuth Publishing DIN (2019). https://dx.doi.org/10.31030/3048531
14. Baltrusaitis, T., Ahuja, C., Morency, L.: Multimodal Machine Learning: A Survey and Taxonomy. IEEE Trans. Pattern Anal. Mach. Intell. **41**(2), 423–443 (2019). https://doi.org/10.1109/TPAMI.2018.2798607
15. Alpaydin, E.: Classifying multimodal data. In: Oviatt, S., Schuller, B., Cohen, P.R., Sonntag, D., Potamianos, G., Krüger, A. (eds.) The Handbook of Multimodal-Multisensor Interfaces, In Association for Computing Machinery and Morgan & Claypool, NY, pp. 49–69 (2018)
16. Noman, N.A., Nasr, E.S.A., AlShayea, A., Kaid, H.: Overview of predictive condition based maintenance research using bibliometric indicators. J. K. Saud Univ. Eng. Sci. **31**(4), 355–367 (2019)
17. Oates, B.J.: Researching Information Systems and Computing. Sage Publications Ltd., Thousand Oaks (2006)
18. Peffers, K., Tuunanen, T., Rothenberger, M., Chatterjee, S.: A design science research methodology for information systems research. J. Manag. Inf. Syst. **24**(3), 45–77 (2007). https://doi.org/10.2753/MIS0742-1222240302
19. Bunks, C., McCarthy, D., Al-Ani, T.: Condition-based Maintenance of machines using hidden Markov Models. Mech. Syst. Sign. Process. **14**(4), 597–612 (2000). https://doi.org/10.1006/mssp.2000.1309
20. Deuszkiewick, P., Radkowski, S.: On-line condition monitoring of a power transmission unit of a rail vehicle. Mech. Syst. Sign. Process. **17**(6), 1321–1334 (2003). https://doi.org/10.1006/mssp.2002.1578
21. Hao, Y., Sun, J., Yang, G., Bai, J.: The application of support vector machines to gas turbines performance diagnosis. Chinese J. Aeronaut. **18**(1), 15–19 (2005). https://doi.org/10.1016/S1000-9361(11)60276-8

22. Baraldi, P., Zio, E., di Maio, F.: Unsupervised clustering for fault diagnostics in nuclear power plants components. Int. J. Comp. Intell. Syst. **6**(4), 764–777 (2014). https://doi.org/10.1080/18756891.2013.804145

23. Merkt, O.: On the Use of Predictive Models for Improving the Quality of Industrial Maintenance: an Analytical Literature Review of Maintenance Strategies. In: Ganzha, M., Maciaszek, L., Paprzycki, M. (eds.) Proceedings of the 2019 Federated Conference on Computer Science and Information Systems FedCSIS, 1–4 September, pp. 693-704. Leipzig University, Leipzig, Germany (2019). https://dx.doi.org/10.15439/2019F101

24. Alexandru, A.: Using Expert Systems for Fault Detection and Diagnosis. Industrial Applications (1998)

25. Krishnakumari, A., Elayaperumal, A., Saravanan, M., Arvindan, C.: Fault diagnostics of spur gear using decision tree and fuzzy classifier. Int. J. Adv. Manuf. Technol. **89**(9–12), 3487–3494 (2017). https://doi.org/10.1007/s00170-016-9307-8

26. Jaramillo, V.H., Ottewill, J.R., Dudek, R., Lepiarczyk, D., Pawlik, P.: Condition monitoring of distributed systems using two-stage Bayesian inference data fusion. Mech. Syst. Sign. Process. **87**, 91–110 (2017). https://doi.org/10.1016/j.ymssp.2016.10.004

27. Liu, C., Li, Y., Zhou, G., Shen, W.: A sensor fusion and support vector machine-based approach for recognition of complex machining conditions. J. Intell. Manuf. **29**(8), 1739–1752 (2018). https://doi.org/10.1007/s10845-016-1209-y

28. Diez, A., Khoa, N.L.D., Alamdari, M.M., Wang, Y., Chen, F., Runcie, P.: A clustering approach for structural health monitoring on bridges. J. Civil Struct. Health Monit. **6**(3), 429–445 (2016)

29. Li, C., Sánchez, R.-V., Zurita, G., Cerrada, M., Cabrera, D.: Fault diagnosis for rotating machinery using vibration measurement deep statistical feature learning. Sensors **16**(6), 895, 1–19 (2016)

30. Widmer, T., Klein, A., Wachter, P., Meyl, S.: Predicting Material Requirements in the Automotive Industry Using Data Mining. In: Abramowicz, W., Corchuelo, R. (eds.) BIS 2019. LNBIP, vol. 354, pp. 147–161. Springer, Cham (2019). https://doi.org/10.1007/978-3-030-20482-2_13

31. Mosallam, A., Medjaher, K., Zerhouni, N.: Data-driven prognostic method based on Bayesian approaches for direct remaining useful life prediction. J. Intell. Manuf. **27**(5), 1037–1048 (2016). https://doi.org/10.1007/s10845-014-0933-4

32. Alsina, E.F., Chica, M., Trawinski, K., Regattieri, A.: On the use of Machine Learning methods to predict component reliability from data-driven industrial case studies. Int. J. Adv. Manuf. Technol. **94**(5–8), 2419–2433 (2018). https://doi.org/10.1007/s00170-017-1039-x

33. Cristaldi, L., Leone, G., Ottoboni, R., Subbiah, S., Turrin, S.: A comparative study on data-driven prognostic approaches using fleet knowledge. In: Arpaia, A., Catelani, M., Cristaldi, L. (eds.) Proceedings of the 2016 IEEE International Conference on Instrumentation and Measurement Technology (I2MTC), 23–26 May, 2016, Taipei, Taiwan, pp. 1-6 (2016). https://doi.org/10.1109/I2MTC.2016.7520371

34. Liu, Q. (C.), Wang, H.P. (B.): A case study on multisensory data fusion for imbalanced diagnosis of rotating machinery. AI EDAM 15(**3**), 203–2010 (2001)

35. Xenakis, A., Karageorgos, A., Lallas, E., Chis, A.E., Gonzalez-Velez, H.: Towards distributed IoT/cloud based fault detection and maintenance in industrial automation. In: Shakshuki, M.E., Yasar, A.-U.-H. (eds.) Proceedings of the 10th International Conference on Ambient Systems, Networks and Technologies (ANT 2019), April 29 - May 2, 2019, Leuven, Belgium, pp. 683–690 (2019). https://doi.org/10.1016/j.procs.2019.04.091

36. Sobaszek, Ł., Gola, A., Kozłowski, E.: Application of survival function in robust scheduling of production jobs. In: Ganzha, M., Maciaszek, L., Paprzycki, M. (eds.) Proceedings of the 2017 Federated Conference on Computer Science and Information systems FedCSIS, 3–6 September 2017, pp. 575-578. Czech Technical University in Prague, Prague (2017). http://dx.doi.org/10.15439/2017F276

37. Sobaszek, Ł., Gola, A., Kozłowski, E.: Job-shop scheduling with machine breakdown prediction under completion time constraint. In: Ganzha, M., Maciaszek, L., Paprzycki, M. (eds.) Proceedings of the 2018 Federated Conference on Computer Science and Information Systems FedCSIS, 9–12 September 2018, pp. 437-440. Adam Mickiewicz university Poznan, Poland (2018). http://dx.doi.org/10.15439/2018F83

38. Khaleghi, B., Karray, F., Khamis, A., Razavi, S.N.: Multisensor data fusion: a review of the state-of-the-art. Inf. Fusion **14**, 28–44 (2013). https://doi.org/10.1016/j.inffus.2011.08.001

39. Bengio, Y., Courville, A., Vincent, P.: Representation learning: a review and new perspectives, Technical report. Univ. Montreal, **35**(8), 1798–1828 (2013). https://doi.org/10.1109/TPAMI.2013.50

40. Baban, C.F., Baban, M., Suteu, M.D.: Using a fuzzy logic approach for the predictive maintenance of textile machines. J. Intell. Fuzzy Syst. **30**(2), 999–1006 (2016). https://doi.org/10.3233/IFS-151822

41. Cui, W., Lu, Z., Li, C., Han, X.: A proactive approach to solve integrated production scheduling and maintenance planning problem in flow shops. Comput. Ind. Eng. **115**, 342–353 (2018). https://doi.org/10.1016/j.cie.2017.11.020

42. Seidgar, H., Zandieh, M., Mahdavi, I.: An efficient metaheuristic algorithm for scheduling a two-stage assembly flow shop problem with preventive maintenance activities and reliability approach. Int. J. Ind. Syst. Eng. **26**(1), 16–41 (2017). https://doi.org/10.1504/IJISE.2017.083180

43. Chou, C.-A., Jin, X., Müller, A., Ostadabbas, S.: MMDF 2018 Multimodal Data Fusion Workshop Report. Northeastern University, Boston (2018)

Framework for Project Management in Agile Projects: A Quantitative Study

Gloria J. Miller[(⊠)] (iD)

maxmetrics, Heidelberg, Germany
g.j.m@ieee.org

Abstract. Recent studies have confirmed the efficacy of agile methodologies in project success, but can projects skip several project management tasks and still deliver the expected results? How are traditional project managers engaged in agile projects? Who executes what project management tasks in projects applying agile methodologies? The aim of this study was to define a framework for project management tasks in agile projects. The results quantify subjective and theoretical speculation on who performs the project management tasks in agile projects. Project managers are engaged in agile projects, and the team, the product owner, and the project sponsor are significantly involved in project management tasks. The agile coach is not a substitute for the project manager. This study identifies areas where agile methodologies should be updated to clarify team responsibilities for project management activities.

Keywords: Project management · Agile · Scrum · ISO · Product owner · Agile coach · Scrum master · Project manager

1 Introduction

While the adoption of agile project management methodologies is widespread [1], the project management tasks in agile projects are uncertain, and this lack of clarity causes confusion in practice [2–4]. Agile methodologies provide events, processes, and artifacts that should allow projects to be flexible to change and deliver results in an iterative, incremental fashion. Some of the most popular agile project management frameworks—such as scrum, extreme programming (XP), and lean/Kanban processes—do not explicitly include a project manager role or project management tasks. For example, scrum includes three roles: a scrum master, product owner, and the team [5].

Shastri, Hoda, and Amor [6] found that the project manager, by all means, still exists in agile projects; however, their study left open the questions as to what activities the project manager performs. "The implementation of agile methods can have a very significant impact on the role of the project manager, but a better understanding of the circumstances under which the project manager role changes and how it changes is needed" [4, p. 11]. Even the *Agile Practice Guide* issued by the Project Management Institute (PMI) in 2017 states that the "role of the Project Manager in an agile project is somewhat unknown" [7, p. 37].

© Springer Nature Switzerland AG 2020
E. Ziemba (Ed.): AITM 2019/ISM 2019, LNBIP 380, pp. 155–174, 2020.
https://doi.org/10.1007/978-3-030-43353-6_9

Several research articles start with the premise that there is an agile project manager, who is a facilitator or coach [8–11]. Noll, Razzak, Bass, and Beecham [2], however, found that tension was created when the scrum master, a coaching role in scrum, was expected to perform the project management tasks and coach the team. In addition, the boundary between the role of the project manager and that of the team is blurred and leads to difficulty at the team level [3, 12]. There is some speculation that the project manager is better suited to assume the product owner role [2] than the agile coach. This option, however, is not transparent in the methodology description [5, 13] and has not been addressed in the literature. While other studies have investigated agility in projects or the effects of specific practices on the success of projects applying agile methodologies [1, 14, 15], they have not clarified the project management activities.

The success rate for projects using agile methodologies is on a par with, if not better than, the success rate for projects managed under a traditional methodology [1]. In agile methodologies, some but not all of the typical project management responsibilities have been assigned to other roles [11]. Thus, if agile methodologies are followed rigorously and exclude a project manager, then the project manager role and some project management tasks may be obsolete. The literature provides conflicting information on the role of the project manager in agile projects, and it is limited in explaining how the other project roles are engaged in the project management activities. Thus, the question of who performs what project management activities in agile projects remains unanswered. Therefore, this study addresses the questions of *how are traditional project managers engaged in agile projects and who executes what project management tasks in projects applying agile methodologies?*

First, we performed a literature review to penetrate project management and the role of the project manager in project work under agile methodologies. We mapped the project management tasks under an agile methodology to the project management knowledge areas and processes from the International Organization for Standardization (ISO) project management standards. Next, we defined and conducted a survey to ascertain which project roles perform which project management tasks. Finally, we quantitatively analyzed the survey results using a case-controlled match analysis to answer the research questions.

The results from this study quantify subjective and theoretical speculation on who performs the project management tasks in agile projects. By providing a framework for the project management activities and the project manager's role in agile projects, the results contribute to the project management literature on agile methodologies.

The next section reviews the literature. Section 3 describes the research methodology. Section 4 presents the data analysis and results. Section 5 provides a discussion of the results. The final section of this paper discusses the conclusions and implications.

2   Literature Review

2.1   Traditional Project Management Methodologies

"A project is a temporary organization to which [human, material, or financial] resources are assigned to do work to bring about beneficial change" [16, p. 1], and "project management is the means by which the work of the resources assigned to the temporary organization is managed and controlled to deliver the beneficial change desired by the owner" [17, p. 93]. Project management lifecycles, activities, and roles are codified in project management methodologies. The traditional, waterfall and plan-driven methodologies are lifecycles that follow a stage-gate or phased lifecycle. These methods have in common the creation of an upfront plan, where the time is limited, with the limitation and termination conditions known from the beginning [18]. The methodologies and frameworks for traditional projects are codified in the project management standards and frameworks, such as "ISO 21500:2012, Guidance on Project Management" [19], *APM Body of Knowledge 6th Edition* [20], and *A Guide to the Project Management Body of Knowledge* (PMBOK guide) [21]. There is a positive relationship between the use of a project management methodology and project success. This is the case if the methodologies are comprehensive—including tools, techniques, process capability profiles, and knowledge areas—or if they need to be supplemented with some elements [22].

2.2 Agile Project Management Methodologies

The *Agile Manifesto* is a set of four values and 13 principles that provide a framework for managing technology projects in a flexible way that responds to dynamic project situations [1, 23, 24]. The principles and values from the *Agile Manifesto* offer a framework on how people should work [24]. Consequently, the manifesto does not explicitly establish who should do the work. Several methodologies or frameworks can be considered to follow the values and principles described in the *Agile Manifesto*. Each agile methodology has its own set of rules, events, and practices; however, in general, they all encourage iterative and incremental development lifecycles, self-organizing teams, and evolutionary product development. Scrum, XP, lean, and Kanban are the most frequently referenced agile methodologies in surveys on agile adoption and in the project management literature [6].

2.3 Project Manager

The project manager is the authorized person who leads and manages project activities and is accountable for project completion [25]. The role is defined in ISO, Association for Project Management (APM), and PMI project management standards and frameworks. In addition, the standards describe subject areas in which a project manager is expected to be knowledgeable and processes that should be led or executed as part of managing a project. The project management literature agrees that the project manager has sole responsibility for planning and managing projects [25]. The project manager should direct the performance of the planned project activities and manage the various technical, administrative, and organizational interfaces within the project [19, 21].

The project manager role is not explicit in the agile methodology. Noll, Razzak, Bass, and Beecham [2] found that the scrum master, a coaching role in the scrum agile methodology, in practice combines project management activities with coaching; however, tension is created, since the scrum master is expected to balance management activities with coaching the team. The inherent suggestion in studies on project managers in agile projects is that the leadership style or skills, knowledge, personal attributes, and behavior of the project manager must be adapted [10, 11, 26, 27].

2.4 Project Management Tasks

In the ISO project management standards, 39 processes in 10 subject areas that cover five process groups are described for the project management role [19, 24]. The project management tasks in plan-driven methodologies are centralized to the project manager role.

In agile methodologies, some of the project management responsibilities are inherent in the methods, while other project management activities or tasks are not explicitly identified. Studies on project managers in agile projects have identified conflicts with other agile roles or assumed that project managers must adapt to manage agile projects [3, 5, 12, 13]. Binder, Aillaud, and Schilli [24] correlated the 12 agile principles to the ISO processes to establish a hybrid model for managing agile projects. They identified gaps and practice modifications that would need to occur to enable effective management of agile projects [3, 12]; however, they did not take a position on who performs the tasks. Shastri, Hoda, and Amor [28] describe the activities for an agile project manager from the project manager's perspective without considering how other roles or the method assumes some of the project management responsibilities.

2.5 Summary

The project management tasks in plan-driven methodologies are centralized to the project manager role. In agile methodologies, some of the project management responsibilities are inherent in the methodological processes, while other project management activities or tasks are not explicitly identified. Research suggests that project managers are engaged in agile projects; however, the engagement of project managers engenders conflict and confusion. We could not identify any studies that show a view of project management tasks across all roles within an agile project. This deficiency in the literature means there is no clear guidance for project sponsors on the management of agile projects.

2.6 Research Questions

The goal of this research was to define a framework for project management tasks in agile projects. Therefore, this study addresses the questions of *how are traditional project managers engaged in agile projects and who executes what project management tasks in projects applying agile methodologies?*

To answer the research questions, we needed to investigate projects for the engagement and interaction of the methods and project roles in project management tasks. We used a mixed-method methodology, including a qualitative assignment of project roles to project management tasks, a quantitative study using a survey instrument to identify field practices, and a matching study to analyze the results.

3 Research Methodology

We performed a literature review to define the project management boundaries, authority, tasks, and roles in projects using agile methodologies. Next, we used quantitative analysis to determine how the project management tasks are practiced in agile projects. Finally, based on the case-controlled match analysis, we defined the project management task framework.

3.1 Theoretical Framework

We used the boundary, authority, role, and task (BART) system to investigate and define the project management task framework for agile projects. The BART system is used in Tavistock or in group relations and conferences as a method of individual learning through experience and reflection [29, 30]. Psychoanalyst Wilfred R. Bion developed the theory that an individual should be studied as a member of the group to which he or she belongs [29]. Bion's seminal work and experiments lead to viewing a group as a collective entity. Given that the objective was to study the project management roles and activities within a temporary organization of group work, we identified the BART system as an effective framework for investigating the project management roles and responsibilities in projects.

The components of the BART system are as follows. The *boundary* is the container for group work, and it must be clearly specified, agreed upon, and adhered to [30]. *Authority* is the right to complete work. It assumes there is responsibility for activities and accountability for actions [30]. Authority should be clearly defined by the granter and should be understood, acted upon, and empowered with the right tools by the receiver [30]. The formal authority may be given to the group or body through delegation of responsibilities by the granter. The personal authority, or the way an individual assumes formal authority, may exert influence by inhibiting or exaggerating the execution of the authority. There are formal and informal *roles*. The formal role defines the duties, parameters, people and processes for interaction, and the outcomes or deliverables that define the performance expectations [30]. Formal roles are usually defined by written descriptions, such as job descriptions or contracts. Informal roles are defined when people fill gaps in authority and are assumed implicitly. The *tasks* are the work to be completed and include activities to support the mission of the group, activities to enable the group to survive as a group, and activities to manage the collective activities of the group [30].

3.2 Mapping Tasks and Roles

First, to identify project managers' activities in agile projects, we evaluated peer-reviewed journal publications from 2006 to 2018. Given the lack of literature in this area, we created a task construct. We mapped the 10 project management knowledge areas and 39 processes from the "ISO 21500:2012, Guidance on Project Management" [19] standard to the agile principles according to the correlation matrix from [24] and to the scrum roles, artifacts, and events according to [5]. We chose the scrum methodology, as it is the most popular agile methodology in practice [6]. The areas without a mapping represented the gaps between processes in the ISO project management standards and those suggested by the agile principle and scrum. The gaps included processes in the stakeholder, cost, risk, procurement, and communications subject areas.

Where there were gaps for the project management tasks, we developed measurement items. Thus, we used a web-based survey to request information on who performs these tasks in agile projects.

3.3 Survey

Second, we used a web-based survey to collect data on the roles engaged in projects and the project management tasks they perform. To explore the difference between the theoretical and practical applications of project management tasks, we employed a quantitative analysis method.

The population for the survey was comprised of project sponsors, project managers, and project team members who had executed agile and non-agile projects in the past 10 years. The number of potential projects is unknowable. Nevertheless, we noted that approximately 24,728 people were certified as agile by PMI at the time of the study [31].

We collected data from members of social media agile and project management groups. We sent invitations to complete a web-based questionnaire to social media groups on LinkedIn, Xing, and Twitter. To gather information from as many projects as possible without regard to project methodology, we chose a wide selection of project management and agile groups (e.g., PMI, Scrum Alliance). The membership numbers for the groups are in the hundreds of thousands; however, there is no method to determine how many people saw or read the invitations. It was, therefore, not possible to determine the response rate.

To ensure proper technical functioning, we tested the survey operations using different devices (i.e., PC and iPad). The survey was available over a 10-day period in January 2019. Respondents were asked to provide information on their last project. The respondents were promised confidentiality and anonymity. A total of 120 respondents started and completed the survey. We checked the responses for extreme responses (all zeros, all fives for a five-point Likert scale, or all sevens for seven-point scale). We performed checks to determine whether there were missing data for mandatory fields or all the same values had been selected for the matrix questions. If we had encountered such a situation, we would have classified the associated data as bad data and removed it. We found no bad data. We analyzed the survey data as described in the following sections.

Measurement Instrument. This paper is concerned with the relationship between the roles in the project and the project management tasks they perform in agile projects; however, the effect of the role on task assignment should be evaluated against a performance criterion. To evaluate the impacts of the task assignment, we selected project efficiency and success. Furthermore, the importance of the task should be judged against a benchmark. In this study, we compared the task executions between agile and non-agile projects.

We used a measurement instrument to collect demographic data, project size attributes, project performance measures, project roles, and responsibility for project management tasks. We created the constructs based on project management literature and standards. Where possible, we used existing constructs. This section describes the survey questions used to collect the data and the derived measurement items.

Project Roles. To elicit the project roles that were engaged in the project, the following two questions were used. *What roles were involved in the project? (Select all that apply, including yours). What was your major role in the project? (Select one).* For the analysis, we created five derived measures. We created a binary variable for role combinations as follows: *agile coach* when agile coach or scrum master was selected; *team role* when IT members, business members, hardware or software vendors, or others were selected; *project sponsor role* when investors in or sponsors of the project were selected; *program management office role* for program managers or members of project/program management; and the *project manager role* for the project manager. We created an additional variable, *full scrum,* for the situation where all scrum roles were present: product owner, agile coach, and at least one team member.

Methodologies. To elicit the methodology used in the project, the following question was used: *What methodology or framework most closely describes the one used in the project?* In addition, we used the measure to create a derived measure for the methodology type to group the methodologies into agile, mixed, or plan-driven using the following assignment: (1) *agile* methodologies include scrum, XP, scrum/XP hybrid, Kanban, lean, scaled agile methods (SAFe, LESS, APM, DAD, RAGE, NEXUS, and scrum of scrums), custom hybrid-agile (multiple agile methodologies), and other agile methodologies (Feature-Driven Development, Dynamic Systems Development Method Atern, AgileUP, or others); (2) *plan-driven* methodologies include waterfall and other plan-driven methodologies (spiral or staged methodologies); and (3) *mixed* methodologies include iterative and custom hybrid-mixed methodologies (agile and non-agile methodologies).

Tasks. Who was responsible for performing these tasks? Select one role per task. This was a matrix question used to identify which of the following six roles were responsible for the following 10 tasks:

- *Roles*: project sponsor, project manager, agile coach/scrum master, product owner, team, and other; not applicable (N/A) was included as an option.
- *Tasks*: establish project team; manage stakeholders; manage project team; control resources; establish budget; control costs; identify risks; assess, treat, and control risks; plan and administer procurements; and select suppliers.

We selected the tasks based upon tasks that were identified in the ISO standards as being applicable to project management but lacked a corresponding definition of a responsible role in the agile principles or scrum methodology. We created a matrix that identified the role that undertook the tasks and verified that the role was also selected as a project role during data entry.

Project Performance. Following the model used in Serrador and Pinto [1], we created a composite variable for project efficiency. We created the variable as the mean value from responses to the following three questions. *How did the project do in meeting the project budget goals? How did the project do in meeting the project time goals? How did the project do in meeting the project scope and requirement goals?* Each question was based on a seven-point scale that ranged from under-performing to over-performing.

These questions and scales were used in previous project management research [1]. In addition, each question resulted in a measure that we used in the comparative analysis: *budget performance*, *time performance*, and *requirement performance*, respectively. The *overall success* variable was based upon the following question: *How successful was the project overall? (Select one)*. The question had a five-point scale that was previously used in project management research [1].

Control Data. Demographic data on the project was used as control data and included the industry of the sponsoring organization and the country of the survey respondent. Similarly, the project attributes included the duration of the project in months and the number of team members. We transformed the control data into scale data for use in the comparative analysis.

Participant Profile. The survey sample comprised 120 usable responses: 33% of the respondents had a project manager role; 11% were program managers; 9% were from a project management office; 9% were agile coaches or scrum masters; 8% were product owners; 24% were project team members from IT, business, software vendors, or others not in the selection list; and 3% were project sponsors. Less than 2% of the respondents were end-users. The participants had the option of specifying another role. The results seemed to fall into the categories of project management or a specialized team member. The organizations sponsoring the projects were distributed throughout 20 different industries. The participants were relatively evenly distributed across geographic regions: Europe (25%), Asia (19%), Africa (18%), Latin America and the Caribbean (18%), North America (16%), and Oceania (3%). Most of the projects had started within the past five years (81%) and lasted for more than one year (56%). Most of the projects (81%) had fewer than 21 team members.

3.4   Descriptive Statistics

We used SAS® Studio (Release 3.6, basic edition) to perform the statistical analysis, produce the tables and figures, the descriptive statistics, mean rankings, and Wilcoxon scores, and to explore the characteristics, establish the validity and reliability, and explain the relationship between the variables. The descriptive statistics provided insight into the content and structure of the projects, the involvement of the different project roles, and the relationship between the involved roles and the methodology. We used the Wilcoxon test to compare the means of variables between the three types of methodologies (agile, plan-driven, and mixed) and to establish the significance of the comparison. Wilcoxon scores with a p-value of less than 0.05 indicated that there were significant differences between the methodologies in terms of that variable. We conducted a correlation analysis to determine the association between the characteristics of the project, the roles within the project, and the project outcomes. We used the Kendall correlation coefficient to evaluate the strength and direction of the relationships between the variables. We elected to use the Kendall correlation coefficient due to the small sample size.

3.5 Case-Controlled Match Analysis

To evaluate the existence of project management tasks in agile projects, we conducted a case-controlled match analysis, using plan-driven projects as the control group. A case-controlled match analysis pairs cases in a treatment group with cases in a control group based upon a number of individual characteristics. This type of analysis is often used in observational studies to approximate a randomized trial and to reduce bias [32, 33]. For this study, this type of analysis had the advantage of providing a basis to explain the difference between agile and plan-driven projects.

In this study, we used the methodology type (plan-driven or agile) to define the target and control groups. We used a SAS® program from [33] to create a propensity score using multivariate logistic regression. We used the tasks and role assignments as the observational variables for the comparison. There was a 1:1 relationship between the observations, yielding 24 cases in each group. Afterward, the mean rankings and Wilcoxon scores were produced for the analysis. The results provided descriptive information on whether each task was executed in more or fewer agile cases than in plan-driven cases, represented in Table 3 by a plus or minus sign, respectively. A p-value less than 0.05, represented by asterisks in the table, identifies the significance of the difference between the two methodology types.

3.6 Validity and Reliability

We assessed the survey responses for scope, completeness, consistency, ambiguity, missing data, and extreme responses. For external validity, we used the existing constructs (with some modifications) and the literature to develop new constructs. For internal consistency, we conducted a correlation analysis to determine whether the items were significantly related to one another ($p < 0.05$).

In designing the measurement instrument and collecting the data, we took steps to limit common method bias (CMB). Item characteristic effects and context effects were mitigated by using existing constructs in the literature. Measurement context effects were mitigated by measuring the predictor and criterion at various locations in the measurement instrument. Nevertheless, because self-reports from a single source were used to garner information on the dependent and independent variables and the data were collected at the same point in time, the risk of CMB persisted. The measurements could have been affected by CMB due to respondents attempting to provide consistent responses across a number of variables [34]. We, therefore, performed a post-hoc statistical test to check for CMB: Harman's single-factor test, which is considered the minimally acceptable test for CMB. To perform Harman's single-factor test, we analyzed all the independent and dependent variables using unrotated factor analysis. A single factor explained 17.59% of the variance. The premise is that, if there is CMB, "one general factor will account for the majority of the covariance among the measures" [34, p. 889]. That the variance was lower than the heuristic of 50% suggests that CMB was not an issue [34].

The data were collected from multiple social media sites, some of which specialized in project management while others specialized specifically in agile practices. To determine whether there was a significant difference between the groups in terms of their responses, we used the Kruskal-Wallis test (for comparing several conditions from different respondents) to compare the means of the organizational performance variables [35]. There was no significant difference between the two groups (H (2) = 5.7643, p = 0.5675). No bias was uncovered; therefore, the data were reliable and valid.

4 Data Analysis and Results

4.1 Project Efficiency

Table 1 presents the mean comparisons between the methodology types; significant differences are based on the Kruskal-Wallis test scores being less than .05 for 95% confidence. We combined project cost, time, and quality performance into a single project efficiency variable by taking the mean value of the variables. We used Cronbach's alpha to assess scale reliability; the .658 alpha was judged reliable for this exploratory research. [35]. There was no significant difference between the methodology types in terms of the composite project efficiency measure or the individual performance measures. Unlike in some other research, the mixed and plan-driven methods exhibited higher mean project efficiency than the agile methods [1].

4.2 Methodology

Scrum and waterfall were the most frequently used methodologies, at 22% and 20%, respectively. Of the agile methodologies, scrum combined with scrum/XP was the most

Table 1. Comparative analysis with means and Kruskal-Wallis test scores

Theme	Measurement item	Mean			Kruskal-Wallis
		Agile N = 74	Plan-driven N = 29	Mixed N = 17	p-Value
Demographics	Team size	3.57	3.06	3.41	0.26
	Duration	2.42	2.29	2.48	0.82
Performance	Requirements	5.01	5.06	5.31	0.60
	Project efficiency	4.43	4.39	4.89	0.34
	Budget	4.33	4.35	4.97	0.48
	Time	3.95	3.76	4.38	0.43
	Overall	3.59	3.53	3.66	0.78
Roles	Team role	0.74	0.76	0.79	0.87
	Project manager	0.58	0.82	0.79	0.04
	Product owner	0.53	0.41	0.14	0.00
	Sponsor	0.38	0.53	0.38	0.50
	Agile coach	0.49	0.18	0.10	0.00

widely used, at 24%. This finding is consistent with the results of other studies, which have found scrum to be the most popular agile methodology in widespread use [1, 6]. The methodology types and methodologies were not significantly correlated with any of the individual performance measures or the project efficiency factor. The methodology types were not significantly different in terms of team size or project durations.

4.3 Roles

The project manager role was involved in 67% of the projects, including 58% of the agile projects, 82% of the mixed methodology projects, and 79% of the plan-driven projects. The agile coach role was included in 35% of all projects, and the product owner role was included in 42% of all projects. There was no significant difference between methodology types in terms of other roles. The agile coach, product owner, and team combination, a full scrum team, was not present in all scrum-related projects. This implies that scrum is not being rigorously applied in practice. The project manager was more prominent in the plan-driven and mixed methodologies, and the agile coach and product owner were more prominent in the agile methodologies. Otherwise, there was no significant difference between the methodology types in terms of the roles. Table 2 illustrates that the presence of the agile coach role was significantly correlated with the time, requirements, and efficiency measures.

4.4 Tasks

Table 3 presents the results of the case-controlled match analysis and provides an overview of the project roles engaged in project management processes. In general, project management tasks were performed in all methodology types with no significant difference. The project manager was overwhelmingly responsible for the project management tasks in all types of methodologies.

Table 2. Kendall Tau-b correlation coefficients

$N = 96$~Prob > |tau| under H0: Tau = 0

Role	Budget	Time	Requirements	Overall	Efficiency
Project manager	0.03	0.07	0.03	−0.01	0.05
Agile coach	0.17	0.28**	0.24**	0.11	0.26**
Team	−0.11	0.06	0.06	−0.01	−0.03
Product owner	0.08	0.12	0.14	0.06	0.12
Sponsor	−0.04	0.05	0.05	0.11	0.02

*** $p < .001$, ** $p < .01$, * $p < .05$

Conversely, the team was more often identified as being involved in assessing, treating, and controlling risks in plan-driven methodologies; meanwhile, in agile methodologies, the product owner was more often identified as being involved in these activities.

This finding is consistent with Tavares, Silva, and Diniz de Souza [36] finding that in agile projects the artifacts are responsible for recording risks and their responses, the events for identifying, analyzing, and planning risk responses and monitoring risks, the project team for managing the technical risk, and the product owner for managing the business risks. The product owner was strongly represented in managing stakeholders; neither the team nor the agile coach was significantly engaged in this task. The project team was not at all involved in procurement in agile methodologies.

Figure 1 combines the qualitative results from the literature review with the quantitative results and thereby provides a consolidated view of project management responsibilities in agile projects. The rows represent the 39 ISO processes grouped into the 10 ISO subject areas, the columns represent the scum artifacts or events as method or the project roles considered in the study, and the color represents the relative degree to which the processes were executed. For example, the integration subject area includes seven processes: two of the processes map to five scrum artifacts and events. The scrum master role maps to one process for the subject area, the product owner role maps to

Table 3. ISO process by project role

ISO Process	Spr	Prj Mgr	AC	PO	Team	Oth	N/A
Establish project team	0.17 (+)	0.21* (−)		0.08 (+)	0.08 (+)	0.17* (+)	0.04 (+)
Manage project team	0.04 (+)	0.38* (−)	0.04 (+)	0.08 (+)	0.13 (+)		0.08 (+)
Control resources	0.08 (+)	0.17* (−)	0.13 (+)	0.13 (+)	0.00 (−)	0.08 (+)	0.08 (+)
Establish budget	0.21 (+)	0.17 (−)		0.08 (+)	0.00 (−)	0.17 (+)	0.08 (+)
Control costs	0.04 (+)	0.33 (−)		0.13 (+)	0.04 (−)	0.17 (+)	0.08 (+)
Identify risks	0.04 (+)	0.21* (−)	0.04 (+)	0.13 (+)	0.33 (+)	0.04 (+)	0.04 (+)
Assess, treat, and control risks	0.04 (+)	0.33 (−)	0.04 (+)	0.21* (+)	0.08* (−)	0.04 (−)	0.04
Plan and administer procurements		0.38 (+)	0.08 (+)	0.04	0.00** (−)	0.17 (+)	0.13 (+)
Select suppliers	0.00 (−)	0.17 (+)		0.08 (+)	0.17	0.21 (+)	0.17 (+)
Manage stakeholders		0.29* (−)	0.04 (+)	0.29* (+)	0.04 (+)	0.04 (+)	0.08 (+)

Significance: *** $p < .001$, **$p < .01$, *$p < .05$; $N = 24$ agile; $N = 24$ plan-driven
Cases: (+) more or (−) less in agile cases than in plan-driven cases
Spr-Sponsor; Prj Mgr-Project Manager; AC-Agile Coach; PO-Product Owner; Oth-Other

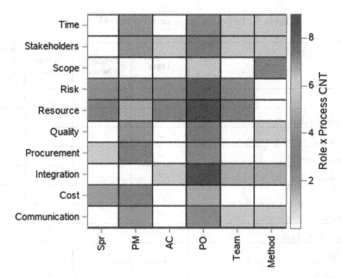

Fig. 1. Heatmap of ISO process groups by project roles

two, the team role maps to five, and the project manager and sponsor role map to none. The details are presented in Tables 4 and 5.

Table 4 presents the qualitative results from the literature review combined with the quantitative results. It depicts the scrum artifacts, roles, and events aligned to the ISO project management subject areas and processes. The checkmark (✓) notes alignment based upon a formal reading of the methodologies; the plus (+) confirms that knowledge based on the results from the survey. The results signified that responsibilities have shifted from the project manager to the agile roles. Table 5 indicates the shift in responsibility from the project manager with a negative sign (−) and indicates the shift in responsibility toward the sponsor or other roles with a plus (+). Such a shift has occurred in most cases; however, the project manager remains significantly responsible for procurement activities.

4.5 Summary

For agile methodologies, some of the project management responsibilities are inherent in the frameworks. The analysis clarified how the project management activities are distributed among the project roles.

Table 4. Project management framework: Scrum

	Team	Product Owner	Scrum Master	Scrum Artifacts & Events
Integration				
Develop project charter		✓		
Develop project plans	✓			✓
Direct project work	✓			
Control project work	✓			✓
Control changes				✓
Close project phase or project	✓	✓		✓
Collect lessons learned	✓		✓	✓
Stakeholder				
Manage stakeholders	(+)	✓(+)	✓(+)	✓
Scope				
Define scope		✓		✓
Control scope		✓		
Create work breakdown structure				✓
Define activities				✓
Resource				
Establish project team	(+)	(+)		
Develop project team	✓		✓	
Control resources		(+)	(+)	
Manage project team	✓(+)	(+)	(+)	
Time				
Estimate activity durations	✓			✓
Costs				
Develop budget		(+)		
Control costs		(+)		
Risk				
Identify risks	(+)	(+)	(+)	
Assess, treat, control risks		(+)	(+)	
Quality				
Perform quality assurance				✓
Procurement				
Select suppliers		(+)		
Communication				
Manage communications	✓	✓		✓

✓- based upon literature mapping; (+)-based on survey analysis

Table 5. Project management framework

	Project Manager	Sponsor	Other
Stakeholders			
Identify stakeholders	✓		
Manage stakeholders	✓ (-)		(+)
Resources			
Establish project team	✓(-)	(+)	(+)
Estimate resources	✓		
Define project organization	✓		
Control resources	✓(-)	(+)	(+)
Manage project team	✓(-)	(+)	
Time			
Develop and control schedule	✓		
Cost			
Estimate costs	✓		
Develop budget	✓(-)	(+)	(+)
Control costs	✓(-)	(+)	(+)
Risk			
Identify risks	✓ (-)	(+)	
Assess, treat, control risks	✓(-)	(+)	(-)
Quality			
Plan quality	✓		
Perform quality control	✓		
Procurement			
Select suppliers	✓ (+)	(-)	(+)
Plan and administer procurements	✓ (+)		(+)
Communication			
Plan communications, distribute info	✓		

✓- based upon literature mapping; (+) more or (-) less based on survey analysis

5   Discussion

First, while agile project methodologies are gaining in popularity, traditional methodologies continue to be in widespread use. Regardless of the methodology, the project management tasks as identified in the ISO standards for managing projects remain relevant. Project managers are engaged in agile projects to a greater degree than agile coaches or product owners. Project managers continue to perform management tasks and do not only act as a "gatekeeper," as described by Taylor [3]. In this study, the sponsors and product owners undertook some management activities, whereas the agile coaches did not. Thus, this partially supports the proposition by Noll, Razzak, Bass, and Beecham [2] that assigning a former project manager to the product owner role rather than the scrum master role will result in a higher degree of project success.

In practice, the project manager focuses on team management and risk identification tasks, while the product owner focuses on scope and stakeholder management activities. The product owner is responsible for the scope before the project starts, during the project, and after the project is completed. A project manager is a transitory role and is not typically engaged in the market and withdrawal phases of a product lifecycle. Stated differently, the boundary for the product owner is the product features, whereas the boundary for the project manager is the project process. Thus, the pairing of sponsor and product owner represents a logical combination for both long-term product success and short-term project success. The agile coach's boundary is the team, and the team's boundary is the project work during an iteration.

For agile projects, the authorization to perform the work is given to the product owner [5]; for plan-driven methodologies, it is given to the project manager [21]. For plan-driven methodologies, the project termination criteria are defined at the start of the project; for agile methodologies, the endpoints emerge over time. This emergence enables flexibility to terminate projects early or to continue beyond an originally planned closing date [5]. The project management tasks in plan-driven methodologies are centralized to the project manager role. In agile methodologies, some of the project management responsibilities are inherent in the framework or distributed to the agile roles, although others are practiced by a project manager or other roles.

From this study, it became clear that the agile coach has a much more limited set of tasks than the project manager. The agile coach has two primary responsibility areas: developing the team and supporting all stakeholders, helping them to understand and apply the methods. In this regard, the management style suggested for an agile coach is that of an effective leader, facilitator, or coach [26]. This recommendation corresponds with studies that argue that a project manager capable of adopting a facilitator leadership style could lead an agile project [10, 11, 26, 27]; however, it is not suggested that the project manager also fill the coaching role as there is likely to be conflict related to the delegation and management styles required by the different sets of responsibilities [2]. Furthermore, the results indicated that the presence of an agile coach was correlated with project efficiency; however, correlation is not causation.

6   Conclusions

Although the tasks that would typically be executed by a project manager are not (explicitly) addressed by agile methodologies, they continue to be practiced. The team, product owner, and project sponsors are assuming the informal role in some project management tasks. The project manager, however, continues to be engaged, albeit with an altered task distribution and leadership style. Table 6 presents a summary of the scope of each role.

Table 6. Boundary, Authority, Role, and Task (BART) analysis for Agile methodologies

Boundary	Project	Product	Iteration	Team
Role	Project manager, Sponsor	Product owner	Team	Agile coach
Who authorizes	Sponsor	Sponsor	Product owner	Sponsor
Tasks	Table 5	Table 4	Table 4	Table 4

6.1 Contributions to Knowledge

The results of this study quantify subjective and theoretical speculation on who performs the project management tasks in agile projects. By empirically defining the project manager's tasks in agile projects, the results of this study contribute to the project management literature on agile methodologies. Although agile methodologies are in widespread use, this information was missing in practice and under-researched in academia.

6.2 Implications for Practice

The practical implication is that project sponsors should consider the project manager an essential role in all project types; however, at the same time, project managers should recognize their reduced role and acknowledge that the product owner is a co-equal partner. In addition, when staffing decisions require a trade-off in role assignments, the project manager role is closer to the product owner role than the agile coach role. Agile coaches add value and increase efficiency by focusing on the team.

The agile methodology authors should update their practices to identify the role the project team and product owner play in assessing, treating, and controlling risks and in selecting suppliers. Furthermore, they should update their practices to reflect the project management tasks that may be outside of the team operations but necessary for project sponsors or project managers to execute. Tables 4 and 5, and Fig. 1 provide a guideline for mapping specific project roles to project management activities.

Since the rigorous application of method artifacts, roles, and events is responsible for some typical project management activities, care should be taken to consider project governance when tailoring agile methods. Next, the agile coach plays a key role that can improve the productivity of project operations. Thus, the role should be formalized into traditional methodologies as a role separate from the project manager. Finally, the project management standards from ISO [19], PMI [21], and APM [20], as well as the PMI *Agile Practice Guide* [7], should be updated to reflect the findings from this study.

6.3 Implications for Research

In future studies, researchers investigating agile methodologies should consider the participants within the overall projects. We determined that fewer than half of the projects following the scrum methodology incorporated all the scrum roles. Thus, the actual results from project studies may inappropriately attribute successful outcomes to the methodology. The role of the "agile project manager" referenced in some studies in the literature is inconsistent with some agile methodologies and with practices. Specifically, in some cases, methodologies that describe the agile project manager do not specify whether the project manager is assuming the responsibilities of an agile coach combined with a project manager, nor do they mention whether an agile coach is present alongside the agile project manager. Thus, the construct of the agile project manager should be formalized in line with the results of this study.

6.4 Limitations and Further Research

The results of this study are not generalizable beyond the methodologies studied in this research. Specifically, software development projects have been the most active in applying agile methodologies. There were no measures to determine whether the project type skewed or biased the results. We lacked financial or factual data to measure project efficiency and performance; thus, we could only evaluate the perception of project performance as judged by the participants. Furthermore, the findings are limited due to the small sample size. Future research could focus on a qualitative study of the agile project organizations, seek to quantify the engagement of the separate roles or use strategies to avoid the limitations of this study.

References

1. Serrador, P., Pinto, J.K.: Does agile work? — A quantitative analysis of agile project success. Int. J. Proj. Manag. **33**(5), 1040–1051 (2015). https://doi.org/10.1016/j.ijproman.2015.01.006
2. Noll, J., Razzak, M.A., Bass, J.M., Beecham, S.: A study of the scrum master's role. In: Felderer, M., Méndez Fernández, D., Turhan, B., Kalinowski, M., Sarro, F., Winkler, D. (eds.) PROFES 2017. LNCS, vol. 10611, pp. 307–323. Springer, Cham (2017). https://doi.org/10.1007/978-3-319-69926-4_22
3. Taylor, K.J.: Adopting Agile software development: the project manager experience. Inf. Technol. Peopl. **29**(4), 670–687 (2016). https://doi.org/10.1108/ITP-02-2014-0031
4. Hobbs, B., Petit, Y.: Agile methods on large projects in large organizations. Proj. Manag. J. **48**(3), 3–19 (2017). https://doi.org/10.1177/875697281704800301
5. Schwaber, K., Sutherland, J.: The Scrum Guide: The Definitive Guide to Scrum: The Rules of the Game (2017)
6. Shastri, Y., Hoda, R., Amor, R.: Does the "Project Manager" still exist in agile software development projects? In: 2016 23rd Asia-Pacific Software Engineering Conference (APSEC), pp. 57–64, Hamilton, New Zealand (2016). https://doi.org/10.1109/APSEC.2016.019
7. PMI: Agile Practice Guide. Project Management Institute, Inc., Newtown Square, Pennsylvania, United States (2017)
8. Mansor, Z., Arshad, N.H., Yahya, S., Razali, R.: The competency of project managers in managing agile cost management. Adv. Sci. Lett. **22**(8), 1930–1934 (2016). https://doi.org/10.1166/asl.2016.7750
9. Conboy, K., Morgan, L.: Combining open innovation and agile approaches: implications for IS project managers, In: ECIS 2010 Proceedings 21 (2010). https://aisel.aisnet.org/ecis2010/21. Accessed 1 Dec 2018

10. Sutling, K., Mansor, Z., Widyarto, S., Letchmunan, S., Arshad, N.H.: Agile project manager behavior: the taxonomy. In: 2014 8th Malaysian Software Engineering Conference (MySEC), pp. 234–239. IEEE, Langkawi, Malaysia (2014). https://doi.org/10.1109/MySec.2014.6986020
11. Sutling, K., Mansor, Z., Widyarto, S., Lecthmunan, S., Arshad, N.H.: Understanding of project manager competency in agile software development project: the taxonomy. In: Kim, K.(ed.) Information Science and Applications. LNEE, vol. 339, pp. 859–868. Springer, Heidelberg (2015). https://doi.org/10.1007/978-3-662-46578-3_102
12. Hoda, R., Murugesan, L.K.: Multi-level agile project management challenges: a self-organizing team perspective. J. Syst. Softw. **117**, 245–257 (2016). https://doi.org/10.1016/j.jss.2016.02.049
13. Sverrisdottir, H.S., Ingason, H.T., Jonasson, H.I.: The role of the product owner in scrum-comparison between theory and practices. Procedia Soc. Behav. **119**, 257–267 (2014). https://doi.org/10.1016/j.sbspro.2014.03.030
14. Mayfield, K.M.: Project Managers' Experience and Description of Decision Uncertainty Associated with the Agile Software Development Methodology: a Phenomenological Study, vol. 3427057, p. 106. Capella University, Ann Arbor (2010)
15. Sheffield, J., Lemétayer, J.: Factors associated with the software development agility of successful projects. Int. J. Proj. Manag. **31**(3), 459–472 (2013). https://doi.org/10.1016/j.ijproman.2012.09.011
16. Turner, J.R.: Towards a theory of project management: the nature of the project. Int. J. Proj. Manag. **24**(1), 1–3 (2006). https://doi.org/10.1016/j.ijproman.2005.11.007
17. Turner, J.R.: Towards a theory of project management: the nature of the project governance and project management. Int. J. Proj. Manag. **24**(2), 93–95 (2006). https://doi.org/10.1016/j.ijproman.2005.11.008
18. Lundin, R.A., Söderholm, A.: A theory of temporary organization. Scand. J. Manag. **11**(4), 437–455 (1995). https://doi.org/10.1016/0956-5221(95)00036-U
19. ISO: ISO 21500: 2012 Guidance on project management. International Standards Organization, Geneva, Switzerland (2012)
20. APM: APM Body of Knowledge 6th Edition. Association for Project Management, Buckinghamshire, United Kingdom (2012)
21. PMI: A Guide to the Project Management Body of Knowledge (PMBOK Guide). Project Management Institute, Inc., Newtown Square, Pennsylvania, United States (2017)
22. Joslin, R., Müller, R.: Relationships between a project management methodology and project success in different project governance contexts. Int. J. Proj. Manag. **33**(6), 1377–1392 (2015). https://doi.org/10.1016/j.ijproman.2015.03.005
23. Beck, K., et al.: Manifesto for Agile Software Development. http://agilemanifesto.org/
24. Binder, J., Aillaud, L.I.V., Schilli, L.: The project management cocktail model: an approach for balancing Agile and ISO 21500. Procd. Soc. Behv. **119**, 182–191 (2014). https://doi.org/10.1016/j.sbspro.2014.03.022
25. Zwikael, O., Meredith, J.R.: Who's who in the project zoo? The ten core project roles. Int. J. Oper. Prod. Manag. **38**(2), 474–492 (2018). https://doi.org/10.1108/IJOPM-05-2017-0274
26. Bonner, N.A.: Predicting leadership success in agile environments: an inquiring systems approach. Acad. Inf. Manag. Sci. J. **13**(2), 83–103 (2010)
27. Yang, H., Huff, S., Strode, D.: Leadership in software development: comparing perceptions of agile and traditional project managers. In: Proceedings of the 15th Americas Conference on Information Systems, AMCIS 2009, 6–9 August 2009, pp. 184–196, San Francisco, California, USA (2009)
28. Shastri, Y., Hoda, R., Amor, R.: Understanding the roles of the manager in Agile project management. In: 10th Innovations in Software Engineering Conference, pp. 45–55, Jaipur, India (2017). https://doi.org/10.1145/3021460.3021465

29. Hayden, C., Molenkamp, R.J.: Tavistock Primer II. AK Rice Institute for Study of Social Systems, Jupiter (2002)
30. Green, Z.: Boundary, Authority, Role and Task (2015)
31. PMI: PMI Fact File. PMI Today, pp. 4. Project Management Institute, Inc., Newtown Square, Pennsylvania, United States (2019)
32. Stuart, E.A.: Matching methods for causal inference: a review and a look forward. Stat. Sci. **25**(1), 1–21 (2010). https://doi.org/10.1214/09-STS313
33. Parsons, L.S.: Using SAS® Software to Perform a Case-Control Match on Propensity Score in an Observational Study. SUGI 29. SAS Institute, Inc., Le Palais des congrès de Montréal Québec, Canada (2004)
34. Podsakoff, P.M., MacKenzie, S.B., Lee, J.-Y., Podsakoff, N.P.: Common method biases in behavioral research: a critical review of the literature and recommended remedies. J. Appl. Psychol. **88**(5), 879–903 (2003). https://doi.org/10.1037/0021-9010.88.5.879
35. Field, A.: Discovering Statistics: Using IBM SPSS Statistics. SAGE Publications Ltd., Thousand Oaks (2013)
36. Tavares, B., Silva, C., Dinizde Souza, A.: Practices to improve risk management in agile projects. Int. J. Softw. Eng. Know. **29**(03), 381–399 (2019). https://doi.org/10.1142/S0218194019500165

Aspects of Implementing Information Technology

Discovery of Customer Communities
– Evaluation Aspects

Jerzy Korczak[1]($\boxtimes$) (iD), Maciej Pondel[2]($\boxtimes$) (iD), and Wiktor Sroka[2]($\boxtimes$) (iD)

[1] International University of Logistics and Transport,
ul. Sołtysowicka 19B, 51-168 Wrocław, Poland
`jerzy.korczak@ue.wroc.pl`
[2] Wroclaw University of Economics and Business,
ul. Komandorska 118-120, 53-345 Wrocław, Poland
`maciej.pondel@ue.wroc.pl, wiktor.sroka@gmail.com`

Abstract. In the paper, a new multi-level hybrid method of community detection combining a density-based clustering with a label propagation method is evaluated and compared with the k-means benchmark and DBSCAN (*Density-based spatial clustering of applications with noise*). In spite of the sophisticated visualization methods, managers still usually find clustering results too difficult to evaluate and interpret. The article presents a set of key assessment measures that could be used to evaluate internal and external qualities of discovered clusters. The approach is validated on real life marketing database using advanced analytics platform, Upsaily.

Keywords: Clustering · Customer communities · Customer segmentation · Cluster evaluation · Marketing

1 Introduction

Discovery of customer communities is one of the important problems in modern data analysis of decision support systems. In marketing information systems, a community can be defined as a densely connected group of customers having similar profile or behavior that is only loosely connected to the rest of the network [1]. Many approaches and clustering algorithms have been published in network literature [2–8]: from the classical k-means, through density-based partitioning, self-organizing maps, graph-based, grid-based, to combinational and hybrid solutions.

In marketing analysis, discovery of accurate and business focused partitions using a single algorithm in isolation is becoming highly complex. The aim of this paper is to present an approach for evaluating the results of clustering that show that some algorithms are better and efficient for very large datasets while others generate results difficult to accept by managers. There are many reasons for these difficulties: sensitivity to initial values, unknown quantity of expected clusters, non-spherical datasets, sensitivity to noise and outliers, varying densities of clusters, or difficulties of business interpretation. In spite of that, there is no one algorithm that can achieve the best performance on all

© Springer Nature Switzerland AG 2020
E. Ziemba (Ed.): AITM 2019/ISM 2019, LNBIP 380, pp. 177–191, 2020.
https://doi.org/10.1007/978-3-030-43353-6_10

measurements for any given dataset [5, 9–11], and at the same time obtain the best results.

To strengthen business outcomes and reduce weaknesses of the single algorithm approaches, a new hybrid multi-level method of community discovery was proposed in our previous paper. It combined a density-based clustering with business-oriented label propagation method. Five basic algorithms have been integrated into this method: DBSCAN, RFM (*Recency, Frequency, Monetary Value*), k-NN (*k-Nearest Neighbors algorithm*), UMAP (*Uniform Manifold Approximation and Projection*), and LPA. As a reminder, the DBSCAN is an efficient algorithm that identifies clusters by measuring density as the number of observations in a designated area [9–11]. If the density is greater than the density of observations belonging to other clusters, then the defined area is identified as a cluster. Usually, in business application, DBSCAN creates a lot of small and difficult to interpret clusters. To improve cluster quality and interpretation, a second algorithm has been proposed that enriches the results of DBSCAN and is able to form communities. After analysis of various community detection methods, the label propagation algorithm (LPA) has been selected due to its simplicity to detect communities in large networks and to low computational complexity [12, 13]. The idea of label propagation is as follows: before beginning computation, some nodes of the network possess assigned labels. During process execution, the labels are propagated iteratively throughout the network according to the formula below.

$$g_i = argmax_g \sum_j A_{ij}\delta(g_j, g) \tag{1}$$

where A_{ij} is an element of the adjacency matrix of the network, and δ is equal to 1 when its arguments are the same, 0 otherwise. There are many extensions of original label propagation algorithm [8, 14, 15]. In our approach, a weighted network is assumed, so formula (1) is rewritten as:

$$g_i = argmax_g \sum_j W_{ij}\delta(g_j, g) \tag{2}$$

where W_{ij} is the sum of weights on the edges between nodes i and j of the adjacency matrix of the network, *and* δ is equal to 1 when its arguments are the same, 0 otherwise.

In other words, the nodes sequentially adopt the labels shared by most of their neighbors, taking into consideration the weights of the edges. The propagation ends when the labels no longer change.

It is important to note that, in our case study, the nodes were represented by clusters of customers created by DBSCAN. Neighborhoods of clusters were defined individually by the distance between the centers of clusters. The upper limit of neighboring was predefined by the manager or analysts, so the number of neighboring clusters varied.

The business goal of the study is to obtain a higher quality of definition of customer communities from the marketing viewpoint. Therefore, in the approach the RFM method has been integrated with graph clustering to give clusters of higher quality than the traditional mono-algorithm clustering. Various data sources, different quality measures, and business orientation provide more up-to-date, richer information for decision makers and marketing analysts.

The paper has been structured as follows: in the next section, the theoretical and contextual foundations are detailed. The third section describes a research methodology outlining the process of clustering of customers of the internet store and the measures used to evaluate the quality of the results. Modeling and computation were performed on Upsaily platform [16]. The fourth section details the results of the case study on real life database. A general conclusion summarizes the outcomes of the proposed approach.

2 Theoretical and Contextual Backgrounds

Currently, analysis of customer behavior in e-commerce is carried out on highly efficient analytical platforms using diverse and rich information sources. Today e-commerce applications collect data on every single action undertaken by the customer (visit, transaction, search, and many more) [17, 18]. In general, such systems concentrate on a delivery of the best fitting proposal for a customer concerning the selected customer segment, desired product, and conditions under which the product is offered. Those issues were examined by the authors in [12, 19] using customer clustering based on the RFM method, considering customer recency, frequency of purchases, and monetary value of orders.

This paper is an extension of the research presented in [19] and concentrates on quality evaluation issues of the generated cluster segments. The segmentation has been done in the same manner as in [19], and e-commerce managers were focused on discovery of specific, money-generating customer communities. In the presented case study, two segments were retrieved and characterized. The first was composed of fashion-driven customers (they focus on new and fashionable items). Second one contained "bargain hunters" – discount-driven customers who were ready to purchase products present on a market for a longer period of time. This segmentation was, in short, referred to as "fashion vs. discount".

The experiment extended in this paper is also based on database originating from B2C store. Sample data being the input to the experiment included 264127 rows (customers). In the database, not only are all customer transactions stored, but also the basic data about their demographic and behavioral profile. Due to the large number of tables and attributes in the source database, only relevant information was aggregated and extracted for the case study, notably:

- Value – as a quantity of items multiplied by unit price.
- Discount – as a percentage the difference between the highest transactional price of a specific item and its price in the current transaction.
- Days after first item sell – as the number of days from the first transaction of a given item to the current transaction.
- Loyalty – expressed in the number of orders. Such an attribute differentiates the one-off buyer customer from the loyal customers.

This information was used to compute the following characteristics of customers:

- Average discount of client's transaction – for some customers, discount drives purchase decision, while others don't mind paying catalog price. Higher percentage discounts are typical for bargain hunters.

- Average number of days after first product sell – it distinguishes new fashionable products from those launched in the past. It determines whether a customer is interested in new (fashionable) items or accepts purchasing items launched in previous seasons.
- Average order value – determines the amount of money the customer can spend on a single purchase.

For each generated segment one can prepare tailored offer, adjusting set of recommended products to the predicted customer expectations. It is assumed that the better the clusters, the better adjusted are the offers and the higher the possibility of offer acceptance.

Several methods for cluster evaluation have been proposed in the literature [9, 20–22]. In this study, a few key business-oriented internal and external measures of cluster quality will be applied, notably Davies-Bouldin index [23], Dunn index [24], Calinski-Harabasz index [25] and Silhouette index [26]. Those measures have been selected because they are comprehensible for marketing analysts, and authors consider them to be well adjusted to customer segmentation business problem. Definitions of the applied measures are provided below:

- **Davies-Bouldin index**

$$DB = \frac{1}{n} \sum_{i=1}^{n} max_{j \neq i} \frac{\sigma_i + \sigma_j}{d(c_i, c_j)} \tag{3}$$

where n is the number of clusters, c_i and c_j are clusters, σ_i and σ_j are the standard deviations, and $d(c_i, c_j)$ is a distance between centroids of c_i and c_j clusters.
According to this measure, the best algorithm is one that generates the lowest value of the DB index.

- **Dunn index**

$$D = \frac{min \, d(c_i, c_j)}{max \, d(c_k)} \tag{4}$$

where c_i and c_j are clusters, $d(c_i, c_j)$ is a distance between centroids of clusters c_i and c_j, and $d(c_k)$ is the diameter of the cluster c_k calculated as the largest distance between two elements in the cluster.
Dunn's index focuses on cluster density and the distance between clusters. Distance between clusters can be measured as the distance between their nearest points or the farthest. Algorithms preferred by the Dunn index are those that reach high values of the measure.

- **Silhouette index**

$$S = \frac{1}{n} \sum_{i=1}^{n} \frac{d(c_i) - d(c_i, c)}{max\{d(c_i), d(c_i, c)\}} \tag{5}$$

where n is the number of clusters, $d(c_i)$ is an average distance between elements within the cluster c_i, $d(c_i, c)$ is the minimum distance of the cluster c_i to all other clusters.

The Silhouette index measures how similar an object is to its own cluster (cohesion) compared to other clusters (separation). The measure is obtained by calculating the difference between two values: the average distance within the cluster and the minimum distance between the clusters. Index value ranges from -1 to $+1$, where high values indicate good matching of the object to its own cluster and poor matching to neighboring clusters. Low and negative values may indicate too few or too many clusters in the model.

- **Calinski-Harabasz index**

$$CH = \frac{BCD(n)(N - n)}{WCD(n)(n - 1)} \tag{6}$$

where n is the number of clusters, N is the total number of all customers, $BCD(n)$ is the inter-cluster dispersion[1] (an overall between-cluster variance), $WCD(n)$ is the intra-cluster dispersion[2] (an overall within-cluster variance).

The Calinski-Harabasz index is an evaluation index calculated as a ratio of the within-cluster dispersion to the between-cluster dispersion. The higher the ratio, the better the clustering effect. This index is best suited for clustering solutions based on k-means methods based on Euclidean distances.

In external evaluation methods, clustering results are assessed using the external data not taken into account during the clustering process. For instance, such data relate to the customers who were previously assigned to the clusters by experts. In this case, the clustering results generated by the algorithm are compared with the clusters determined by the experts. Apart from the mentioned metrics, other measures can be also applied, such as F-score, Fowkes-Mallows index, etc.

The Upsaily analytical platform has been used to carry out the computation. Functionally, the platform can be classified as a Customer Intelligence system, i.e. one whose primary interest is current customers. The aim is not to help in acquiring new customers, but to increase customer satisfaction that translates into increased turnover. This could be achieved by customers making follow-up purchases, increasing the value of individual orders (cross-selling), or more valuable products (up-selling).

3   Research Methodology

The research study is a continuation of our previous project on the multi-level approach to discover customer communities [19, 27]. The objective was to evaluate the discovered communities of the most profitable customers. A profitable customer was one whose order values were high and at the same time they didn't seek discounts. As a reminder, the discovery process was composed of the following steps:

---

[1] Between-Cluster Dispersion can be calculated as $BCD(n) = \sum_i \overline{c_i} \cdot d^2(c_i, c)$, where n is the number of clusters, $d(c_i, c)$ is the distance between centroid of the cluster c_i and the global center of all clusters, $\overline{c_i}$ is the number of elements in the cluster c_i.

[2] Within-Cluster Dispersion can be calculated as $WCD(n) = \sum_i \sum_{x \in c_i} d^2(x, c_i)$, where n is the number of clusters, x is an element of the cluster c_i, $d(x, c_i)$ is the distance between centroid of the cluster c_i and the element x belonging to the cluster c_i.

1. Customers clustering using Hierarchical DBSCAN (HDBSCAN) algorithm.
2. Dimensions reduction using Uniform Manifold Approximation and Projection (UMAP) method in order to base next steps on two dimensions.
3. Centroid calculation for each cluster according to UMAP result.
4. Graph generation with k-NN algorithm.
5. Communities detection according to LPA algorithm.
6. Cluster evaluation.
7. Marketing interpretation.

To begin the process, HDBSCAN method was selected because of its marketing usage in effective discovery of clear patterns in given set of observations. The specification of HDBSCAN has been explained in [19, 28]. HDBSCAN generates a number of clusters based on the number of patterns found in the data. Compared to DBSCAN, HDBSCAN is a hierarchical clustering algorithm, and it constructs a cluster hierarchy of connected components based on minimum cluster size. It is worth noticing that some observations remain without assigning them to any cluster.

Source data included 264127 rows describing customers. 140 segments were generated. Figure 1 presents visualization of 7 selected clusters of the most profitable customers. Customers assigned to clusters (indicated by color) are presented in left hand side. Distribution of order characteristics is presented in right hand side.

In the second step, to reduce the space dimension, UMAP method was used [29]. The cluster centroids coordinates were then computed.

From initial 264127 rows describing customers, 174297 were assigned to clusters by HDBSCAN algorithm. The remaining customers (89830) were assigned to "−1" cluster, which meant that insufficient density was found in the area they were located (no pattern was detected). 2046 small but very consistent clusters were discovered. Such quantity of clusters was too high to effectively address managers' needs; hence the reason was to aggregate small clusters into customer communities.

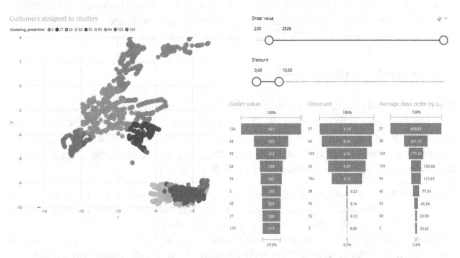

Fig. 1. Most profitable customers in k-means segmentation. (Color figure online)

In [30], communities are defined as, "groups of vertices within which connections are dense, but between which connections are sparser". According to [31], such communities can be considered as fairly independent spaces of a graph, sharing common properties and/or playing similar roles within it.

In our case study, communities are groups of customer clusters whose elements share common properties and allow managers to apply the same measures to them or to identify strong similarities between groups in the same community.

Label Propagation Algorithm has been proposed for detecting communities in networks represented by graphs [12]. The specification of LPA can be found in [12, 19]. In [32], the LPA has been compared with other clustering algorithms: Louvain algorithm [33], Smart Local Moving (SLM) [34], and Infomap algorithm [35]. The main idea behind LPA is to propagate labels throughout the graph, from a node to its neighbor nodes. As a result, the groups of nodes sharing the same label and whose nodes have more neighbors than nodes in other groups are classified as communities. The algorithm, due to its linear time complexity of $O(m)$ for each iteration, simplicity, and ease of implementation, is commonly used to identify communities in large-scale Manhattan real-world networks, such as social media. An advantage of the algorithm is that it does not require prior information on number of communities or their cardinalities to run, neither does it require any parameterization. The number of iterations to convergence is barely dependent on the graph size, but it grows very slowly.

It is important to note that Label Propagation Algorithm operates on graphs, hence the input data must be converted into a graph. In our experiment, it was necessary to perform a dimension reduction with UMAP on "fashion vs. discount" case study, grouping customers with similar properties into clusters and determining centroids of each cluster accordingly.

In order to create a graph, the k-Nearest Neighbors algorithm (known as k-NN), that is one of the simplest, but perfectly fitting into the experiment context, was used, and, as a non-parametric method, it is commonly used for classification and regression. For classification, the centroids with Euclidean distance between them are used and transformed into the normalized distances for all nodes while filtering out all that is above a given threshold.

A graph was created, where the nodes represent clusters generated by HDBSCAN and edges are weighted links connecting clusters, determined by applying k-NN algorithm from the previous step and representing normalized distances between clusters. It should be added that the centroids defined while executing UMAP method were crucial in the creation of a proper graph for LPA method.

Finally, using the data from the previous steps, a large graph consisting of 2046 clusters (vertices) and 15364 links was created. More detailed information about the graph structure will be given further.

To sum up the discovery process: HDBSCAN created numerous clusters, UMAP reduced the dimensions, k-NN formed graph, and finally LPA found communities. The graph is illustrated in Fig. 2. The densest groups of clusters have been marked in color on the graph. They form communities characterized by common attributes. Results of that experiment favor LPA to be used with large scale data, as it outperforms other algorithms in case of well-defined clusters.

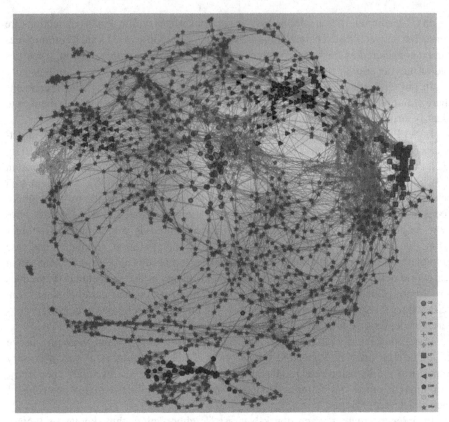

Fig. 2. Graph of clusters with highlighted communities. (Color figure online)

In general, densely connected groups reach a common label quickly. When many such dense groups are created throughout the network, they continue to expand outwards until it becomes impossible to do so. Randomization of the order the clusters are processed has consequences: it may not deliver a unique solution, or the final solution might not be found at all (due to fluctuations in label assignment, adjacent clusters can interchange their labels in every iteration, preventing the convergence criteria from being achieved).

In retail businesses, managers would want to know about the customers in order to efficiently tailor offers for targeted groups, and to increase efficiency and also customer satisfaction. This in turn increases business profitability. On the other hand, there might be a group of customers that may abuse the system, searching for system weaknesses and resulting in a loss or very small benefit for the retailer. The aim of this experiment was to find clusters of the most profitable customers, which has been already mentioned, and to provide marketing manager or analyst with appropriate knowledge about customer behavior in respect to the value of products, discount, and "age" of the product.

If a manager is interested in clusters of customers with the highest order values (as potentially the most beneficial customers), they filter clusters using the order-values. For example, selected clusters of customers who buy goods valued at more than 350

PLN are presented in Fig. 3. There are 133 groups (communities) created by LPA out of 2052 clusters generated by HDBSCAN. On the left-hand side of visualization one dot represents one HDBSCAN cluster and the color of the dot represents LPA cluster (after community detection by LPA).

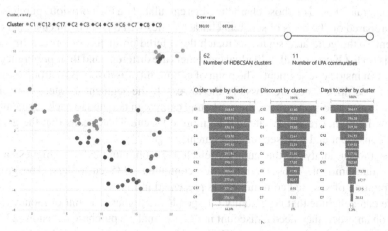

Fig. 3. Graphical representation of analyzed clusters meeting manager's criteria. (Color figure online)

If managers are interested in some specific clusters, they could observe the distribution of each feature in clusters. If one takes into consideration clusters C2 and C7 presented in Fig. 3, one can observe that these are customers not looking for discounts (they buy with 0% discount), they buy new products (launched respectively 31 and 20 days before purchase). The difference between those clusters is in the average order value (respectively 452 and 385 PLN). Having such knowledge, the recommendation system makes it possible to tailor the offer in order to meet customer's expectations. The chart on the left-hand side presents these clusters (one dot one cluster) and color of dots represents a final community.

4 Evaluation Measures and Research Findings

As mentioned earlier, the case study is focused on the communities of customers with the highest average order value. Those customers are the most beneficial to the retailer. They buy highest-margin products. In addition, their buying power is the most significant, so they deserve a special treatment in order to gain their loyalty. The aim of undertaken operation is to select relatively consistent segments for those clients and provide them with tailored offers. The offer should be adjusted to customer preferences based on explained earlier characteristics:

- amount of money customer might spend,
- discount from catalog price,

• product availability period (it distinguishes new fashionable products from those launched in the past). It is also one of key decision drivers for specific segments.

The authors assume that product price, discount, and product availability period presented in an offer influence the purchase decision. That is why segments of customers were generated based on those characteristics calculated on their previous purchases. An offer prepared on the basis of segment characteristics will be sent to all customers in the segment. If the generated segments match the offered products, the probability of purchase is high. Of course, all individual customers are different, and their preferences may differ even inside one segment. The point of community discovery is to group customers where those differences are possibly the lowest. If the segment is internally coherent and well separated from others, the marketing campaign targeted to each segment might achieve the higher response rate and be more efficient. That means that the goal is to define consistent and well separated segments.

For further analysis, the authors selected 7 communities with highest average order value amount. Those communities contained 1485 customers. The graphical interpretation of selected communities is presented in Fig. 4.

We can conclude that community C1 spends the highest amount of money (548.62 PLN) on an order, they need a discount in order to make a purchase decision (23%) and they buy relatively new products (117 days after a product launch). Another segment C2 – those customers buy relatively less expensive products, but still average order value is high (452.91 PLN), they buy the newest products (31 days after product launch) and they do not search for discounts – they buy in catalog prices (0% discount). It is obvious that clients from each of those segments need a different offer that matches their individual preferences. Finally, the key question of this study is to demonstrate whether those communities generated by the presented method are better than those generated using other methods.

To verify the quality of those methods, the authors performed clustering on the same dataset using two well-known algorithms: k-means and HDBSCAN. The authors clustered whole set 264127 customers and selected top N clusters with the highest average order values. Those experiments were repeated several times in order to return

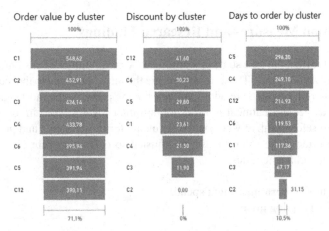

Fig. 4. Interpretation of selected clusters.

similar number of clusters (7) with comparable number of customers (1485). k-means based clustering returned 6 clusters with 1994 customers and HDBSCAN returned 6 clusters and 1473 customers.

Due to a fewer number of clusters, authors also generated another HDBSCAN sample with 7 clusters and 2153 customers. In order to maintain the same conditions to the final evaluation, a sample generated by proposed method with 8 clusters and 1924 customers was included. Samples with numbers of clusters and customers are presented in Table 1. To evaluate communities Dunn[3], Davies–Bouldin[4], Silhouette[5], and Calinski-Harabasz[6] indices were calculated for all samples.

Table 1. Samples with number of clusters and customers

Sample name	Number of clusters	Number of customers
LPA 1	7	1485
LPA 2	8	1494
k-Means	6	1994
HDBSCAN 1	7	2153
HBDSCAN 2	6	1473

The results are presented in Table 2.

Table 2. Evaluation of clusters with Dunn and Davies–Bouldin indices

Sample name	Dunn	Davies-Bouldin	Silhouette (Euclidean)	Silhouette (Manhattan)	Calinski-Harabasz
LPA 1	0.0059	2.0108	0.0115	0.0745	407.8
LPA 2	0.0059	1.7444	0.0140	0.0682	511.1
k-Means	0.0006	3.1805	0.0173	0.0484	1035.3
HDBSCAN 1	0.0006	2.5879	−0.0028	0.0261	973.1
HBDSCAN 2	0.0014	2.2580	0.0512	0.0836	861.2

---

[3] The code for Dunn index calculation was found on GitHub: Dunn index for clusters analysis - https://gist.github.com/douglasrizzo/cd7e792ff3a2dcaf27f6. Computing of Dunn index is relatively simple, authors verified published code before it was used in order to prove its validity.

[4] Implementation of Davies–Bouldin index was taken from Scikit learn library: https://scikit-learn.org/stable/modules/generated/sklearn.metrics.davies_bouldin_score.html.

[5] Implementation of Silhouette index was taken from Scikit learn library: https://scikit-learn.org/stable/modules/generated/sklearn.metrics.silhouette_score.html.

[6] Implementation of Calinski-Harabasz index was taken from Scikit learn library: https://scikit-learn.org/stable/modules/generated/sklearn.metrics.calinski_harabasz_score.html.

A higher value of Dunn index indicates better clustering, so for both LPA samples this index is the highest. As regards Davies–Bouldin index, a lower value means better clustering. Using this index, LPA samples also are ranked the best. From this evaluation we can conclude that the method presented in this paper returned better clusters than other algorithms.

In reference to Silhouette index, the best value is 1 and the worst is -1. The Authors calculated this index twice using two available methods of distance calculation: Euclidean and Manhattan. For Euclidean distance, the proposed method returned poor result in comparison to others. Both HDBSCAN and k-means algorithms use Euclidean distance for calculation of observation closeness. These algorithms favor more circular clusters where observations are located around a centroid. For the proposed method grouping clusters of customers whose elements share common properties, Manhattan distance is more natural because it favors observations with the same values of a specific feature. When calculating Manhattan distance, LPA samples are ranked 2nd and 3rd, which shows that the algorithm gives better result than k-means.

Calinski-Harabasz index shows that the proposed method gives worse results than well-known algorithms. One must remember that this index is mostly used to evaluate the optimal number of clusters. This index favors k-means algorithm because it applies the criterion of minimum within-cluster sum of squares. Using this index k-means is ranked the best.

According to managers, Davies-Bouldin and Dunn indices are best matched to the business problem of customer communities detection. In addition to other methods, determining distances using Manhattan function can be considered to meet the business criteria.

5   Conclusions and Future Research

The primary objective of the presented research was to develop a method to evaluate customer communities discovered by data mining algorithms. The pilot study was carried out on a new multi-level hybrid method for community discovery, implemented and validated on the Upsaily experimental platform. The research methodology is composed of seven, closely integrated steps. In the first place, relevant information on customers is extracted from large marketing databases and partitioned by the clustering algorithm (HDBSCAN), secondly, the space dimensions are reduced into two dimensions using the Uniform Manifold Approximation and Projection (UMAP) method, and thirdly, the centroids are computed for each cluster. The graph is generated in the step four using the k-NN algorithm. To discover customer communities, the Label Propagation Algorithm (LPA) is applied. These experiments demonstrated that the "customer communities discovery" compared against "segmentation with k-means algorithm", gave much more precise identification of group of customers and enables managers and data analysts to better understand clusters. A number of quality measures demonstrated very high performance of the multi-level hybrid clustering. The final step, most important for decision makers, concerned marketing interpretation of discovered customer communities.

The multi-level clustering approach described in this paper has proven its advantage over single method clustering. Numerous small clusters were turned into communities sharing common properties. Specifically, running HDBSCAN alone against the data describing customer's purchases resulted in a high number (2046) of dense, but small clusters, making it elusive to predict customer's needs or address tailored offerings. It is important to mention that using the simplest PCA method for dimensions reduction did not live up to the expectations: the clusters did not form homogenous communities, which in turn could not provide managers with reliable tools to support decision making processes. When the PCA method was replaced by the UMAP method, the clustering results lived up to the expectations, making it possible to calculate meaningful centroids for each cluster. Afterwards, the label propagation method was applied, providing the means to determine customer communities, grouping them based on business needs.

The Upsaily platform used in the experiment allows for parameterization of the multi-level approach to clustering described in the paper, through defining the features used for clustering, business-oriented cluster identification, defining data range, or specifying the size of expected clusters. The advantage of this customized approach is that it can be widely applied to any type/category of customers and it provides the means to perform advanced analytics on the business data.

The results obtained so far on real marketing data are very encouraging; in addition, they have been positively validated by managers of internet shops. However, many algorithmic and business-oriented issues remain to be expanded and fine-tuned. For instance, a desirable extension of the approach will be to refine a method of feature construction describing a customer profile. An interesting future improvement could focus on implementation of the collective and cooperative clustering with built-in business-oriented quality measures. One, but not the last, ambitious work will be focused on the dynamics and evolution of customer communities.

References

1. Wu, Z.H., et al.: Balanced multi-label propagation for overlapping community detection in social networks. J. Comput. Sci. Technol. **27**(3), 468–479 (2012). https://doi.org/10.1007/s11390-012-1236-x
2. Barber, M.J.: Modularity and community detection in bipartite networks. Phys. Rev. E **76**(6), 066102 (2007). https://doi.org/10.1103/PhysRevE.76.066102
3. Codaasco, G., Gargano, L.: Label propagation algorithm: a semi-synchronous approach. Int. J. Soc. Netw. Min. **1**(1), 3–26 (2011). https://doi.org/10.1504/IJSNM.2012.045103
4. Gregory, S.: Finding overlapping communities in networks by label propagation. New J. Phys. **12**, 103018 (2010). https://doi.org/10.1088/1367-2630/12/10/103018
5. Han, J., Li, W., Su, Z., Zhao, L., Deng, W.: Community detection by label propagation with compression of flow. e-print arXiv:161202463v1 (2016). https://doi.org/10.1140/epjb/e2016-70264-6
6. Liu, W., Jiang, X., Pellegrini, M., Wang X.: Discovering communities in complex networks by edge label propagation. Sci. Rep. **6** (2016). https://doi.org/10.1038/srep22470
7. Rossetti, G., Cazabet, R.: Community discovery in dynamic networks: a survey. arXiv:1707.03186 (2017). https://doi.org/10.1145/3172867
8. Subelj, L., Bajec, M.: Group detection in complex networks: an algorithm and comparison of the state of the art. Physica A **397**, 144–156 (2014). https://doi.org/10.1016/j.physa.2013.12.003

9. Aggarwal, C.C., Reddy, C.K.: Data Clustering: Algorithms and Applications. Chapman & Hall/CRC, New York (2013). ISBN 978-1466558212
10. Gan, G., Ma, C., Wu, J.: Data Clustering: Theory, Algorithms, and Applications. SIAM Series (2007). https://doi.org/10.1137/1.9780898718348
11. Witten, I.H., et al.: Data Mining: Practical Machine Learning Tools and Techniques. Morgan Kaufmann, Burlington (2016)
12. Pondel, M., Korczak, J.: Recommendations based on collective intelligence – case of customer segmentation. In: Ziemba, E. (ed.) AITM/ISM 2018. LNBIP, vol. 346, pp. 73–92. Springer, Cham (2019). https://doi.org/10.1007/978-3-030-15154-6_5
13. Raghavan, U.N., Albert, R., Kumara, S.: Near linear time algorithm to detect community structures in large-scale networks. Phys. Rev. E **76**, 036106 (2007). https://doi.org/10.1103/PhysRevE.76.036106
14. Rosvall, M., Bergstorm, C.T.: An information-theoretic framework for resolving community structure in complex networks. Proc. Natl. Acad. Sci. **104**, 7327–7331 (2007). https://doi.org/10.1073/pnas.0611034104
15. Xie, J.R., Szymanski, B.K.: LabelRank: a stabilized label propagation algorithm for community detection in networks. In: Proceedings of the IEEE, Network Science Workshop, pp. 386–399 (2014). https://doi.org/10.1109/NSW.2013.6609210
16. Korczak, J., Pondel, M.: Kolektywna klasteryzacja danych marketingowych - System rekomendacji UPSAILY. Przegląd Organizacji **1**, 42–52 (2019)
17. Applebaum, W.: Studying customer behavior in retail stores. J. Mark. **16**(2), 172–178 (1951). https://doi.org/10.2307/1247625
18. See-To, E., Ngai, E.: An empirical study of payment technologies, the psychology of consumption, and spending behavior in a retailing context. Inf. Manag. **56**(3), 329–342 (2019). https://doi.org/10.1016/j.im.2018.07.007
19. Korczak, J., Pondel, M., Sroka, W.: An approach to customer community discovery. In: Proceedings of Federated Conference on Computer Science and Information Systems (FedCSIS), ACSIS, vol. 18, pp. 675–683 (2019). https://doi.org/10.15439/2019F308
20. Rodriguez, M.Z., et al.: Clustering algorithms. A comparative approach. PLoS ONE **14**(1), e0210236 (2019). https://doi.org/10.1371/journal.pone.0210236
21. Abbas, O.A.: Comparisons between data clustering algorithms. Int. Arab J. Inf. Technol. **5**(3), 320–325 (2008)
22. Rossetti, G., Cazabet, R.: Community discovery in dynamic networks: a survey. Pre-print arXiv:1707.03186v2 [cs.SI] (2017). https://doi.org/10.1145/3172867
23. Davies, D., Bouldin, D.: A cluster separation measure. IEEE Trans. Pattern Anal. Mach. Intell. **PAMI-1**(2), 224–227 (1979). https://doi.org/10.1109/TPAMI.1979.4766909
24. Dunn, J.C.: Well-separated clusters and optimal fuzzy partitions. J. Cybern. **4**(1), 95–104 (1974). https://doi.org/10.1080/01969727408546059
25. Calinski, T., Harabasz, J.: A dendrite method for cluster analysis. Commun. Stat. Theory Methods **3**(1), 1–27 (1974). https://doi.org/10.1080/03610927408827101
26. Rousseeuw, P.J.: Silhouettes: a graphical aid to the interpretation and validation of cluster analysis. Comput. Appl. Math. **20**, 53–65 (1987). https://doi.org/10.1016/0377-0427(87)90125-7
27. Pondel, M., Korczak, J.: A view on the methodology of analysis and exploration of marketing data. In: Proceedings of Federated Conference on Computer Science and Information Systems (FedCSIS), pp. 1135–1143. IEEE (2017). https://doi.org/10.15439/2017F442
28. Schubert, E., Sander, J., Ester, M., Kriegel, H.P., Xu, X.: DBSCAN revisited, revisited: why and how you should (still) use DBSCAN. ACM Trans. Database Syst. (TODS) **42**(3), 19 (2017). https://doi.org/10.1145/3068335
29. McInnes, L., Healy, J.: UMAP: uniform manifold approximation and projection for dimension reduction. Preprint arXiv:1802.03426 (2018). https://doi.org/10.21105/joss.00861

30. Newman, M.E.J.: Detecting community structure in networks. Eur. Phys. J. B **38**(2), 321–330 (2004). https://doi.org/10.1140/epjb/e2004-00124-y
31. Fortunato, S.: Community detection in graphs. Preprint arXiv:0906.0612 (2004). https://doi.org/10.1016/j.physrep.2009.11.002
32. Emmons, S., Kobourov, S., Gallant, M., Börner, K.: Analysis of network clustering algorithms and cluster quality metrics at scale. PLoS ONE **11**(7), e0159161 (2016). https://doi.org/10.1371/journal.pone.0159161
33. Blondel, V.D., Guillaume, J.L., Lambiotte, R., Lefebvre, E.: Fast unfolding of communities in large networks. J. Stat. Mech. Theory Exp. (2008). https://doi.org/10.1088/1742-5468/2008/10/P10008
34. Waltman, L., Eck, N.J.: A smart local moving algorithm for large-scale modularity-based community detection. Eur. Phys. J. B **86**(11), 1–14 (2013). https://doi.org/10.1140/epjb/e2013-40829-0
35. Rosvall, M., Bergstrom, C.T.: Maps of random walks on complex networks re-veal community structure. Proc. Natl. Acad. Sci. **105**(4), 1118–1123 (2008). https://doi.org/10.1073/pnas.0706851105

Perspectives on Industrial Symbiosis Implementation: Informational, Managerial, and IT Aspects

Linda Kosmol and Christian Leyh[✉]

Technische Universität Dresden, 01062 Dresden, Germany
{linda.kosmol,christian.leyh}@tu-dresden.de

Abstract. Industrial symbiosis is a favored approach to balancing an industry's economic growth with its environmental impact on a regional scale. Although the scientific literature reports numerous examples of industrial symbiosis around the world, this approach and its related concepts are not considered to be widespread in practice, due to various barriers.

Informational and managerial barriers are seen as significant obstacles to industrial symbiosis, but they have not yet been adequately investigated. Empirical research is needed to understand how industrial actors perceive these barriers, and especially supporting information technologies (IT). Therefore, in this paper, we first examine the barriers to industrial symbiosis through a literature review, focusing on informational and managerial barriers. In a second step, we develop a study involving an online questionnaire in order to investigate the extent of managerial and informational barriers that prevent industrial symbiosis, as well as the perception of corresponding IT support. Finally, we present the results of our pre-study.

Keywords: Industrial symbiosis · Barriers · Information · Management · IT

1 Introduction

In today's world, sustainability is important. The demand for sustainable development continues to increase, and the term 'sustainability' has come to be an omnipresent, central issue in discussions on industrial development. Companies face growing economic, ecological, and social challenges, as do their business partners. Hence, sustainability has become a key strategic task for many businesses, which are now concerned with the challenges of sustainability management [1–3]. One approach to sustainable industrial development that has begun to attract research attention is industrial symbiosis. Industrial symbiosis aims to balance industrial activities with their impact on the environment. It consists of regional, cross-sectoral, and cross-company cooperation to increase resource efficiency and to ecologically and economically benefit all parties involved [4, 5].

To address these aspects, a growing number of uncovered and facilitated examples of industrial symbiosis, from all over the world, have been described in the scientific literature [6–8]. These examples contribute to sustainable development economically

E. Ziemba (Ed.): AITM 2019/ISM 2019, LNBIP 380, pp. 192–213, 2020.
https://doi.org/10.1007/978-3-030-43353-6_11

(e.g., reduced waste disposal and input costs), environmentally (e.g., reduced waste production and resource use), and socially (e.g., community awareness). Nevertheless, despite these success stories, other reports show that industrial symbiosis practices are not widely implemented, due to various barriers [9, 10]. According to [11], less than 0.1% of 26 million active companies in Europe are engaged in industrial symbiosis.

In particular, barriers that are managerial (e.g., limited commitment) and informational (e.g., lack of information sharing) in nature are regarded as significant obstacles to industrial symbiosis [9–14], since these barriers must be overcome for symbiotic opportunities to be identified and subsequently utilized. If these barriers are not addressed, subsequent processes—such as feasibility studies on identified opportunities—cannot be carried out, and other related barriers (such as technical or financial issues) cannot be identified. Since informational and managerial barriers are easier to overcome than technical or regulatory barriers and can be alleviated with appropriate IT support, we focus on these barriers in this paper.

Currently, industrial symbiosis research needs more empirical and quantitative studies, which it lacks (as stated by [15]). In recent years, some surveys have been conducted on industrial symbiosis activities, both to examine the interest in and maturity of industrial symbiosis in a specific region as well as to capture the perception of barriers to adopting symbiotic practices (Table 1). The surveys typically target companies (general or environmental managers) or policymakers but rarely the managers of industrial parks, despite wide recognition of the latter's potential role as facilitators of industrial symbiosis [16, 17].

Table 1. Industrial symbiosis surveys

Year	Article	Region	Focus[1]	Sample[2]
2016	[18, 19]	Philippines	Barrier interdependencies (10)	10
2017	[20]	Brazil	Social barriers (4)	29
	[16]	Europe	Symbiosis activity, barriers (5)	92
	[17]	Europe	Symbiosis activity, barriers (10)	N/A
2018	[21]	Slovenia	Symbiosis activity (-)	50
	[22]	Sweden	Symbiosis activity, maturity, barriers (4)	20 (50)
	[23]	Spain	Symbiosis activity, barriers (9)	95
2019	[24]	Europe	Symbiosis activity, impacts, barriers (12)	22 (25)

[1] No. in brackets = No. of barrier categories
[2] No. in brackets = No. of follow-up interviews

The perceived relevance of informational and managerial barriers varies considerably across different studies. These differences can be caused by region and context but also by the diverse barrier categorizations proposed in the different studies. Informational, managerial, and social aspects are not clearly separated from each other: informational barriers in particular are often linked with social factors like trust, cooperation, and community. According to [14] and [15], managerial barriers are a cause factor and informational barriers are an effect factor; however, although a cause-effect relationship might exist, the inconsistencies in barrier categorization and the lack of a uniform allocation of underlying aspects make it difficult to compare the studies, reducing their reliability and validity. Only [21] and [23] considered informational barriers separately from social aspects, albeit exclusively with reference to information systems. The survey of [21] shows that 49 out of 50 respondents would use an online platform to implement industrial symbiosis if one was available, while the survey in [23] reveals that some companies consider inadequate information management systems to be a barrier. However, neither study gave further information regarding the information system/online platform (information types, functionality, access, users, etc.). Therefore, the extent of informational barriers and their causes remain unknown.

The absence of an empirical foundation can also be seen in efforts to support industrial symbiosis with information technology (IT) in order to mitigate informational issues. These tools appear to be primarily research-driven, and it remains unclear how much they are known, used, and perceived as useful by companies [12, 25]. Therefore, we decided to set up a long-term research project to address this research gap. We have observed that research needs to further explore the readiness of corporate management to engage in industrial symbiosis, as well as to investigate opinions on informational issues and IT support. In particular, an investigation of informational aspects in terms of information availability, confidentiality, and relevance—as well as of the perception of IT support—will contribute to understanding and exposing gaps between research efforts and practice.

Therefore, the aim of this paper (an extended version of [26]) involves the first step of our research project: to identify and clarify the aspects of informational and managerial barriers and of IT support that need to be addressed for industrial symbiosis. In addition, we will present the results of a pre-study and outline the steps of our ongoing research.

This paper is structured as follows. Section 2 presents a short theoretical background on industrial symbiosis. Section 3 describes our overall research approach. In Sect. 4 the procedure and the results of the literature review of the various barriers to industrial symbiosis are presented. Section 5 describes the design of the survey and presents the preliminary findings. Finally, Sect. 6 concludes the paper with a discussion and future steps.

2 Theoretical Background

Although industrial symbiosis research has increased significantly in recent years, the concept is not new; extensive literature reviews [8, 15, 27, 28] trace its origins to the 1990s. Originally, 'industrial symbiosis' dealt with the physical exchange of materials, energy, water, and by-products between geographically-close companies in order to reap economic and environmental advantages [1]. Today, the term encompasses all business models of inter-firm exchange or sharing of under-utilized resources, including materials, energy, logistics, capacities, space, expertise, and knowledge [5]. These business models (synergies) are either exchange-based or sharing-based and are commonly divided into three categories [29–31]: by-product exchange and reuse; utility and infrastructure sharing; and service sharing.

'By-product exchange' refers to one company's residual outputs (e.g., waste, and by-products) being used as another company's inputs (e.g., water, material, waste heat). The exchanged resources replace either raw materials that are part of a product or operating materials required for production. Here, the principle of circular economy is followed. 'Utility and infrastructure sharing' refers to joint use and/or operation of technical infrastructure and decentralized plants, such as a combined heat and power plant, water treatment plant, or district heating grid. 'Service sharing' refers to cross-company management or joint provision of common services, such as joint disposal/procurement, logistics and warehousing, staff training, and knowledge exchange.

Depending on the business model and the role of the company (supplier or consumer), various economic and ecological advantages can occur for the parties involved and for the corresponding region. These include reduced resource consumption and waste generation, eco-innovation, revenues from residues and by-products, less raw material and disposal costs, new business and market opportunities, and more [32].

The development mechanisms of industrial symbiosis can be divided into three categories: self-organized, facilitated, and planned/designed. The degree of involvement of coordinating/mediating third parties (research institutes, governmental agencies, park management) increases with each category [33]. Intermediaries are regarded as vital to supporting contact initiation, collecting necessary information and knowledge, and facilitating exchanges between companies [34].

Industrial symbiosis is often associated with eco-industrial parks (EIPs), in which companies adopt symbiotic behavior and commit to sustainable development [35, 36]. Through this collaboration, a community of co-located businesses becomes an industrial ecosystem [37, 38]. The concepts of industrial symbiosis and EIPs are often equated, but they differ in terms of geographical scope, actors, and practices [8, 15, 39]. This differentiation is important, as it implies differences in the platform required or suitable, in terms of users, functionality, governance, etc. Park managers are considered to be the best candidates to provide such social and informational infrastructure to the companies in an industrial park [9].

3 Research Methodology—Overall Research Approach

In this research project, we aim to design an IT tool (IT artifact) to mitigate and overcome informational and managerial issues in industrial symbiosis. Therefore, we follow the design science paradigm [40]; the steps of design science research in information systems are shown Table 2.

Currently, we are in the first stages of a long-term research project concerning industrial symbiosis. We initiated our research by identifying the problem (managerial and informational barriers) and a solution space (IT) through a comprehensive literature review (described in Sect. 4). Additionally, to gain practical insights into the problem space of industrial symbiosis, in the first phase of our research project we conducted an extensive survey with industrial actors. In Sect. 5, we present the survey design and the preliminary results.

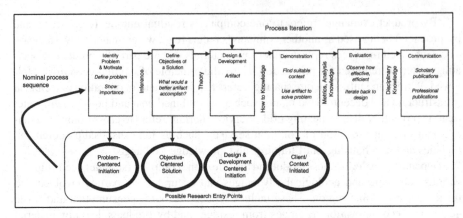

Fig. 1. Design science research methodology [40]

The information in the following sections shows that managerial and informational barriers persist and that IT solutions encounter a number of problems. Furthermore, both research and industry lack design guidelines and best practices for IT solutions that enable/support industrial symbiosis [41]. Like other researchers, we think that IT tools—particularly digital platforms—can help overcome managerial and informational barriers [12, 42], but only if their designs are tailored to the needs, circumstances, and restrictions of the intended users. Understanding these aspects requires capturing the general attitude of management towards industrial symbiosis, along with the associated exchange of information and knowledge, together with the corresponding IT; this will be done by means of a survey administered to relevant industrial players in industrial symbiosis. This problem-centered approach highlights the relevance of the topic and clarifies the problems addressed in this research project (Fig. 1).

Based on the answers to the survey, as well as the information obtained in subsequent interviews, we aim to deduce where an IT tool could/should be applied and how it could enable industrial symbiosis. By conducting empirically-grounded problem identification and aligning it with the existing solution space, we endeavor to confirm the research gap and to ensure that the proposed IT tool is designed in such a way that it is tailored to and accepted by the target users, thus enabling it to be embedded in existing strategies and processes so as to address this important issue [25].

4   Literature Review

4.1   Methodology

In order to identify the barriers to industrial symbiosis, we conducted a systematic literature review, in line with [43].

Due to the interdisciplinary character of industrial symbiosis, databases of different scientific disciplines were searched. AISeL and IEEE Xplore were selected to represent information systems, and Scopus and EBSCOhost were selected to represent engineering and natural sciences.

Our search query—(("industrial symbiosis" OR "eco-industrial park") AND (barrier OR obstacle OR limiter)) within title, abstract, and keywords—led to 88 non-duplicate records. For each record, the title and abstract were read and assessed independently by two researchers to identify eligible articles. Forty articles met the inclusion criteria (at least partial focus on barriers to industrial symbiosis). The full texts of these remaining articles were then examined independently by both researchers for their relevance. This resulted in 23 articles that were included in the final in-depth literature analysis.

All included articles were analyzed using Mayring's approach to qualitative content analysis [44]. The analysis was performed collaboratively by both researchers. The barriers described in the literature were recorded in a list and were subsequently categorized inductively with a bottom-up approach, with no pre-existing categories. Similar barriers (e.g., missing technical knowledge and lack of market knowledge) were first assigned to a subcategory (e.g., lack of knowledge). Then, similar subcategories (e.g., lack of knowledge and knowledge sharing) were assigned to categories (e.g., knowledge) describing a whole cluster of barriers. Finally, the categories were grouped into factors (e.g., soft factors), which represent the underlying patterns triggering an individual barrier. This categorization process was conducted for each barrier until all barriers were categorized. Whenever the existing categories were inadequate, a new category was introduced. More detailed information on the procedure can be found in [45].

4.2 Results

Various barriers were extracted from the 23 articles, with the following distribution:

- 49% were assigned to the categories 'cooperation', 'management', 'knowledge', and 'information'. These are difficult to quantify, as they address personal aspects; they have been termed *soft factors*.
- 32% refer to 'economic', 'financial', and 'technological' issues. These categories have been termed *hard factors*, as they tend to be tangible and easily quantifiable.
- 19% are related either to 'policy/regulation' or to 'public/market' barriers, representing *contextual factors* around the symbiosis.

Figure 2 shows the number of barriers contained in each subcategory of the various categories. This analysis examines only the number of mentions of these barriers in the literature and does not infer their impact or relevance. Although some studies have measured perceptions of barriers through interviews and surveys [24, 46], the results are mixed, and their actual impact on the implementation of industrial symbiosis has not been investigated.

In the following paragraphs, we focus on the soft factors, namely information- and knowledge-related, management, and cooperation barriers. For a detailed analysis of all barriers, see [45].

A glance at the barriers that fall under 'soft factors' reveals that they are strategic in nature. These barriers account for 49% of all barriers, indicating that the business strategy of the involved companies is a crucial element in industrial symbiosis. Accordingly, an examination is needed into how new processes that support sustainable development and industrial symbiosis can be integrated as easily as possible into existing businesses

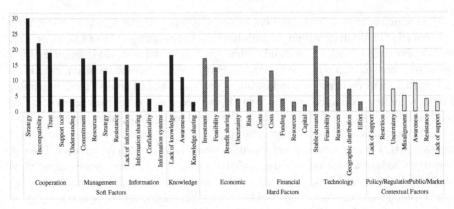

Fig. 2. Implementation barriers of industrial symbiosis [45]

and industrial networks, especially in the context of limited personnel, time, budget, etc. Particular attention must be paid to the allocation of responsibilities as well as personnel and time resources.

In the context of information systems research, it is striking that these four barrier categories (cooperation, management, information, knowledge) can be addressed using IT tools (e.g., business process modeling and groupware). However, current IT tools primarily support information and knowledge, detached from management and cooperation. These tools could allow partners to integrate approaches for project management or for designing business processes and models. Furthermore, current IT tools for industrial symbiosis focus more on information and knowledge exchange and less on their strategic embedding within the process of implementing industrial symbiosis and coordinating information and knowledge flows [25].

Informational Barriers. Within the category information, *lack of information*—i.e., limited information on or accessibility to resource quality and quantity [10, 16, 47], collaboration methods [47], or inefficient information flows [9]—is the most prevalent barrier. Other barriers include: *information sharing*—i.e., general lack of information sharing [10, 18, 48], and resistance [9] or difficulty [49, 50] to do so; *confidentiality issues*—i.e., limited information disclosure due to confidentiality [51–53], even unnecessary confidentiality [54]; and *information systems*—i.e., absent or inadequate sustainability or management of information systems [23, 51].

Knowledge Barriers. First and foremost under the knowledge category is *lack of knowledge* to identify and utilize industrial symbiosis opportunities—whether technical [47], market [47], or environmental knowledge [48], or a lack of expertise or experts [9, 10, 49] and/or a lack of training [48, 49, 54]. This barrier is followed by *awareness*, characterized by unfamiliarity with industrial symbiosis concepts [18, 49], lack of recognition of waste as potential input [55], or unknown benefits [46]. Difficult or absent *knowledge sharing*—i.e., lack of mechanisms and methods to educate or learn [18, 50]—can also hinder industrial symbiosis efforts.

The availability of information and knowledge, and the willingness to share these benefits with others, are essential to identifying and evaluating synergy opportunities for industrial symbiosis. For example, in the case of a potential by-product exchange, what is relevant/important is information on the incoming and outgoing resource flows of companies, as well as knowledge of relevant compatibility criteria and technical expertise to implement synergies. However, lack of trust, confidentiality issues, and motivational issues may lead to an unwillingness to share pertinent information and knowledge [9, 34, 56]. Lack of internal information, lack of contacts with whom to share information and knowledge, communication issues, and difficulty in sharing knowledge further limit available information and knowledge sources [10, 12, 57]. Confidentiality issues in particular have not been investigated in industrial symbiosis research.

Since we aim to determine the extent to which informational barriers exist, we need to keep these barriers separate from social aspects, such as trust and relationships. We consider the following to be informational barriers to industrial symbiosis:

- Lack of awareness of principles and benefits of industrial symbiosis;
- Lack of available information and knowledge;
- Unwillingness to and/or difficulty in sharing information and knowledge;
- Non-transparent, inefficient exchange of information and knowledge;
- Lack of information-sharing mechanisms and infrastructure.

IT support is seen as promising in terms of alleviating informational barriers and providing a space for interaction and exchange between companies [13, 14]. Generally, these tools are online repositories (e.g., ISData) and/or platforms (e.g., eSymbiosis) that provide myriad ways to disseminate and share information and knowledge as well as facilitate by-product exchanges via waste market functions and automatic matching engines.

However, industrial symbiosis IT tools face a number of barriers [41, 58]. Currently, these tools are not provided with enough data and information to be used effectively. This may be caused by unwillingness to use the tools, confidentiality issues, manual effort required for data entry, ignorance of the existence of such tools, and access restrictions— all leading to a low number of potential users. Social networking approaches [34, 59] have addressed criticized early tools for not taking sufficient account of the social context [12]. In addition, many tools are limited in their functionality to the early stages of industrial symbiosis (synergy identification and assessment) [12, 14]. Moreover, many tools are not easily/publicly accessible, not operational, or still in the concept or development stages [12, 14]. Hardly any information can be found on the operational tools about the contexts in which they are used, the extent to which they are used, how and by whom they are used, and which specific functions they provide to (potential) users. Therefore, it is difficult to assess how useful the current IT support tools are to industrial symbiosis.

Cooperative Barriers. As industrial symbiosis is comprised of inter-firm partnerships, cooperative issues may arise due to differences in the involved companies' *strategies*— i.e., aversion [18, 47, 49]), unwillingness [60], and discontinuity [51] regarding collaboration; conflicts of interest and objectives [18]; or absent or difficult multi-actor decision making [16, 61]). Organizational *incompatibilities* result from the structure and current situation of the potential partners (e.g., bound by old contracts [60], different cultures [16, 46, 62], or differences in power structure and company size [16, 60, 63]). In addition, a lack of *trust* (e.g., due to competitive attitudes [51, 54] or social isolation [47]), a lack of *support tools* (e.g., information systems for communication, coordination, and collaboration [51, 54, 61]) and a lack of *understanding* (e.g., inconsistency in terminology [18, 46] or no shared understanding [18, 54]) are regarded as important subcategories of this category.

Management Barriers. The management category refers to both a company's and an industrial park's management, the latter of which may be involved in facilitating industrial symbiosis. This category describes barriers that must be overcome internally by the company or park management in order to be ready for synergies. This category consists of the factors *commitment*—i.e., (lack of) interest in and engagement with sustainable development [9, 10, 47] or (lack of) behavioral change [46]; *resources*—i.e., (lack of) time [24, 47, 48] or available and qualified personnel [23, 50, 63]. While the subcategory 'strategy' in the cooperation category refers to the incompatibility of strategies of potential partners, *strategy* in the management category refers to internal company problems that prevent the implementation of industrial symbiosis. This might include such situations as: symbiosis is misaligned with the company's policies [16]; the project is not channeled in the right way through the company [64]; or inappropriate hierarchical organizational structures result in separated responsibilities and require approval of the corporate headquarters [48, 51]. Another subcategory is *resistance* from organizations (e.g., unwillingness to risk existing supply chain [16], or aversion to changing procedures and processes [24, 47]).

In order for businesses to gather and share information and knowledge, there must be a willingness to commit to sustainable business models; to participate in workshops; and to provide time, personnel, and (likely) financial resources. Synergy identification and implementation require resources. Without a commitment to incorporating industrial symbiosis into a holistic strategy and into the business processes of participating companies, the discovered potential synergies may go unused [12]. Since the potential benefits are unknown and difficult to predict at first, and since coordination and exchange of information and knowledge are time-consuming, the commitment and willingness must persist beyond initial meetings and workshops. We consider the following to be managerial barriers to industrial symbiosis:

- Lack of commitment to sustainable business processes and to the community/network;
- Lack of management support;
- Unwillingness to collaborate and communicate.

The attitude of the company and of the park management not only influence informational barriers but can also determine if and how IT tools are used for industrial symbiosis.

5 Survey Design and Pre-study

5.1 Methodology

To address the identified problems/barriers and to investigate them in more detail—thus filling this gap in the literature—we designed a study based on an online questionnaire.

The purpose of this design is to reach a large number of companies and to gather various opinions and perceptions of managerial, informational, and IT-related aspects of industrial symbiosis. The questionnaire will be provided in German for companies in Germany, Austria, and Switzerland and in English for companies in other European countries. Our objective is to gain insights into the (estimated) willingness and ability of companies to engage in industrial symbiosis. The questionnaire is composed of four sections, which we describe in the following paragraphs.

General Data – Participant Characterization. In order for the participants' answers to be accurately analyzed, the participants themselves must be sufficiently characterized. Therefore, the general data section includes the following information:

- Role of the participants' company (media supply/disposal, industry, park management); this determines the opportunities of participating in industrial symbiosis
- Type of company (private, public, public-private partnership); this indicates the incentives to participate in industrial symbiosis or other sustainability practices
- Location (county or federal state); this ensures the preservation of the participants' anonymity, but permits to draw conclusions about different industrial sites
- Length of stay at site (in years); this may influence the number of established contacts and (business) relationships
- Size of company/industrial park (number of employees/companies); this indicates the human resources available and the number of potential synergy partners
- Certification in energy (ISO 50001) and/or environmental (ISO 14001/EMAS) management and acknowledgement of the importance of energy and material consumption and waste; this indicates the relevance of sustainability issues
- Participants' position (employee, executive, general manager)

The characteristics of the companies and the comparisons among them may reveal fundamental differences in readiness and in business attitudes towards industrial symbiosis, from which different conclusions can be drawn (e.g., requirement profiles).

Managerial Aspects – Current Practice, Readiness, and Potentials. The extent of managerial barriers is seen in the company's current practices and in its readiness to adopt industrial symbiosis practices and business models. Therefore, the first block of questions explores the current practices, including the type of business model and the role of the company. This section also examines awareness of the concept of industrial symbiosis, regardless of specific terms.

The survey participants are also asked to assess the readiness, interest, and potential opportunities of the company/companies in terms of practicing industrial symbiosis. Questions related to readiness examine a company's ability to collaborate at the company level, while questions related to potential opportunities assess the company's ability to collaborate at the network level (by asking about the perceptions of other companies in the industrial park). To measure readiness and potential, we use the proposed readiness areas of [65]. These areas include business models of industrial symbiosis (e.g., readiness for by-product exchange) and the company's strategic orientation to industrial symbiosis (e.g., readiness to pursue common goals or to provide time and/or personnel for industrial symbiosis activities). Questions regarding potential help indicate the extent to which companies have information/knowledge of other companies at the same location. Answers are given on a 5-point Likert scale, from low (1) to high (5) readiness/potential.

Informational Aspects – Availability and Sharing. The extent of information-related barriers is seen in concept awareness, internal and public availability of information and knowledge, and willingness to disclose information and knowledge.

These questions first examine the company's policies and practices in terms of internal and external exchange of knowledge. 'Policy' refers to management support for/facilitation of knowledge sharing, while 'practice' refers to existing formal and informal communication channels and actual methods of knowledge sharing. Companies can benefit from improving or qualifying existing channels and practices instead of developing and imposing new ones. An example question on communication channels is given in Fig. 3.

Which communication channels do you mainly use in your company to exchange experiences and knowledge with colleagues and partners?					
	Within your company				
	Never	Rarely	Sometimes	Often	Always
	1	2	3	4	5
Face-to-face communication	☐	☐	☐	☐	☐
Virtual face-to-face communication	☐	☐	☐	☐	☐
E-mail	☐	☐	☐	☐	☐
Internet/Intranet (non-e-mail)	☐	☐	☐	☐	☐
Expert systems	☐	☐	☐	☐	☐

Fig. 3. Example survey question – knowledge sharing

Then, the following questions investigate the availability of needed information. To this end, the participants are asked whether certain information about inputs and outputs is known within the company, whether it is publicly available (e.g., in environmental reports), and whether it is generally subject to confidentiality. The types of information addressed in these questions are listed in Table 2. This information is typically used to identify synergies at a high level of detail [66]. To examine the willingness to share information, questions are included that ask about the relevance of the various types of information, along with questions on the disclosure of information and its level of detail. An example question concerning information confidentiality is given in Fig. 4.

Another important aspect related to information sharing is the type of interaction type in information exchange. In direct interactions, other interested companies in the industrial park can receive or view information (participant model [12]). In indirect interactions, an intermediary receives the information, processes and analyzes it, and passes on the results of the analysis (i.e., a synergy potential is presumed or not) to other companies, without the latter having access to the original information (facilitator model [12]).

Table 2. Necessary information for industrial symbiosis

Information type	Examples/Level of detail
Resource type	Material, energy, water, EWC classification
Resource quantity	Average per year/per month/per day/per hour
Supply pattern	Constant/fluctuating, maximum/minimum, lot size
Resource property	Components/ingredients, pollution, temperature
Resource source	Plant type (e.g., processing/production plant), utilization (e.g., material input, drying, air conditioning, process heat), specific plant (e.g., industrial furnace)
Availability period	All year/seasonal, month details (e.g., April–August), date specification (e.g., 01.04.19–04.12.20), shift system (e.g., Mo–Fr 5:30 to 22:30)
Supplier/customer	Type, name
Price/cost	Total per year/per unit, upper/lower price limit

Are the following types of information classified as confidential in your company and therefore subject to disclosure restrictions to other companies (i.e., non-disclosure agreements)?

	Raw materials		
	Yes	Uncertain	No
Resource type	☐	☐	☐
Resource quantity	☐	☐	☐
Supply pattern	☐	☐	☐
Resource properties	☐	☐	☐
Availability period	☐	☐	☐
Supplier/customer	☐	☐	☐
Price/cost	☐	☐	☐

Fig. 4. Example survey question – information sharing

Companies' preference for one interaction type or the other can provide insight into a suitable mechanism for information exchange within an industrial park and for the design of appropriate IT support.

IT Support – Awareness and Design. This section of the questionnaire addresses the awareness of IT tools and the perception of their usefulness on the basis of provided functions. Based on [13], different types of IT tools (online waste market, synergy identification system, etc.) are presented with examples, in order to assess participants' awareness of them. Then, select functions of these tools (exchange market, matching engine, social applications, etc.) are described, in order to examine whether these functions are considered useful and/or would be used. Here, a question is asked on the preference for direct or indirect exchange of information in the context of IT. Finally, both forms of the questionnaire (for the companies in industrial parks and for the park management) include the question of who should provide and operate such a tool (Fig. 5).

Who do you think should operate/provide such systems or platforms?

□ Park management
□ Focal company
□ Third Party
□ Uncertain

Fig. 5. Example survey question – IT

5.2 Pre-study – Initial Results

The pre-study involved 10 industrial actors: two park operators, two supply/disposal contractors, and six participants from production companies. With the exception of two participants (one park management employee and one industry employee), all participants have been on-site over 15 years. Based on the information regarding the federal state/county, it can be deduced that three participants are located at the same site. From both an economic and ecological point of view, energy consumption, material consumption, and waste generation are relevant for all participants, although ecology is subordinate to economics (Fig. 6).

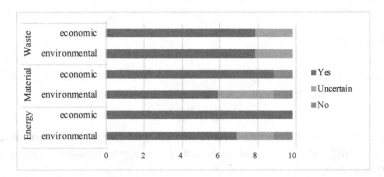

Fig. 6. "Please indicate whether the following topics are important to your company."

Managerial Aspects – Current Practice, Readiness, and Potentials. With regard to current practice, 7 of 10 respondents answered that they already have some experience with industrial symbiosis. Despite the relatively small number and the random selection of survey participants, all business models of industrial symbiosis are represented in the group of respondents, although utility sharing and service sharing dominated (6 out of 7). In this regard, joint disposal and supply is the type of cooperation mentioned most often, while shared logistic services or workshops and knowledge exchange is least frequently mentioned. By-product exchange is only practiced by 2 out of 7 respondents. Cooperation mainly involves non-competitors, although some occurs with competitors from outside the park (1 out of 7) or in a similar industrial sector (2 out of 7).

Both park operator participants already cover the various functions (energy and media supply, environmental services, site development, promotion of information and knowledge exchange, etc.) proposed in the literature for facilitators of industrial symbiosis. However, the extent to which they take on these functions was not investigated.

Figure 7 shows the survey answers regarding readiness to participate in industrial symbiosis, in terms of business models (e.g., replacing raw materials with recycled materials and/or other waste and by-products from another company) and strategic alignment (e.g., being part of a network that is strategically aligned with industrial symbiosis and sustainability). The numbers include the statements of the industrial players as well as the park managers' perceptions about the companies located on-site. Most participants are willing to participate in by-product exchanges (BPE), utility sharing, and service sharing if it is economically beneficial; only one participant was unwilling to participate in any symbiotic activities. The majority favors utility or service sharing. The willingness to strategically reorient themselves is less prevalent. Such a reorientation would include: making personnel and time resources available for industrial symbiosis activities (Management Support); aligning business strategy and corporate policy towards sustainability and industrial symbiosis (Sustainability Orientation); sharing the same goals with other companies, or developing and pursuing common goals (Cooperation); and being part of a network that strategically aligns itself with industrial symbiosis and sustainability (Network). Management support in particular is perceived as lacking.

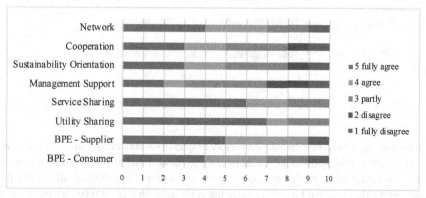

Fig. 7. "Please assess the current willingness of your company to participate in Industrial Symbiosis in terms of business models and strategic orientation, regardless of whether there are actually opportunities. Your company (management) is ready for ..."

The participants' estimated or perceived opportunities for industrial symbiosis activities is depicted in Fig. 8. The opinions are generally conservative, although here too the by-product exchange ranks worse than the other models.

Informational Aspects – Availability and Sharing. Figure 9 shows participants' familiarity with the concepts and business models of Industrial Symbiosis. The answers

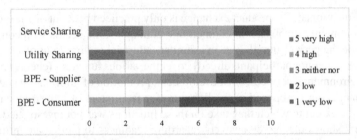

Fig. 8. "Please assess the potential/opportunities for your company with regard to the business models in the industrial estate. Consider existing synergies as well as information and knowledge about resources, needs and the basic attitude of the companies in the industrial estate. How do you assess the potential [for]…"

of the respondents suggest that about half of the actors are not familiar with the concepts 'industrial symbiosis' or 'by-product exchange'. Overall, industrial symbiosis and by-product exchange are less known, while utility and service sharing are more commonly known. The higher awareness of utility and service sharing is almost certainly due to the setting, as industrial parks tend to have shared infrastructures.

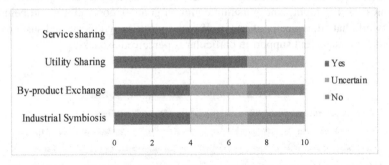

Fig. 9. "Are you familiar with these concepts, regardless of their terminology?"

The participants were also asked a variety of questions concerning internal and external information and knowledge exchange. In general, participants' attitudes towards internal and external exchange of knowledge was positive. For example, all but one participant agree that time for knowledge sharing is allowed, that employees are encouraged and supported in sharing knowledge and experience, and that communication with local companies is advocated.

E-mails are the primary means of both internal and external information exchange and communication. Face-to-face interaction is less prevalent in inter-company communication than in internal communication, even though it is considered important for knowledge exchange. Communication between companies via internet-based platforms or intranet solutions (not based on e-mail) also occurs, but much less frequently.

In general, information on resource inputs and outputs is available internally. In total, 5 out of 8 participants (excluding park management) have information on inputs, and 4 out of 8 participants have information on outputs, in their company. While the inputs were often straightforward "yes" or "no" answers, more uncertainty was observed concerning the outputs. The park management also stated that it had information on the energy and material flows of the local companies. The only information that was considerably less known by all participants was cost information.

Participants were asked what information they would not disclose in an initial evaluation/identification of synergy potentials without non-disclosure agreements. About half of the participants already disclose information on inputs and outputs, such as in environmental reports or online exchanges. However, this openness is limited by the type and quantity of resources. As for other information listed (e.g., resource properties), there was some lack of agreement. Only the suppliers or buyers and the cost information are definitely not disclosed by any participant.

IT Support – Awareness and Design. Existing online tools that support industrial symbiosis are rather unknown to the participants: 3 respondents knew of knowledge repositories, 2 were aware of synergy identification systems, and 4 had heard of online exchange markets. However, half of the respondents use information systems or databases to collect and analyze information from the (other) companies in the park. This is not limited to park management.

A mixed picture emerges regarding the functionalities of possible IT support. The park operators generally hold a positive attitude towards the proposed functions, while the industry members have mixed opinions about their benefits. Figure 10 illustrates the opinions on IT functionalities that are often mentioned in industrial symbiosis tools.

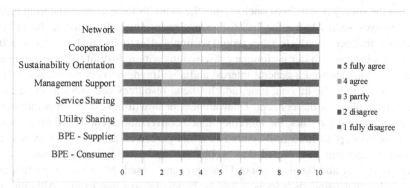

Fig. 10. "Do you consider the following functions, supported by an information (and communication) system, to be useful for your industrial region, provided that access and confidentiality restrictions have been defined, and sufficient information is entered?"

A clear preference can be seen regarding the interaction type, both in general and in terms of IT support (Fig. 11): a direct information exchange is preferred, followed by an approach combining indirect and direct exchange.

Interestingly, 5 out of 10 participants prefer automated data input or import into an online tool, supporting the claim of [58] that manual operation can hinder the use of IT

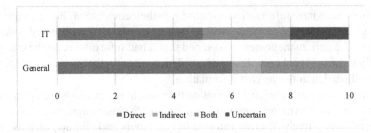

Fig. 11. "What kind of information exchange would you prefer in such a system?"

tools for industrial symbiosis. Of the 10 participants, 3 prefer manual data entry, while 2 are uncertain. Only half of the participants stated that they would use an IT tool, with the condition that its use and operation is economically beneficial.

6 Discussion and Future Steps

The existing industrial symbiosis research does not sufficiently address managerial and informational barriers and associated IT support. In particular, empirical research on industrial actors' perceptions of these barriers and of IT is lacking. In order to develop appropriate and sustainable IT tools to overcome these barriers—the objective of our research—it is necessary to identify the specific underlying problems, needs, and resistances/aversions of potential users.

From the survey results, we conclude that the main obstacle to implementing industrial symbiosis seems to be the lack of management support—namely, the lack of resources (time, personnel, etc.) they would willingly offer to deal with symbiotic activities. This is in line with our preliminary discussions with industrial park members and managers, which showed a general interest and a willingness to cooperate, but no/few attempts to provide the human, time, and financial resources necessary to pursue and adequately implement the concept. Unawareness or unwillingness to cooperate is not evident in the survey results; the aforementioned conversations confirmed this. Awareness of the concept of industrial symbiosis is not perceived as an issue; however, the exchange of information is regarded as problematic and needing improvement.

Knowledge of and opinions about IT support are mixed. Most survey participants acknowledge that using such tools would be beneficial to some extent. Although the majority were in favor of the park management providing these IT tools/platforms, it remains unclear whether the park management has the time and competence to develop and maintain such support. Although no aversion to IT support was seen, we did note a certain reluctance due to concerns about the cost-effectiveness of a potential platform. At present, there is no indication as to how much time and cost would be required to develop and maintain industrial symbiosis platforms.

Since industrial symbiosis implementation is highly context-dependent, small samples are not sufficient for a holistic understanding of the relevance of managerial and informational issues. Therefore, in order to reach as many actors as possible, and to obtain a deeper and more holistic picture of these issues, we designed an online questionnaire targeting relevant players of industrial symbiosis. By sending the online questionnaire to a large set of industrial actors (as the next step in our long-term research project), we aim to expand the understanding of the problems/barriers and the IT solutions identified in the existing literature and in our preliminary results, as presented in Sects. 4 and 5.

At this point in our research, the responses to this new questionnaire are particularly important to providing guidance on how to design and use applicable IT support in industrial parks, and how to coordinate industrial symbiosis activities (e.g., information flow). After the results of the questionnaire have been obtained, the subsequent step in our research will involve discussing these issues in detail with companies in industrial parks and with park management, using qualitative approaches like interviews and focus group discussions. After that, we will use all the results (from both the questionnaire and the qualitative methods) to develop an adequate, suitable concept for an IT support tool for industrial symbiosis in industrial parks, along with an instantiation of the tool. For the final step in our research project, the developed tool will be evaluated via questionnaire by companies in industrial parks and by park management.

References

1. Lo, S.-F., Sheu, H.-J.: Is corporate sustainability a value-increasing strategy for business? Corp. Gov. Int. Rev. **15**, 345–358 (2007). https://doi.org/10.1111/j.1467-8683.2007.00565.x
2. Schaltegger, S.: Sustainability as a driver for corporate economic success: consequences for the development of sustainability management control. Soc. Econ. **33**, 15–28 (2011). https://doi.org/10.1556/SocEc.33.2011.1.4
3. Leyh, C., Rossetto, M., Demez, M.: Sustainability management and its software support in selected Italian enterprises. Comput. Ind. **65**, 386–392 (2014). https://doi.org/10.1016/j.compind.2014.01.005
4. Chertow, M.R.: Industrial symbiosis: literature and taxonomy. Annu. Rev. Energy Env. **25**, 313–337 (2000). https://doi.org/10.1146/annurev.energy.25.1.313
5. Lombardi, D.R., Laybourn, P.: Redefining industrial symbiosis. JIE **16**, 28–37 (2012). https://doi.org/10.1111/j.1530-9290.2011.00444.x
6. Gibbs, D., Deutz, P.: Reflections on implementing industrial ecology through eco-industrial park development. J. Clean. Prod. **15**, 1683–1695 (2007). https://doi.org/10.1016/j.jclepro.2007.02.003
7. Susur, E., Hidalgo, A., Chiaroni, D.: A strategic niche management perspective on transitions to eco-industrial park development: a systematic review of case studies. Resour. Conserv. Recycl. **140**, 338–359 (2019). https://doi.org/10.1016/j.resconrec.2018.06.002
8. Neves, A., Godina, R., Azevedo, S.G., Matias, J.C.O.: A comprehensive review of industrial symbiosis. J. Cleaner Prod. **247**, 119113 (2019). https://doi.org/10.1016/j.jclepro.2019.119113. Corrected Proof
9. Sakr, D., Baas, L., El-Haggar, S., Huisingh, D.: Critical success and limiting factors for eco-industrial parks: global trends and Egyptian context. J. Clean. Prod. **19**, 1158–1169 (2011). https://doi.org/10.1016/j.jclepro.2011.01.001
10. Golev, A., Corder, G.D., Giurco, D.P.: Barriers to industrial symbiosis: insights from the use of a maturity grid. J. Ind. Ecol. **19**, 141–153 (2015). https://doi.org/10.1111/jiec.12159
11. Lombardi, R.: Non-technical barriers to (and drivers for) the circular economy through industrial symbiosis: a practical input. Econ. Policy Energy Environ. (2017). https://doi.org/10.3280/EFE2017-001009

12. Grant, G.B., Seager, T.P., Massard, G., Nies, L.: Information and communication technology for industrial symbiosis. JIE **14**, 740–753 (2010). https://doi.org/10.1111/j.1530-9290.2010.00273.x
13. van Capelleveen, G., Amrit, C., Yazan, D.M.: A literature survey of information systems facilitating the identification of industrial symbiosis. In: Otjacques, B., Hitzelberger, P., Naumann, S., Wohlgemuth, V. (eds.) From Science to Society. PI, pp. 155–169. Springer, Cham (2018). https://doi.org/10.1007/978-3-319-65687-8_14
14. Maqbool, A., Mendez Alva, F., Van Eetvelde, G.: An assessment of European information technology tools to support industrial symbiosis. Sustainability **11**, 131 (2018). https://doi.org/10.3390/su11010131
15. Chertow, M., Park, J.: Scholarship and practice in industrial symbiosis: 1989–2014. In: Clift, R., Druckman, A. (eds.) Taking Stock of Industrial Ecology, pp. 87–116. Springer, Cham (2016). https://doi.org/10.1007/978-3-319-20571-7_5
16. Menato, S., Carimati, S., Montini, E., Innocenti, P., Canetta, L., Sorlini, M.: Challenges for the adoption of industrial symbiosis approaches within industrial agglomerations. In: 2017 International Conference on Engineering, Technology and Innovation (ICE/ITMC), pp. 1293–1299. IEEE, Funchal (2017). https://doi.org/10.1109/ICE.2017.8280029
17. Siskos, I., Wassenhove, L.N.V.: Synergy management services companies: a new business model for industrial park operators. J. Ind. Ecol. **21**, 802–814 (2017). https://doi.org/10.1111/jiec.12472
18. Bacudio, L.R., et al.: Analyzing barriers to implementing industrial symbiosis networks using DEMATEL. Sustain. Prod. Consum. **7**, 57–65 (2016). https://doi.org/10.1016/j.spc.2016.03.001
19. Promentilla, M.A.B., et al.: Problematique approach to analyse barriers in implementing industrial ecology in Philippine industrial parks. Chem. Eng. Trans. **52**, 811–816 (2016). https://doi.org/10.3303/CET1652136
20. Ceglia, D., de Abreu, M.C.S., Da Silva Filho, J.C.L.: Critical elements for eco-retrofitting a conventional industrial park: social barriers to be overcome. J. Environ. Manag. **187**, 375–383 (2017). https://doi.org/10.1016/j.jenvman.2016.10.064
21. Fric, U., Rončević, B.: E-Simbioza – leading the way to a circular economy through industrial symbiosis in Slovenia. Soc. Ekol. **27**, 119–140 (2018). https://doi.org/10.17234/SocEkol.27.2.1
22. Kurdve, M., Jönsson, C., Granzell, A.-S.: Development of the urban and industrial symbiosis in western Mälardalen. Procedia CIRP **73**, 96–101 (2018). https://doi.org/10.1016/j.procir.2018.03.321
23. Ormazabal, M., Prieto-Sandoval, V., Puga-Leal, R., Jaca, C.: Circular economy in Spanish SMEs: challenges and opportunities. J. Clean. Prod. **185**, 157–167 (2018). https://doi.org/10.1016/j.jclepro.2018.03.031
24. Domenech, T., Bleischwitz, R., Doranova, A., Panayotopoulos, D., Roman, L.: Mapping industrial symbiosis development in Europe_typologies of networks, characteristics, performance and contribution to the circular economy. Resour. Conserv. Recycl. **141**, 76–98 (2019). https://doi.org/10.1016/j.resconrec.2018.09.016
25. Kosmol, L.: Sharing is caring - information and knowledge in industrial symbiosis: a systematic review. In: 2019 IEEE 21st Conference on Business Informatics (CBI), pp. 21–30. IEEE, Moscow (2019). https://doi.org/10.1109/CBI.2019.00010
26. Kosmol, L., Leyh, C.: ICT usage in industrial symbiosis: problem identification and study design. In: Proceedings of the 14th Federated Conference on Computer Science and Information Systems, pp. 685–692. IEEE, Leipzig (2019). https://doi.org/10.15439/2019F323
27. Yu, C., Davis, C., Dijkema, G.P.J.: Understanding the evolution of industrial symbiosis research: a bibliometric and network analysis (1997–2012). JIE **18**, 280–293 (2014). https://doi.org/10.1111/jiec.12073

28. Zhang, Y., Zheng, H., Chen, B., Su, M., Liu, G.: A review of industrial symbiosis research: theory and methodology. Front. Earth Sci. **9**, 91–104 (2015). https://doi.org/10.1007/s11707-014-0445-8

29. Mirata, M., Emtairah, T.: Industrial symbiosis networks and the contribution to environmental innovation: the case of the Landskrona industrial symbiosis programme. J. Clean. Prod. **13**, 993–1002 (2005). https://doi.org/10.1016/j.jclepro.2004.12.010

30. Chertow, M.R.: "Uncovering" industrial symbiosis. JIE **11**, 11–30 (2007). https://doi.org/10.1162/jiec.2007.1110

31. Massard, G., Erkman, S.: A regional industrial symbiosis methodology and its implementation in Geneva, Switzerland (2007)

32. Fraccascia, L., Mango, M., Albino, V.: Business models for industrial symbiosis: a guide for firms. Procedia Environ. Sci. Eng. Manag. **3**, 83–93 (2016)

33. Boons, F., Spekkink, W., Mouzakitis, Y.: The dynamics of industrial symbiosis: a proposal for a conceptual framework based upon a comprehensive literature review. JCP **19**, 905–911 (2011). https://doi.org/10.1016/j.jclepro.2011.01.003

34. Ghali, M.R., Frayret, J.-M., Robert, J.-M.: Green social networking: concept and potential applications to initiate industrial synergies. J. Clean. Prod. **115**, 23–35 (2016). https://doi.org/10.1016/j.jclepro.2015.12.028

35. Lowe, E.A., Evans, L.K.: Industrial ecology and industrial ecosystems. J. Clean. Prod. **3**, 47–53 (1995). https://doi.org/10.1016/0959-6526(95)00045-G

36. Park, H.-S., Rene, E.R., Choi, S.-M., Chiu, A.S.F.: Strategies for sustainable development of industrial park in Ulsan, South Korea—from spontaneous evolution to systematic expansion of industrial symbiosis. J. Environ. Manage. **87**, 1–13 (2008). https://doi.org/10.1016/j.jenvman.2006.12.045

37. Ehrenfeld, J., Gertler, N.: Industrial ecology in practice: the evolution of interdependence at Kalundborg. J. Ind. Ecol. **1**, 67–79 (1997). https://doi.org/10.1162/jiec.1997.1.1.67

38. Lowe, E.A.: Creating by-product resource exchanges: strategies for eco-industrial parks. J. Clean. Prod. **5**, 57–65 (1997). https://doi.org/10.1016/S0959-6526(97)00017-6

39. Lowe, E.A., Moran, S.R., Holmes, D.B.: Fieldbook for the Development of Eco-Industrial Parks. Indigo Development, Oakland (1996)

40. Peffers, K., Tuunanen, T., Rothenberger, M.A., Chatterjee, S.: A design science research methodology for information systems research. J. Manag. Inf. Syst. **24**, 45–77 (2007). https://doi.org/10.2753/MIS0742-1222240302

41. Benedict, M., Kosmol, L., Esswein, W.: Designing industrial symbiosis platforms – from platform ecosystems to industrial ecosystems. In: Proceedings of the 22nd Pacific Asia Conference on Information Systems, Yokohama, Japan, pp. 26–30 (2018)

42. Isenmann, R.: Bringing together environmental informatics and industrial ecology – the role of ICT in industrial symbiosis projects. In: Wohlgemuth, V., Page, B., Voigt, K., Gesellschaft für Informatik (eds.) Environmental Informatics and Industrial Environmental Protection: Concepts, Methods and Tools, EnviroInfo 2009, pp. 213–216. Shaker, Berlin (2009)

43. Fettke, P.: State-of-the-art des state-of-the-art. Wirtschaftsinformatik **48**, 257–266 (2006)

44. Mayring, P.: Qualitative content analysis. Forum Qual. Soc. Res. **2**, 1–10 (2000)

45. Kosmol, L., Otto, L.: Implementation barriers of industrial symbiosis: a systematic review. In: Proceedings of the 53rd Hawaii International Conference on System Sciences, Maui, HI, USA, pp. 6052–6060 (2020)

46. Stubbs, W.: Exploration of barriers to mainstreaming industrial ecosystems in Australia. PIE **8**, 319 (2014). https://doi.org/10.1504/PIE.2014.066814

47. Aid, G., Eklund, M., Anderberg, S., Baas, L.: Expanding roles for the Swedish waste management sector in inter-organizational resource management. Resour. Conserv. Recycl. **124**, 85–97 (2017). https://doi.org/10.1016/j.resconrec.2017.04.007

48. LeBlanc, R., Tranchant, C., Gagnon, Y., Côté, R.: Potential for eco-industrial park development in Moncton, New Brunswick (Canada): a comparative analysis. Sustainability **8**, 472 (2016). https://doi.org/10.3390/su8050472

49. Madsen, J.K., Boisen, N., Nielsen, L.U., Tackmann, L.H.: Industrial symbiosis exchanges: developing a guideline to companies. Waste Biomass Valorization **6**(5), 855–864 (2015). https://doi.org/10.1007/s12649-015-9417-9

50. Zhu, Q., Geng, Y., Sarkis, J., Lai, K.-H.: Barriers to promoting eco-industrial parks development in China: perspectives from senior officials at national industrial parks. J. Ind. Ecol. **19**, 457–467 (2015)

51. Fichtner, W., Tietze-Stöckinger, I., Frank, M., Rentz, O.: Barriers of interorganisational environmental management: two case studies on industrial symbiosis. Prog. Ind. Ecol. **2**, 73–88 (2005). https://doi.org/10.1504/PIE.2005.006778

52. Mauthoor, S.: Uncovering industrial symbiosis potentials in a small island developing state: the case study of Mauritius. J. Clean. Prod. **147**, 506–513 (2017). https://doi.org/10.1016/j.jclepro.2017.01.138

53. Van Beers, D., Corder, G., Bossilkov, A., Van Berkel, R.: Industrial symbiosis in the Australian minerals industry: the cases of Kwinana and Gladstone. J. Ind. Ecol. **11**, 55–72 (2007). https://doi.org/10.1162/jiec.2007.1161

54. Teh, B.T., Ho, C.S., Matsuoka, Y., Chau, L.W., Gomi, K.: Determinant factors of industrial symbiosis: greening Pasir Gudang industrial park. IOP Conf. Ser. Earth Environ. Sci. (2014). https://doi.org/10.1088/1755-1315/18/1/012162

55. Patricio, J., Axelsson, L., Blomé, S., Rosado, L.: Enabling industrial symbiosis collaborations between SMEs from a regional perspective. J. Clean. Prod. **202**, 1120–1130 (2018). https://doi.org/10.1016/j.jclepro.2018.07.230

56. Fraccascia, L., Yazan, D.M.: The role of online information-sharing platforms on the performance of industrial symbiosis networks. Resour. Conserv. Recycl. **136**, 473–485 (2018). https://doi.org/10.1016/j.resconrec.2018.03.009

57. Kosmol, L., Esswein, W.: Capturing the complexity of industrial symbiosis. In: Bungartz, H.-J., Kranzlmüller, D., Weinberg, V., Weismüller, J., Wohlgemuth, V. (eds.) Advances and New Trends in Environmental Informatics. PI, pp. 183–197. Springer, Cham (2018). https://doi.org/10.1007/978-3-319-99654-7_12

58. Halstenberg, F.A., Lindow, K., Stark, R.: Utilization of product lifecycle data from PLM systems in platforms for industrial symbiosis. Procedia Manuf. **8**, 369–376 (2017). https://doi.org/10.1016/j.promfg.2017.02.047

59. Ghali, M.R., Frayret, J.-M.: Social semantic web framework for industrial synergies initiation. J. Ind. Ecol. **23**, 726–738 (2018). https://doi.org/10.1111/jiec.12814

60. Wolf, A., Eklund, M., Söderström, M.: Towards cooperation in industrial symbiosis: considering the importance of the human dimension. Prog. Ind. Ecol. **2**, 185–199 (2005). https://doi.org/10.1504/PIE.2005.007187

61. Yedla, S., Park, H.-S.: Eco-industrial networking for sustainable development: review of issues and development strategies. Clean Technol. Environ. Policy **19**, 391–402 (2017). https://doi.org/10.1007/s10098-016-1224-x

62. Li, J., Pan, S.-Y., Kim, H., Linn, J.H., Chiang, P.-C.: Building green supply chains in eco-industrial parks towards a green economy: barriers and strategies. J. Environ. Manage. **162**, 158–170 (2015). https://doi.org/10.1016/j.jenvman.2015.07.030

63. Walls, J.L., Paquin, R.L.: Organizational perspectives of industrial symbiosis: a review and synthesis. Organ. Environ. **28**, 32–53 (2015). https://doi.org/10.1177/1086026615575333

64. Päivärinne, S., Hjelm, O., Gustafsson, S.: Excess heat supply collaborations within the district heating sector: drivers and barriers. J. Renew. Sustain. Energy **7**, 033117 (2015). https://doi.org/10.1063/1.4921759

65. Pigosso, D.C.A., Schmiegelow, A., Andersen, M.M.: Measuring the readiness of SMEs for eco-innovation and industrial symbiosis: development of a screening tool. Sustainability **10**, 2861 (2018). https://doi.org/10.3390/su10082861
66. Cecelja, F., et al.: e-Symbiosis: technology-enabled support for Industrial Symbiosis targeting Small and Medium Enterprises and innovation. J. Clean. Prod. **98**, 336–352 (2015). https://doi.org/10.1016/j.jclepro.2014.08.051

How to Extract Workflow Privacy Patterns from Legal Documents

Marcin Robak[(✉)] and Erik Buchmann

Hochschule für Telekommunikation Leipzig, Leipzig, Germany
{robak,buchmann}@hft-leipzig.de

Abstract. The General Data Protection Regulation (GDPR) strengthens the importance of data privacy and protection for enterprises offering their services in the EU. An important part of intensified efforts towards better privacy protection is enterprise workflow (re)design. In particular, the GDPR has strengthened the imperative to apply the *privacy by design* principle when (re)designing workflows. A conforming and promising approach is to model privacy relevant workflow fragments as Workflow Privacy Patterns (WPPs). Such WPPs allow to specify abstract templates for recurring data-privacy problems in workflows. Thus, WPPs are intended to support workflow engineers, auditors and privacy officers by providing pre-validated patterns that comply with existing data privacy regulations. However, it is unclear yet how to obtain WPPs systematically with an appropriate level of detail.

In this paper, we show our approach to derive WPPs from legal texts and similar normative regulations. The proposed structure of a WPP, which we derived from pattern approaches from other research areas. We also introduce a framework that allows to design WPPs which make legal regulations accessible for persons who do not possess in-depth legal expertise. We have applied our approach to different articles of the GDPR, and we have obtained evidence that we can transfer legal text into a structured WPP representation. If a workflow correctly implements a WPP that has been designed that way, the workflow automatically complies to the respective fragment of the underlying legal text.

Keywords: Privacy · Patterns · Workflows

1 Introduction

Privacy and data protection are within the scope of interest of enterprises since years. Most current privacy related efforts in enterprises are driven by the General Data Protection Regulation (GDPR) [1] which came into action in May 2018 at the EU level. The regulation describes a set of imperatives enterprises have to consider in their workflows. A workflow is a business process automation, where information and tasks are transferred between participants according to business rules. Regarding GDPR, special attention should be paid to the Article 25 ('data protection by design and by default'). It obliges businesses to implement

© Springer Nature Switzerland AG 2020
E. Ziemba (Ed.): AITM 2019/ISM 2019, LNBIP 380, pp. 214–234, 2020.
https://doi.org/10.1007/978-3-030-43353-6_12

privacy-aware data management processes in all workflows that handle personal data. This is a complex and challenging task, because all respective workflows must be reconsidered from a privacy perspective. These requirements can originate from privacy norms written in national and international law texts. They also can result from a company's Binding Corporate Rules.

Workflow Privacy Patterns (WPPs) have been introduced by [2]. The idea of WPPs is to compile complex data privacy norms into a compact representation which support workflow creators and analysts with designing and verifying workflows. WPP have to be pre-validated by data privacy experts and must be understandable for a wider audience. Workflow engineers without legal expertise shall be able to assess if the implementation of a particular WPP allows to create a privacy-compliant workflow. The implementation of a WPP shall not require legal expertise. Also, it shall be easier for a workflow analyst to find out if a workflow contains a WPP, than to conduct a privacy assessment unassisted. Thus, the WPP approach is promising. However, what is currently missing is a library of validated WPP designs. This is due to the fact that there is no approach to obtain WPPs from legal sources. In this paper, which is an extended version of [3] we introduce our approach to derive WPPs from complex legal texts containing data privacy norms.

Our research method is based on the design science [4] approach. We start with a problem statement, then we systematically compile a set of requirements for 'good' WPPs. Based on the structure of legal documents, we deduce which information must be represented in a WPP, and we provide a framework to extract this information from documents such as binding corporate rules, national and international law texts or compliance rules. We show applicability of our approach with two different use cases.

Our work indicates that it is possible to create WPPs in a structured way, resulting in WPPs with practical potential. This could foster companies in fulfilling privacy obligations which promote customer privacy protection.

The next section describes fundamentals and legal concepts related to our work and serves as a starting point for our research. In Sect. 3 we define a structure of a WPP, and in the Sect. 4 we describe how to fill it with content derived from legal documents. This section also shows exemplarily how this framework can be applied to a fragment from the GDPR. Finally, Sect. 6 concludes.

2 Related Work

In this section we discuss legal and research foundation related to data privacy. We will also describe the concept of patterns which is in use in the computer science and other industry areas.

2.1 Privacy Concepts

The GDPR describes several requirements on privacy; most of them are well-proven concepts. The GDPR has an impact on workflow designs on three different levels of abstraction:

On a global level, the GDPR obligates the enterprises to take care about data protection already *while planning and designing* their workflows. Specifically, Article 25 requires that the processing of personal data shall be planned and executed always in a way which supports privacy. This requirement is known also as privacy (or data protection) by design and by default [5]. It results from postulate of instant protection, and from the observation that effective data protection should not be realized only by reactive or retrospective actions [6]. To obtain privacy by design, other two levels must be taken care of. We describe them below.

The second level of the GDPR's impact on workflows is the *requirement for particular actions* in specific situations. Several Articles describe situations for which particular actions must be taken. For example, Article 15 ('right of access') calls for businesses that provide information about the amount of personal data, the purposes of the processing, its storage period, etc., as soon as a person files a request for information. Other articles describe further situations the enterprises must be prepared for. It can be changing or erasing personal data, if a person asks for it in line with the Article 16 ('right for rectification') or Article 17 ('right to be forgotten').

The third level is constituted by the *principles* relating to the processing of personal data. They do not describe specific actions or workflow fragments, but they still affect workflows. Some of these principles are described in the Article 5. For example 'purpose limitation' principle requires that the data collected to fulfill one particular business task should not be used for other purposes. The data minimization principle specifies that the amount of personal data which is collected or handled should be limited to the minimum required to finish the business task.

2.2 Patterns

Design patterns are reusable solutions for recurring problems. Design patterns have been proposed in several fields. Already in 1977 Alexander [7] wrote "Each pattern describes a problem which occurs over and over again in our environment, and then describes the core of the solution of the problem, in such way that you can use this solution a million times over, without ever doing it the same way twice". The same kind of thinking was adapted in the fields of software engineering [8] and IT architecture [9].

In the field of workflow modeling, workflow patterns have been introduced [10]. Different perspectives of workflow models can be considered [11], depending on the intended use of the model. Well-known perspectives are 'control flow', 'data', 'resources', 'functional' and 'operational'. Most workflow patterns [12] focus on the first three perspectives. For example, [13] lists 43 different control-flow patterns ranging from the synchronization of parallel workflows to the explicit termination of workflows. Patterns regarding the data perspective [14] consider the visibility of data, data-driven interactions, the transfer of data and its transfer routes. Patterns like 'Role-based allocation' [15] address life cycles of work items from the resources perspective. [16,17] present exception handling patterns.

In the area of data privacy, collections of software design patterns have been already proposed [18,19]. Such collections include options to collect, process and share personal data in a legal way, e.g., by using anonymization, onion routing or implied consent. However, a structured collection of design patters for the data-privacy perspective in workflows does not exist so far.

2.3   Representation of Privacy Requirements

In general, three approaches exist to integrate privacy requirements into workflows. They vary in the degree of abstraction and the degree of formalization.

Numerous 'best practice' *implementation guides* have been written by privacy authorities, privacy officers and law firms. Such guides contain textual descriptions of steps needed to handle legal obligations. For example, a guide could translate a GDPR Article into an intuitive description of steps which have to be performed. In many cases the guides are tailored to specific industry sectors. However, such guides are less structured than the legal articles. This induces some degree of freedom when implementing them into workflows. Thus, it is difficult to ensure that a workflow designed on basis of a guide is indeed compliant with the regulation.

Checklists allow to perform a target-actual comparison in a structured way. A checklist reduces the effort needed to incorporate legal requirements into workflows. A legal article is distilled to a list of capabilities which must be implemented. However, it is difficult to express some legal obligations only in form of one-dimensional checklists. For example, it would be confusing to represent the right of access as a checklist. This is because the right of access is interwoven with other articles of the GDPR, depending on aspects such as data transfers into third countries or conflicts with the rights of other persons.

Finally, industry-specific *reference models* provide optimized workflow models in a semi-formal language such as EPC [20] that handle typical privacy obligations. For example, a domain expert could define a reference model for handling incoming requests for access in a typical retailer scenario. Thus, the reference model contains best practices in a specific application domain. A workflow engineer could adapt this model to the workflows of his company. However, a reference model does not ensure that its implementation into the workflows of a company is correct regarding the privacy obligation. This has two reasons: Firstly, languages such as EPC or BPMN do not allow to model all obligations mentioned in privacy regulations, e.g., storage periods or data transfers to foreign countries with less developed privacy standards. Secondly, the workflow engineer has a high degree of freedom when adapting the reference model to his company.

3   Deriving Workflow Privacy Patterns

Workflow models automate business processes that execute specific business tasks. To design a workflow model, a workflow engineer analyzes business objectives, company structure, key performance indicators, etc. But also legal obligations must be met. This is where data privacy requirements come into play. They have an impact on workflow design and are involved in several aspects of workflows. For example, the order of activities (the sequence flow order) in a workflow is vital for privacy. A natural person must give consent *first*, before his data is stored or processed. The data flow within workflows is another important aspect. Authorization and authentication for gaining data access must be carefully planned. Also execution exceptions have the potential to violate data privacy regulations, say, if an activity on personal data cannot be completed without involving third parties.

Consider Text 1, which we will use as a running example in this paper. It shows a typical article from the GDPR.

Text 1 (Fragment of GDPR's Article 15 - Right of access)

1. The data subject shall have the right to obtain from the controller confirmation as to whether or not personal data concerning him or her are being processed, and, where that is the case, access to the personal data and the following information:
   (a) the purposes of the processing;
   (b) the categories of personal data concerned;
   (c) the recipients or categories of recipient to whom the personal data have been or will be disclosed, in particular recipients in third countries or international organisations;
   (d) where possible, the envisaged period for which the personal data will be stored, or, if not possible, the criteria used to determine that period;
   (e) the existence of the right to request from the controller rectification or erasure of personal data or restriction of processing of personal data concerning the data subject or to object to such processing;
   (f) the right to lodge a complaint with a supervisory authority;
   (...)
2. Where personal data are transferred to a third country or to an international organization, the data subject shall have the right to be informed of the appropriate safeguards pursuant to Article 46 relating to the transfer.
3. The controller shall provide a copy of the personal data undergoing processing. (...)

Staying compliant with such legal regulations implies many consequences for a company's workflows. Enterprises must be prepared for the case when a customer places such access enquiry and they must be able to react accordingly.

3.1   Problem Statement

A WPP is a translation of one or more privacy obligations into a semi-formal specification, which can be integrated into a workflow model [2]. WPPs support enterprises to be compliant with data privacy regulations. In particular, WPPs shall foster planning, implementing and auditing of workflows handling personal data. In order to find out how such a WPP must be structured and how it can be obtained in a systematic way, we need to consider the capabilities of the WPP users, and we need to define requirements that a WPP must fulfill in order to be applicable.

User Roles. We have analyzed which different roles are involved in creation and use of WPPs. Our focus was on the functions the roles must fulfill, and which knowledge and which skills are needed in this regard. We have identified three distinct user roles:

WPP creator This role develops a WPP from a particular data privacy norm. This role has legal expertise needed to identify all information from various legal sources, that must be considered in order to implement privacy-compliant workflows. This skill is needed to be able to mirror the legal norm(s) semantically. The WPP creator needs background knowledge on workflow modeling to provide syntactically correct WPPs.

Workflow engineer This role models workflows with the help of WPPs. The workflow engineer implements WPPs into existing workflows or creates new workflows according to a WPP specification. This role needs domain knowledge on the workflow domain and workflow modeling skills, but it doesn't need to possess legal knowledge.

Privacy officer This role verifies and documents if workflows are compliant with data privacy norms. In this role can be a employee or an external auditor. A privacy officer has sufficient domain knowledge and legal expertise to find out, if existing workflow model meets certain privacy obligation.

Requirements for WPPs. From the intended use of the WPPs and the expertise of the user roles, we have derived three requirements for WPPs:

R1 WPPs are a variant of design patterns. Thus, WPPs have to meet all *general requirements for design patterns*, e.g. completeness, understandability and reusability.

R2 Because the workflow engineer may lack legal expertise, a WPP must contain *all information necessary* to model or validate a certain privacy obligation. For example, if a WPP is a specification for the implementation of the 'right of access' - as shown in Text 1, then it must be possible to create a privacy-compliant workflow on the basis of this WPP only, i.e., without having to consider additional legal texts.

R3 WPPs must be modular to enable *linking of WPPs*. This is particularly important, as privacy obligations often are spread over several articles or multiple legal texts.

Given these requirements, we will now explore options to structure WPPs. We start by deriving an information model to express information from legal norms in a WPP. In the next section, we propose our framework to compile WPPs from legal texts.

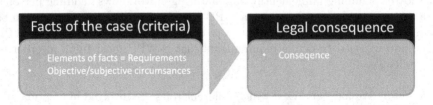

Fig. 1. Structure of legal texts

3.2   Structures of Legal Texts and Design Patterns

In this subsection we compare the structures of legal texts and design patterns. Obligations in legal texts typically follow a well-defined structure, as shown in Fig. 1. A legal obligation is described by

(1) **the facts of the case** and
(2) **the legal consequences.**

The facts of the case specify

(1a) the *general criteria* for the applicability of the norm and
(1b) the *circumstances* under which a certain legal norm shall be applied.

The facts of the case result in an if-then form. Thus, the legal norm or corporate rule can be always interpreted as 'if all prerequisites are met, then the consequences apply'. The consequences in turn can be either

(2a) a *course of action* that must be taken or
(2b) a *yes/no-conclusion* in the sense 'if all prerequisites are met, then the regulated action is lawful'.

In a case of our running example, the general criteria for the applicability of the norm (1a) are described in Art. 2, 3 GDPR (Text 2, 3). The norm applies if the company handles personal data related to activities in the EU.

Text 2 (Fragment of Article 2 GDPR) Material Scope

> 1. This Regulation applies to the processing of personal data wholly or partly by automated means and to the processing other than by automated means of personal data which(...)

Text 3 (Fragment of Article 3 GDPR) Territorial Scope

> 1. This Regulation applies to the processing of personal data in the context of the activities of an establishment of a controller or a processor in the Union, (...)

The circumstances (1b) for a person claiming access rights are described in the first paragraph of Art. 15 GDPR (Text 1). It says that the company must actually possess information about this person. The legal consequence (2) is described in the subsequent paragraphs of Art. 15. The consequence requires the company to provide certain information (2a), according to further dependencies.

Design patterns consist of three components, as described in the previous subsection: (i) the *context* the pattern can be applied to, (ii) the *problem* description that allows the engineer to decide, if the pattern is useful for specific design problem, and (iii) a generic *solution* for the described problem [21]. Observe that the general structure of design patterns is similar to the structure of obligations in legal texts; this is shown in Fig. 2. Thus, it seems appropriate to define a WPP alike. To this end, we distinguish **activity patterns** where the consequence is a course of action (2a), and **check pattern** that result in a yes/no-conclusion (2b).

3.3 Options to Represent Legal Texts

In order to obtain evidence on approaches to structure a WPP, we have conducted a series of preliminary experiments. In particular, we have asked a class of master's students to model the facts of the case and the legal consequences of various articles of the GDPR. The students had a professional background on data privacy and security and attended an extra-occupational education class on workflow modeling.

The students have observed that the general criteria for the applicability of the norm (1a) refer to domain knowledge of the workflow that cannot be easily

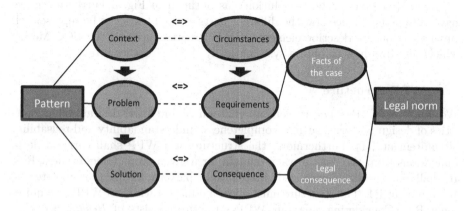

Fig. 2. Relation between legal texts and design patterns

represented as a check list or a BPMN-style workflow model. We think that describing the criteria textually is the most appropriate option. Furthermore, our students have reported that the set of circumstances for the applicability of a specific article (1b) does not have an inherent order. Therefore it makes no sense to represent the circumstances as a workflow model fragment with a graphical language. A simple check list is sufficient and was preferred by the students. Our students also found out, that the legal consequence (2a) can be represented as workflow model. This model can be defined in a semi-formal language such as BPMN or EPC. If the consequence is a straightforward yes/no-conclusion (2b), this part can be cut down to a simple event 'Processing is lawful'. The final observation of the experiment was, that only such articles can be represented in a proposed way, which do not contain uncertain legal concepts. For example, consider Text 4. It requires legal expertise to decide for each workflow instance individually if the interests of the controller are overridden by the rights of a person.

Text 4 (Frag. of Art. 6 GDPR) Lawfulness of processing

> 1. Processing shall be lawful only if (...)
>   (f) processing is necessary for the purposes of the legitimate interests pursued by the controller or by a third party, except where such interests are overridden by the interests or fundamental rights and freedoms of the data subject (...)

4   The CCC Model

In this section, we introduce our CCC model. It structures fragments of legal texts into Context, Condition and Consequence.

In the previous section, we have observed a similarity between the structure of legal texts (the circumstances for applicability of an article, the legal requirements named in the article and the legal consequence) and three elements of a pattern (context, problem, solution), as outlined in Fig. 3. Furthermore, we have obtained evidence how the different parts of legal texts can be represented. In this section, we describe elements of a WPP structure and the CCC Model, which describes how to obtain systematically WPPs from legal texts.

4.1 WPP Structure

We aimed for WPP structure elements that mirror and foster desirable characteristics of design patterns, such as completeness, understandability and reusability (Requirement R1). Furthermore, the structure of a WPP shall carry all legal obligations from the data privacy domain for a given scope (Requirement R2). It shall not result in oversized, inapplicable pattern forms, that violate the Requirement R1. The structure must allow modular stacking of WPPs (Requirement R3). Considering this, our WPP structure consists of *Header, Context, Condition* and *Consequence*:

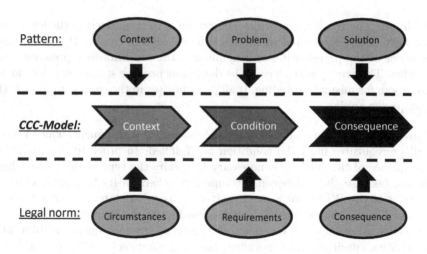

Fig. 3. CCC-model

Header. The header contains meta-information of the pattern. It describes essentials like name, type, legal focus of the WPP and relation to other WPPs. Further meta-information as an unique database ID, date or the name of the WPP creator, may be added.

WPP Name A pattern. It makes the pattern easily recognizable, and allows searching for it in a pattern catalog. The name of the WPP shall indicate the objective of the pattern.

WPP Type WPPs can be distinguished into check patterns and activity patterns, as observed in the last section.

Legal Focus Specifies all legal texts (articles, paragraphs, etc.) which were used to derive the pattern. It declares which legal obligation is covered (entirely or partly) with this WPP.

Relation to other WPPs WPPs can build upon each other. When implementing multiple WPPs into a workflow, sometimes the relation between WPPs needs to be specified. For example, a WPP creator might decide to split the legal obligation to delete data into multiple WPPs. One WPP keeps records of the data used, a second one ensures that the data is deleted at the specified time. WPPs might also exclude each other. For example, a WPP to execute a business task anonymously might exclude a WPP for the deletion of personal data. Since new WPPs might be created at any time, information on the relation to other WPPs may be incomplete.

Context. The context of a WPP contains an intuitive textual description of the situation and of the resulting problem, which is addressed by the WPP. The user must clearly understand when and for which objectives the WPP can be applied, and if the application of the WPP results in further legal obligations.

Condition. The condition provides all prerequisites mentioned in the legal texts that have been enumerated in the 'legal focus' field of the WPP header. Since the order of the prerequisites is insignificant, the condition is represented as a checklist. The prerequisites have to be defined as positive statements that do not leave room for misunderstanding. If all prerequisites in the checklist are met, the consequence applies.

Consequence. The consequence of a check pattern is a statement, which is true, if all prerequisites from the condition are fulfilled. In order to determine the consequence of the WPP, it is necessary to specify the type of the pattern first. This is, because the consequence component differs in its form depending on the type of the WPP. For a check pattern it is (a) a statement that the case described in the context field is lawful, according to the legal norms specified in the header. Alternatively - for an activity pattern - the consequence is (b) a chain of activities, specified with a workflow modeling notation like EPC (event-driven process chain) or BPMN (Business Process Model and Notation). This chain of activities has to be executed, if all the prerequisites described in condition component are met.

4.2   The CCC Model

Typically, modeling a new WPP is triggered by a workflow engineer or a privacy officer, who has identified a recurring, challenging problem which has no corresponding pattern. Recall that the WPP creator must be familiar with legal texts (Requirement R2), but the workflow engineer does not necessarily possess such knowledge. Thus, a model for deriving WPPs must ensure, that all legal obligations are included in the resulting WPP.

We will now outline the six steps needed to derive a WPP. They constitute our CCC Model. For this we use the structure described in previous subsection. We use Text 1 to illustrate these steps. Note that Text 1 refers to an activity pattern. An example for a check pattern can be found in the Appendix.

Define the Scope. At first, the WPP creator sets the outline of the new WPP. He decides which legal articles and paragraphs will be in the scope. By setting the scope, he must ensure that the resulting WPP meets the requirements of design patterns (R1). In particular, the WPP must be not too complex or too simple to be useful. He also has to ensure that the new WPP can be combined with already existing WPPs (R3). Furthermore, the WPP creator has to consider that the legal texts in the scope do not contain uncertain legal concepts that are unsuitable for a WPP, as shown in Text 4. Scoping of a WPP can be supported with four questions:

- Is the scope suitable to create a WPP that is non-trivial?
- Is the scope understandable for the workflow engineer?
- Does the scope overlap with a WPP that already exists?
- Does the scope include legal texts that need to be interpreted individually by a legal expert?

Example 1 The scope of the WPP is the implementation of the 'right of access' according GDPR for customer data. The company doesn't collect data from and doesn't transfer data to third parties, but it uses automated means for data processing of customer data in the EU. Furthermore, the WPP addresses only requests that arrive electronically.

Define the Header. In this step, the meta-data of the WPP is defined. The meta-data of the pattern is the *Name*, the *Type*, the *Legal focus* and the *Relations to other WPPs*. The WPP name should be intuitively understandable and reflect the WPP type. A name beginning with 'Processing' would indicate an activity pattern, while a name starting with 'Lawfulness of' would refer to a check pattern. The articles and paragraphs specified in 'Legal Focus' mirror the scope of the WPP. 'Relations to other WPPs' contains information if the scope of this WPP depends on, overlaps with or contradicts with existing WPPs.

Example 2
WPP Name Processing the Right of Access from the Inventory of Processing Activities
WPP Type Activity Pattern
Legal Focus Art. 15 Par. 1a-d, Par. 3; Art. 2 Par. 1; Art. 3 Par. 1 GDPR
Relation to other WPPs dependency to WPP 'Update Inventory of Processing Activities'

Define the Context. The context describes the situation and the purpose of the pattern in a plain language that is clearly understandable without legal expertise. It must answer the following questions:

- Which business activities are in concern of this WPP?
- When does the privacy pattern apply?
- Which activities can occur before or after the WPP?

Example 3 A business unit has received a request from a customer. The customer asks if personal data concerning him is processed. If this is the case, the customer must be given access to his personal data.

Define the Condition. The condition translates legal requirements into prerequisites for the applicability of a WPP. The prerequisites have to be defined as positive statements that do not leave room for misunderstanding for a person without legal expertise. Thus, we discourage citing or referring to legal texts. The following questions serve as a guideline to obtain a check list of conditions:

- Which legal texts are in the 'Legal Focus' of this WPP?
- Do those texts base on other legal definitions?
- Which different requirements exist in each sentence of the legal text?

- Is a certain requirement already excluded by 'Context'?

Example 4

☐ The identity of the requester has been verified.
☐ The requester asks for his or her own data.
☐ The requester does not make use of this right more than three times a year.

Define the Consequence. The Consequence depends on the WPP type. For a check pattern only a state must be defined, which comes into effect when all requirements set in the Condition are met. For an activity pattern, the consequence is a chain of activities which must be specified (e.g. in form of an EPC notation) in this step.

Example 5 Figure 4 describes the activities to process the request for access from a customer as a business process model.

Review the WPP. To ensure that the pattern is correct and useful, it must be reviewed according to the following questions:

- Does the WPP meet the general quality criteria of design patterns?
- Is the WPP applicable for persons without legal expertise?
- Do the components Context, Condition and Consequence represent all information specified in the 'Legal Focus'?

5   Use Cases

In the last section, we have shown by example how the CCC model helps to generate WPPs from legal texts. In this section, we will provide two different use cases to demonstrate that our approach is applicable to very different parts of the GDPR. In particular, we have used the CCC approach in order to map the legal requirements for an electronic consent into a check pattern, and we have transferred the Right to be Forgotten into an activity pattern.

5.1   Lawfulness of an Electronic Consent

In this section, we present a check pattern for the GDPR articles related to the consent for data processing.

Scope

Before an enterprise processes personal data, it must verify the lawfulness of processing. If there is no other legal basis, say, from other laws or a contract, the data subject must have been provided a consent to the processing. The purpose of this WPP is to prove the lawfulness of an electronic consent from an adult according to the GDPR. The consent has been documented.

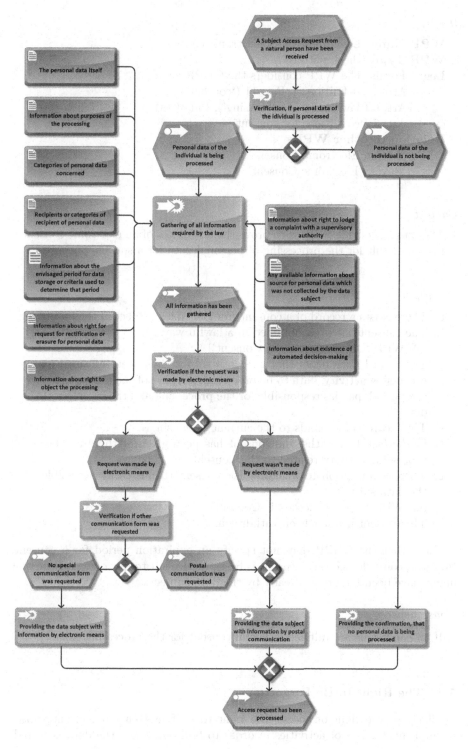

Fig. 4. Workflow to handle a request for access.

Header

WPP Name Lawfulness of an electronic consent
WPP Type Check pattern
Legal Focus The WPP considers the GDPR articles:
  – Art. 4 ('definitions'), Par. 11 ('consent')
  – Art. 6 ('lawfulness of processing'), Par. 1 (a)
  – Art. 7 ('conditions for consent')
Relation to other WPPs
  – 'Obtain Electronic Consent'
  – 'Revoke Electronic Consent'

Context

The purpose of this WPP is to prove the lawfulness of an electronic consent from an adult for the processing of personal data for a specific purpose.

Condition

☐ There exists a record of a consent from the data subject in the database.
☐ The consent has been obtained in a lawful way.
  (cf. WPP 'Obtain Electronic Consent')
☐ The record documents that the data subject has been informed about processing activity, data to be processed, purpose of the processing, storage period, parties responsible for the processing and the receivers of the data.
☐ The record corresponds to the current processing.
☐ In the last 18 months, the consent has been given or there has been a processing activity related to this consent.
☐ There is an option to withdraw the consent that is easily accessible for the data subject.
  (cf. WPP 'Revoke Electronic Consent')
☐ The consent has not been withdrawn.

Note that the GDPR does not specify an expiration period for a consent. However, court decisions say that it is best practice not to rely on a consent that might have been forgotten already by the data subject.

Consequence

If all conditions are fulfilled, a lawful consent for the processing exists.

5.2   The Right to Be Forgotten

Similarly to the right of access, the right to be forgotten requires enterprises to implement series of activities in order to find out where the data is stored.

What makes the deletion of data challenging is that there are circumstances like legal retention periods or required backups which cannot be deleted. This might prevent the deletion of fragments of data.

Scope

The scope of this WPP is the implementation of the 'right to be forgotten' according GDPR for customer data. The company might have transferred such data to third parties, and there might be ongoing business activities or legal claims that prevent data from deletion. The enterprise in the focus of this WPP does not operate in areas of public interest, i.e., aspects such as freedom of speech, public health or scientific research must not be considered.

Header

WPP Name Processing the Right to be Forgotten
WPP Type Activity Pattern
Legal Focus Art. 17 Par. 1-2, Art. 2 Par. 1, Art. 6 Par. 1 GDPR
Relation to other WPPs
  – excludes 'Processing the Right to be Forgotten for public authorities'
  – dependency to 'Update Inventory of Processing Activities'

Context

A business unit has received a personal data erasure request from external source. The purpose of this WPP is to find out which data can be deleted, to handle ongoing business activities that depend on this data, and to forward the request to external receivers of personal data, in a case if it is needed.

Condition

☐ An natural person has filed a request for deletion.
☐ There has been a business activity with the requester in the past.
☐ The identity of the requester has been verified.
☐ The requester asks for his or her own data.
☐ The requester does not make use of this right more than three times a year.

Consequence

Model which is splitted in Figs. 5 and 6 describes the activities to process the request for deletion from a customer as a business process model.

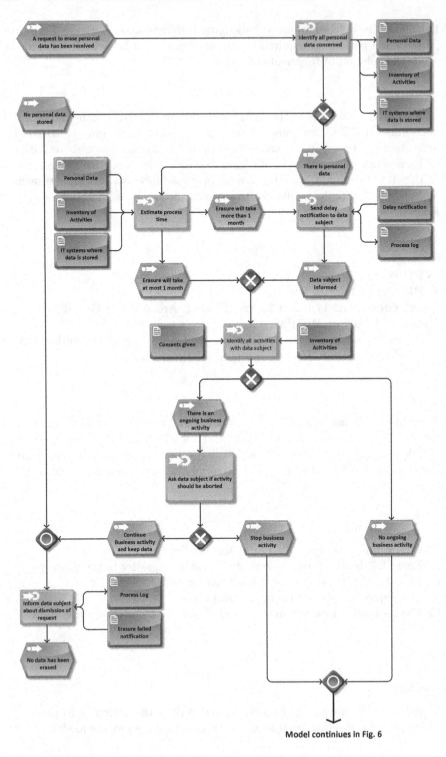

Fig. 5. 1st part of workflow to handle right to be forgotten.

Continuation from Fig. 5

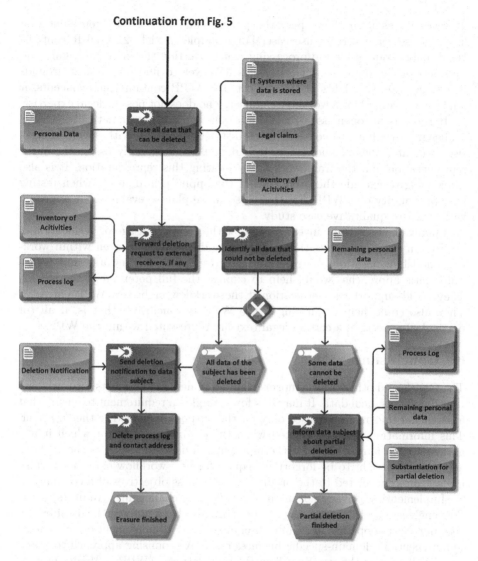

Fig. 6. 2nd part of workflow to handle right to be forgotten.

Note that according to Art. 30 GDPR the Inventory of Processing Activities allows to obtain business activities, retention periods and external receivers of personal data. However, typically it does not contain information regarding particular IT systems where the data is actually stored.

5.3 Discussion

We have derived our WPP representation from the general structure of legal texts. Essentially, we can represent any fragment of a legal article as a WPP.

However, it was not in the scope of this paper to find out if a WPP representation makes sense for a certain use case. For example, Article 21 GDPR contains "legitimate grounds for the processing which override the interests, rights and freedoms of the data subject". It needs a lawyer to find out if such grounds indeed override the rights of the subject. If a WPP contains such concepts, it might not be useful for a workflow engineer, who does not possess legal expertise.

It remains an open issue to evaluate our approach systematically. This is challenging: we have to consider three distinct user roles, with specific expertise areas and domain knowledge. It is difficult to separately assess the WPP representation and the framework for generating this representation. It is also challenging to exclude the properties of the application domain, when testing the applicability of a WPP. For this reasons, we plan to evaluate our approach with a broad, qualitative case study.

Finally, it needs to be investigated how the creation, usage or verification of WPPs can be supported within workflow modeling tools or even within workflow modeling notations. Furthermore, corresponding frameworks and (semi-)automatic approaches would help to express the full potential of the WPPs. They could support the verification if the workflow embeds a WPP correctly. They also could help confirming if the WPP is conclusive, that is, if all (or particular) aspects of a certain legal text are represented within the WPP.

6   Conclusion

The GDPR and other privacy norms resulted in new requirements for workflows that handle personal data. It may be - for example - a requirement to ensure that a particular information is used only for the purpose explained to the customer. This information must be deleted when the original purpose for which it was gathered is no longer valid. Furthermore, individual rights such as the 'right of access' or the 'right to be forgotten' require for new workflow extensions which are not directly related to the original core business objectives of a company.

Implementing privacy norms into workflows is challenging. Auditors, workflow engineers and data privacy officers normally have different fields of expertise, but must cooperate in an interdisciplinary way to implement or verify legal requirements in domain-specific business tasks. A promising approach to tackle such challenges is the use Workflow Privacy Patterns (WPPs). WPPs provide solutions to problems recurring in enterprise workflows. However, existing work on WPPs does not explain how such patterns can be obtained systematically.

In this paper, we have investigated how to derive WPPs from legal texts such as the GDPR. We have defined three distinct user roles that are involved in the creation and use of WPPs. Furthermore, we have compared the characteristics of legal texts with the properties of design patterns. From this point we have developed a formal representation of WPPs that follows the structure of legal norms. Furthermore, we have developed a framework that compiles WPPs in six steps. With two different use cases we have provided evidence that our approach allows to map articles of the GDPR into a formal representation which supports process engineers in designing workflows, which meet legal requirements.

Acknowledgment. We would like to thank Martin Bahr for his work on the CCC Model.

References

1. European Parliament, Council of the European Union: Regulation on the protection of natural persons with regard to the processing of personal data and on the free movement of such data. EU Regulation 2016/679 (2016)
2. Buchmann, E., Anke, J.: Privacy patterns in business processes. In: INFORMATIK 2017, pp. 793–798 (2017). https://dl.gi.de/handle/20.500.12116/4101
3. Robak, M., Buchmann, E.: Deriving workflow privacy patterns from legal documents. In: 2019 Federated Conference on Computer Science and Information Systems (FedCSIS), pp. 555–563. IEEE (2019). https://doi.org/10.15439/2019F275
4. Von Alan, R., Hevner, R.: Design science in information systems research. MIS Q. **28**(1), 75–105 (2004). https://doi.org/10.2307/25148625
5. Schaar, P.: Privacy by design. Identity Inf. Soc. **3**(2), 267–274 (2010). https://doi.org/10.1007/s12394-010-0055-x
6. Information Commissioners Office: Guide to the general data protection regulation (GDPR). https://ico.org.uk. Accessed July 2018
7. Alexander, C.: A Pattern Language: Towns, Buildings, Construction. Oxford University Press, New York (1977). https://doi.org/10.2307/1574526
8. Wolfgang, P.: Design Patterns for Object-Oriented Software Development, vol. 15. Addison-Wesley, Reading (1994). https://doi.org/10.1145/253228.253810
9. Schmidt, D.C., Stal, M., Rohnert, H., Buschmann, F.: Pattern-Oriented Software Architecture, Patterns for Concurrent and Networked Objects, vol. 2. Wiley, Hoboken (2013)
10. Ter Hofstede, A., Kiepuszewski, B., Barros, A., Aalst, W.: Workflow patterns. Distrib. Parallel Databases **14**(1), 5–51 (2003). https://doi.org/10.1023/A:1022883727209
11. Jablonski, S., Bussler, C.: Workflow Management: Modeling Concepts, Architecture and Implementation, vol. 392. International Thomson Computer Press, London (1996)
12. Russell, N., van der Aalst, W.M., ter Hofstede, A.H.M.: Workflow Patterns: The Definitive Guide. MIT Press, Cambridge (2016)
13. Russell, N., et al.: Workflow control-flow patterns: a revised view. BPM Center Report, 06-22 (2006)
14. Russell, N., ter Hofstede, A.H.M., Edmond, D., van der Aalst, W.M.P.: Workflow data patterns: identification, representation and tool support. In: Delcambre, L., Kop, C., Mayr, H.C., Mylopoulos, J., Pastor, O. (eds.) ER 2005. LNCS, vol. 3716, pp. 353–368. Springer, Heidelberg (2005). https://doi.org/10.1007/11568322_23
15. Russell, N., van der Aalst, W.M.P., ter Hofstede, A.H.M., Edmond, D.: Workflow resource patterns: identification, representation and tool support. In: Pastor, O., Falcão e Cunha, J. (eds.) CAiSE 2005. LNCS, vol. 3520, pp. 216–232. Springer, Heidelberg (2005). https://doi.org/10.1007/11431855_16
16. Russell, N., van der Aalst, W., ter Hofstede, A.: Workflow exception patterns. In: Dubois, E., Pohl, K. (eds.) CAiSE 2006. LNCS, vol. 4001, pp. 288–302. Springer, Heidelberg (2006). https://doi.org/10.1007/11767138_20
17. Lerner, B.S., et al.: Exception handling patterns for process modeling. Trans. Softw. Eng. **36**(2) (2010). https://doi.org/10.1109/TSE.2010.1

18. EU FP7 Project PRIPARE: privacypatterns.eu - collecting patterns for better privacy. https://privacypatterns.eu. Accessed Apr 2019
19. Projects by IF: Data permissions catalogue - an evolving collection of design patterns for sharing data. https://catalogue.projectsbyif.com/. Accessed June 2019
20. Vom Brocke, J.: Design principles for reference modeling: reusing information models by means of aggregation, specialisation, instantiation, and analogy. IGI Global (2007)
21. Buschmann, F., Henney, K., Schmidt, D.C.: Pattern-Oriented Software Architecture, on Patterns and Pattern Languages, vol. 5. Wiley, Hoboken (2007)

Exploratory Study of PaaS Adoption Determinants Using Experimentally Augmented Delphi Process

Alalaa Tashkandi[(✉)] [iD]

Saudi Aramco, Information Technology, Al-Midra Tower, Dhahran 31311, Saudi Arabia
alaa.tashkandi@aramco.com

Abstract. Platform as a Service (PaaS) is one of Cloud Computing service models [1]. Adoption factors associated with PaaS specifically are not explored. Management of database systems, middleware and application runtime environments is automated in PaaS [2]. PaaS issues and requirements were collected in three rounds from information technology experts using a novel Delphi technique augmented with experiment. PaaS experiment was required to have understanding of the factors and requirements. In this paper, PaaS adoption factors by an organization are systematically collected and explored. Evaluation of the adoption factors was based on experiment in a private cloud for an organization undergoing a transformation toward PaaS computing. It was found that technology, organization and environment (TOE) factors are relevant in this context. Based on collected data from Delphi process and the associated experiment, TOE adoption model for PaaS is proposed.

Keywords: Platform as a Service · PaaS cloud computing · Adoption determinants · Delphi · Experiment · Exploratory · TOE model

1 Introduction

Based on National Institute of Standards and Technologies, Platform as a Service (PaaS) is one of three service models in Cloud Computing (CC). In this service model, customer does not have control over the infrastructure layer while he/she has control over the application and its configuration [1]. Middleware, application runtime environment and database systems are examples of components in PaaS model [3–6]. PaaS provides self-deployment and lifecycle management of applications and development environments. Monitoring capabilities for PaaS resources are provided to customers [2, 7]. PaaS simplifies application platform provisioning and management.

General CC adoption factors by organizations were explored and validated in several studies [8, 9]. Claiming the uniqueness of adoption factors for all CC types requires scientific evidence for the following reasons. Infrastructure as a Service (IaaS) CC maturity level is higher. IaaS and PaaS models are different in terms of operation management, underlying technologies, users, standardization and adoption level [7, 10–12]. PaaS security requirements are not identical to IaaS. PaaS is functioning on top of IaaS. Securing the interaction between PaaS and IaaS needs exploration. PaaS tools and automation systems require exploration and critical analysis by researchers. PaaS commercial and technology offers are different from IaaS offers. Hence, analysis of adoption factors should focus on specific type of CC.

Systematic exploration of PaaS adoption factors was not achieved based on a literature review. This could be attributed to the nature of PaaS model and its users. It can be argued that finding PaaS experts who are potential users, actual users or service providers as a source of input data is challenging.

The objective of this paper is exploring perceived adoption factors of PaaS in the context of an organization based on Information Systems (IS) experts' inputs. Research scope is limited to PaaS model of CC. Software as a Service (SaaS) is out of the scope of the research.

The paper is organized as follows. Section 2 is a literature review of PaaS, PaaS challenges and PaaS automation. Research questions are provided in this section. Section 3 presents the research methodology by describing Delphi technique, team structure and rounds. Research findings are summarized in Sect. 4 by describing the design of PaaS management system based on experts' perceived requirements and critics and the associated incremental experiment results. Section 5 begins with analysis of experts' highlighted critics and proposes Technology, Organization and Environment (TOE) adoption model. The conclusion of the paper is presented in Sect. 6 which includes research implication, limitations and future work.

2   Literature Review

PaaS provides users with capabilities to develop, manage and operate application platforms. Applications in PaaS context can be classified based on computation model, resource utilization type, resource utilization variability or interactivity level. Examples of PaaS offering include Google App Engine and Amazon Web Services Lambda [2].

2.1   PaaS

The user of PaaS model does not have control over the infrastructure layer while he/she has control over the application and its configuration [13]. Middleware, application runtime environment and database systems are examples of components in PaaS model [3–6]. PaaS provides self-deployment, monitoring and lifecycle management of applications [2, 7]. PaaS offers include middleware services, like Database as a Service (DbaaS), and reusable middleware components. Complex application platforms consist of several middleware components such as database, web application server and gateway. Middleware components include application runtime environments that can be used as part of an application platform [4, 14].

PaaS provides flexibility and agility to developer team. By automating the deployment of application platforms and their components, different setups and configurations can be realized with minimal efforts and time. Interactions between software development team and operation team are minimized through automation and abstraction [3, 10]. Infrastructure is abstracted by PaaS [4]. Automation associated with PaaS should lead to operational cost reduction [4].

Private cloud and multicloud are now the general practice of organizations that need to protect their in-house information technology investment while seeking new technologies and opportunities. Use of resources in multicloud can be sequential or parallel. Support of multicloud minimizes vendor lock-in issue associated with the cloud [2, 10, 15].

Two sets of users represent PaaS consumers. The first set represents software developers in organizations. The other set represents SaaS cloud service providers who needs to focus on software development and services quality [10].

PaaS components can be provisioned in containers by cloud service providers [16]. Alternatively, PaaS can be coupled with IaaS virtualization. Analysis was done to compare between the performance of containers and virtualization. Micro-services concept is evolving with container platforms [17].

2.2 PaaS Challenges

The use of CC in general provides speed and flexibility to organizations. On the other hand, cloud raises challenges in terms of quality and security of services [7, 18]. When CC is evaluated by organization for production and business operation, security and Quality Assurance (QA) are two significant adoption factors. Security factor associated with PaaS model is not completely addressed [18]. Sequence of events and logs of security control and QA must be forensically sound and reliable in case of a security incident or PaaS failure [13].

Service Level Agreement (SLA) is one of the solutions that was studied in several papers to address security and quality requirements [2, 19]. Service level quality is measured based on Service Level Objectives (SLOs). Service Level Agreement (SLA) grants SLOs based on contractual agreement between the service provider or a broker and the customer [2].

Under PaaS service model, wide varieties of technologies exist [7]. Specific applications in PaaS are based on distributed computing. Managing the dependency between distributed components is complex [5]. Vendor lock-in is a risk associated with PaaS [18].

2.3 PaaS Automation

Application deployment automation is an enabler for PaaS [11]. Automation performance can be evaluated qualitatively or quantitatively. Qualitative aspects include automation flexibility, reusability and user input assumption freedom. Quantitative aspects include automation processing time, dependencies between plans which represents the steps required to achieve specific automation case and finally the complexity of automation process that consists of multiple steps [4].

Operation automation approaches were classified into infrastructure management, plan-based configuration management, image-based configuration management, model-based management and platform centric management automation. Plan-based configuration management automation enables deployment and management of middleware in PaaS. UNIX shell scripts are considered artifacts in plan-based configuration. This automation was proposed by DevOps community. Model based automation can be used to orchestrate deployment or management plans on distributed applications [4, 12].

Automation of middleware and application deployment should be decoupled from Infrastructure layer. Encapsulating applications in virtual images reduces the flexibility of updating applications over time [11].

Automation standardizations; such as Topology and Orchestration Specification for Cloud Applications (TOSCA); are emerging. TOSCA has relatively small community. Released automation artifacts are limited [12, 20, 21].

2.4 Research Questions

Comprehensive analysis of using PaaS for mission critical operation is not achieved. Adoption factors specific to PaaS from organizational and environmental perspectives are not explored. In this research project, new Delphi approach is proposed to analyze adoption stages and factors of a new technology in an attempt to answer the following questions:

- Q1: What are the critical adoption factors of PaaS by Organizations?
- Q2: How does cloud service providers manage PaaS technologies and automations?
- Q3: How does the governance, risk and control aspects of PaaS cloud are defined and managed?

3   Research Methodology

Standards in PaaS are emerging [22]. Security and quality control processes in this context are under development. Adoption determinants are not explored comprehensively. In this research project, efforts were devoted to explore perceived adoption factors of PaaS that is suitable for organization mission critical operations. Delphi technique was selected in this context. The experiment in the study augmented Delphi process with an objective of developing an understanding of PaaS requirements and confirming suitability of the requirements of an evolving technology with the real world.

3.1   Delphi Technique

Delphi technique is used when the pool of subject matter experts is relatively small and the problem is not addressed in the scientific or technical literature [23, 24]. It is used in exploratory research when there is a lack of holistic knowledge of adoption motivators or inhibitors [24]. It fits as well in new technology evaluation [24]. The technique supports independent thoughts and new ideas generation [25]. One of Delphi method objectives is achieving an optimal system based on experts' opinions [24].

Delphi process consists of iterative data collection rounds that build on summarized information collected from previous rounds. Consensus or majority is required to end the Delphi process. Otherwise, another round is required to probe for further details and find solutions [24]. Majority agreement was set to at least 80% [23]. Variables definition in Delphi can be defined in the first round or added later [23]. Rounds are labeled differently in the literature. El-Gazzar, Hustad and Olsen [26] rounds were Brainstorming, Narrowing Down, Ranking and Follow-Up Interviews. Other researchers labeled Delphi study stages Projection/Question Development, Expert Selection, First Estimates, Feedback & Revised Estimates and finally Further Analysis and Decision Making [27]. Delphi was classified into four types [28]. The first type is Classical Delphi with an objective to collect facts and create consensus. The applications for this type are natural sciences and engineering problems studies. The second type is Policy Delphi with an objective of generating ideas and differentiating views. Application for this type fits in social and political contexts. The third type is Decision Delphi with an objective to make a decision by an empowered group of decision makers. The last type is called Ranking-Type Delphi in which experts identify and rank key factors [28].

3.2 Delphi Process Formation

Modified Delphi approach was used to collect data and opinions from Information Technology experts within an organization. The type is considered a combination of Classical Delphi and Decision Delphi. Each member of the group is empowered to approve or reject the output of the round. Consensus rather than majority was required to achieve research objective due to variation in experts' specialties, small sample size, and complexity of the system.

A group of information systems experts was formed as listed in Tables 1 and 2. IaaS Systems Security, Application Developer and Information Systems Security specialties were added in round three based on experts' feedback in round two. Below three years of experience was not accepted in experts' panel.

Table 1. Specialties of experts

Information system specialty	Frequency	%
Application Platform Operation Management	4	36%
IaaS Systems Security	2	18%
Operating System Specialist	2	18%
IaaS Operation Management	1	9%
Information Systems Security	1	9%
Application Developer	1	9%

Awareness of PaaS specific requirements compared to the awareness of IaaS CC was limited. The study was augmented with practical experiment within the organization.

3.3 Delphi Rounds

The first round was started with building PaaS automation system without quality and security control in a dedicated computing lab. Several Automation scenarios were tested

Table 2. Years of experience of experts

Years of experience	Frequency	%
>20	5	45%
11–15	3	27%
3–5	1	9%
6–10	1	9%
16–20	1	9%
Total	11	100%

to deploy Database and application servers, and to manage their lifecycle in PaaS context. Insights about technical aspects and organizational fit were collected from experts. The collection was based on survey, one-to-one meeting and open-ended questions. Anonymity was guaranteed through the survey approach. On the other hand, one-to-one meeting was essential to probe for details regarding requirements, motivators and inhibitors of PaaS from organizational perspectives.

The second round of data collection was started with experimenting the control measures highlighted by experts in the Exploring round. The prototype was customized with automation control measures to control Operating System (OS) privileged activities. The control included providing central management of executing privileged commands and logging the activities on central server. The teams in the previous round were approached to provide their feedback after implementing the updates and testing PaaS automation within the same organization.

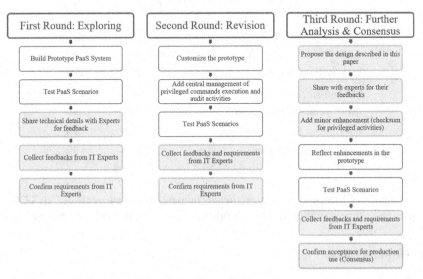

Fig. 1. Modified Delphi rounds

The third round of data collection was triggered after summarizing experts' input and sharing the results of the second round with all participants. The proposed system in this paper was designed and built to address operational, security and quality requirements at organization level. In this round, the design was shared with experts for their feedback. Based on their input, enhancements, that include dual integrity check subsystem, were added and final green light was received from experts to build the system for production operation. Figure 1 provides summaries of the modified Delphi rounds steps.

4 Research Findings

Critical adoption factors were probed in Delphi rounds. Table 5 provides PaaS critics summary. The proposed design in the next section was developed based on the adoption factors and the requirements gathered during the first and second rounds of Delphi process. The design was drafted during the third round of Delphi process. Minor updates were added to the system design in this round. Final design was validated based on experiment and experts' consensus.

4.1 PaaS Management System Design

The design is divided into five layers based on roles and responsibilities to achieve the required operational, quality and security controls identified by experts. PaaS Management System (MS) consists of Security Audit Layer, Infrastructure as a Service (IaaS) Management Layer, PaaS Management Layer, PaaS Automation Developer Layer and PaaS Consumer Layer. Segregation of Duties (SoD) concept is implemented to maximize security and quality control in mission critical systems without losing the opportunity of automating their deployment and routine operational activities. The five layers are reflected in Fig. 2.

Security Audit Layer includes Privileged Activities Management, Security Policies and Security Events systems. Security policies contain Delegated Privileged Commands (DPC)s which give a delegate group the authority to execute privileged commands owned by different entity. IaaS Privileged commands are executed by PaaS in a controlled approach. First of all, IaaS administrator assesses the impact of delegating and automating the command or infrastructure operation. Once assessed and approved, Security Analyst registers them and assigns them to a delegate group, which is PaaS in this context, in a security policy within Security Audit Layer. Thereby, the infrastructure operation required to deploy or manage application is utilized at PaaS layers as a self-service. Privileged Activities Management server enables a secure and central management of privileged commands. Security Events database logs the usage of DPCs.

IaaS Management Layer is where infrastructure resources of the cloud are managed. Infrastructure resources include hypervisors, bare metal hosts [29], storage systems and network components. IaaS administrator manages this layer. The administrator activities as a super user are controlled by Privileged Activities Management server. IaaS resources deployment and management are orchestrated by central IaaS orchestrator tool.

The third layer is PaaS Management Layer. This layer consists of PaaS Development Orchestrator (DO), PaaS Production Orchestrator (PO) and shared storage called

Platform Images (PI). PaaS administrator manages these components to automate the deployment and management of PaaS applications. The administrator also manages containerization platforms in contrast to hypervisors which are managed by IaaS administrator. PaaS DO consists of an application server and OS level Development Area. The application server is used to model PaaS automation processes by PaaS developer. It is also integrated with lab resources to conduct QA tests by PaaS developer in the next layer. Development Area is used to build OS level artifacts. The Orchestrator orchestrates PaaS automation in labs and provides pooling capability to logically isolate lab resources based on projects. Automation is developed and simulated in isolated environment before deploying it in production to verify security, performance and quality factors. PaaS PO is generally similar to the DO. The difference is in the role and integration with cloud resources. PO is connected to consumer assigned tenants and resources.

PI storage in PaaS Management Layer consists of Development Engine, Production Engine, Distributor, Repositories, Images and Shipment areas. PI storage is mounted on all PaaS resources and protected by IaaS privileges. Development and Production Engines store automation artifacts. In order to release new automation artifacts from PaaS Development Area to Development Engine, DPCs are used. PaaS Developer is delegated to update Development Engine using pre-approved delegated commands. These delegated commands verify integrity and analyze automation run time requirements. In addition, the release events and the contents of the developed artifacts are reflected in the Security Events system. The deployment to Production Engine is also protected. Only PaaS administrator is delegated to deploy through DPCs. This is enforced to verify the quality of automation before deploying them for production use.

The fourth Layer of the MS is PaaS Developer which provides a workbench for the QA of automation associated with PaaS. Control of the workbench is enforced by system design through roles assigned to developers at DO Application Server and Operating System file and directory permissions. Developer cannot update an artifact directly in Development or Production Engines. Artifact represents automation logical unit. PaaS automation developers are PaaS automation experts who understand the requirements to deploy and manage applications' platforms.

The fifth layer is PaaS Consumer Layer. PaaS consumer can be SaaS service provider or Organization software developer [10]. PaaS consumer consumes PaaS automated services on his assigned resources. Automation artifacts are deployed for production use after conducting quality assurance and reviewing privileged activities. Only PaaS administrator has the right to achieve production deployment using DPCs.

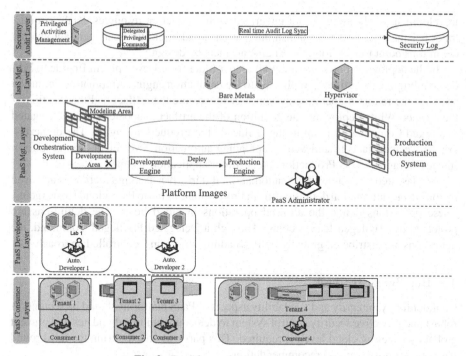

Fig. 2. PaaS layered management system

4.2 PaaS Automation Lifecycle Management

In Fig. 2, PaaS developer works in Development Area of PaaS Development Orchestrator server. Development Area is a multi-user Operating System environment. Automation developer builds Operating System automation logical units in this area while orchestration and modeling of an automation process that consists of multiple logical units is done in the application server layer of the Development Orchestrator server. Automation orchestration modeling are exported from the application server to Operating system in XML format toward Development Area.

Once automation development is finished, Developer utilizes Delegated Privileged Commands to release definitions, artifacts, scripts and models from local file system to Platform Images shared storage. In case the script requires IaaS privileged account, LINUX root account for example, to execute infrastructure operation, IaaS administrator needs to approve it and generate a checksum for it. The checksum is replicated in Platform Images storage and protected by IaaS privileged user. During the execution of Delegated Privileged Command, the required user for execution is verified and the checksum is checked. If successful, definition, script and model are replicated in Platform Images storage and protected by privileged user. The contents of automation units are reflected in Security Events storage.

Once automation is released to Development Engine and definitions are distributed to lab host agents, the developer can start the quality assurance process of automation in isolated environment. The test cannot be conducted in production resources because

Development Orchestrator is not integrated with production resources. PaaS administrator has the privileges to establish integration. In addition, lab host agent automation definitions point to Development Engine artifacts by design.

In the deployment process of automation artifact from Development Engine to Production Engine, the artifact is replicated to the production engine. Automation definition specifies the required operating system user to execute the artifact and the location of the artifact. While deploying, the definition of the artifact is updated by the Delegated Privileged Command to point to the artifact in the Production Engine. The orchestration between artifacts is achieved by uploading automation XML model from Platform Images storage to PaaS Production Orchestrator application server.

The last step of enabling PaaS automation, if it involves IaaS interaction, is achieved by rolling out automation definitions from Production Engine to PaaS cloud Host Agents. These definitions define the allowed operations in cloud hosts. The definitions are protected by privileged IaaS account. Through a Delegated Privileged Command, the definitions are distributed globally by PaaS administrator in a controlled approach.

4.3 Dual-Integrity Check

Confidentiality, integrity and availability aspects of PaaS platforms should be secured. A robust and proactive security control system to detect unauthorized updates and prevent global damages, at cloud level, is required. This part was added during the third round based on security experts' recommendation.

In the system, two privileged roles exist; IaaS administrator and PaaS administrator. PaaS administrator relies on IaaS privileged account to protect automation files integrity. However, an attacker may target the IaaS layer and get access to the privileged account. In order to achieve multilayer protection, integrity of PaaS automation is controlled at PaaS and IaaS Management Layers.

Security can be compromised using PaaS Administrator role or IaaS Administrator role. To mitigate the risk associated with these roles, Dual Integrity Check subsystem is embedded to the overall design as reflected in Fig. 3.

In this subsystem, two secret servers are introduced. The secret servers maintain a shadow of Platform Images storage. The shadow replicate Platform Images filesystem tree structure. Moreover, the leaves represent the automation files in Platform Images storage while they represent files' calculated checksums in the shadow.

During the process of production deployment of a PaaS automation, the shadow is updated with the checksums of authorized files. A scan job in IaaS secret server regularly verifies the integrity of files accessible by cloud servers. If anomaly is detected, the event is reported and the file is quarantined. The scope of IaaS job is monitoring the compliance of artifacts that require execution using IaaS privileged accounts. The scan job identifies such artifacts through the file definition available centrally in Platform Images. IaaS service provider is not entirely protected from unauthorized updates. Unauthorized update may be conducted by an insider within IaaS layer. For that reason, PaaS service provider needs to protect his automated services integrity using PaaS Secret Server. PaaS administrator maintains a shadow of authorized automation in the Secret Server. In case of unauthorized update that was not detected by IaaS secret server, PaaS Secret server detects this update and reports it to PaaS administrator. The automation is

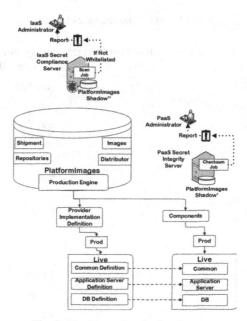

Fig. 3. Dual-integrity check subsystem

disabled at PaaS Production Orchestrator Application Server since PaaS Administrator does not have direct write privileges on Platform Images shared storage at operating system level.

4.4 Experiment

Research findings were internally validated through experiment. It was implemented in a private data center. Consensus is achieved regarding the suitability of the design for production use after experiment validation. Table 3 summarizes IaaS resources used in the lab.

IaaS Management and Security Audit Layers. In Security Audit Layer, security policies for DPCs were created. The policies are assigned to PaaS developers and PaaS administrators based on roles. DPCs include PI management commands to add new components or definitions, commands to deploy from Development Engine to Production Engine, and commands to rollout automation definitions from Engines to Cloud HAs. Contents of automation artifacts and definitions are written to Security Events database during the release, deploy or rollout of these automation units. Management of HAs is also achieved securely using DPCs by PaaS administrator. Events at HAs are monitored and logged in Security Events subsystem.

During the provisioning process of an IaaS server, HA is installed automatically as a sub-provisioning plan and PI NAS is mounted automatically. Artifacts definitions in Production Engine are reflected in the HA as part of the provisioning process to achieve automated and direct integration with PaaS orchestrator.

Table 3. IaaS cloud resources for lab

Infrastructure components	CPUs cores per instance	RAM per instance (GB)	Storage per instance (GB)	# Instances
Lab Servers	2–4	8–32	200–500	14
PO	16	64	500	2
DO	4	32	400	1
PaaS Secret Integrity Server	1	4	200	1
IaaS Secret Integrity Server	1	4	200	1
Privileged Activities Management Server	4	16	1,000	1
Security Log	–	–	20,000	1
PI (zone 1)	–	–	1,000	1
PI (zone 2)	–	–	500	1
Backup	–	–	50,000	1

The hosts are integrated with PaaS PO through Host Agents (HA). HAs are required by PaaS Automation Orchestrator in this MS. Secure Hyper Text Transfer Protocol (HTTPs) is used for the communication between PaaS Orchestrator and IaaS HAs. HAs are started automatically during the booting process of the servers and run with IaaS privileged accounts in the managed consumer servers. The agents digitally trust the orchestrator. Automation artifacts are whitelisted through definitions in the HAs. By that, HAs provide additional layer of control on cloud hosts. Orchestrator is not configured to execute any commands in the target host unless it is whitelisted.

Definitions are rolled out from Platform Images storage to host agents using Delegated Privileged Commands. The rollout process verifies the checksum of the definition and its content against unauthorized activities.

PaaS Layers. PaaS orchestrators in PaaS Management Layer are realized on Java platform with web user interface. Orchestrators are installed on LINUX OS. PI storage is based on Network Attached Storage (NAS). NAS is mounted with read only permissions on Developer and Consumer layers while it is mounted with write permissions on PaaS Management layer. This provides an additional layer of control at storage layer to prevent unauthorized update from a random cloud host. Lab in PaaS Automation Developer Layer consists of 14 servers and is divided into pools to simulate consumer environment and isolate developers' environments. A total of seven PaaS automation developers worked on the lab environment during the experiment. The developer models and defines automation processes to execute artifacts on the target managed cloud servers. Deployment of database, application server and web application server was simulated. Plans and artifacts were developed to patch and update middleware, database systems and application run time environment in PaaS. Summary of PaaS application components utilized in the lab are available in Table 4.

Table 4. PaaS application resources for lab

Application platform	Components	# Instances
PO	Relational Database Management System	2
	Java Web Application Server	2
DO	Relational Database Management System	1
	Java Web Application Server	1
Standalone Database	Relational Database Management System	2
Multitenant Database	Relational Database Management System	1
ERP System	Relational Database Management System	6
	Application Server	8
Web Application Platform	Relational Database Management System	2
	Java Web Application Server	2

5 Discussion of Findings

In this section, data collected as part of Delphi process are analyzed. Observations of the experiment are discussed.

5.1 Analysis of Critics

Critics associated with PaaS, design consideration and experiment observation are summarized in Table 5.

With respect to critic number one, PaaS automation cannot be fully guaranteed as observed in the experiment. QA should minimize the probability of automation failure. PaaS automation failure happened even after verifying and testing the quality in isolated environment. Automation developer support is required to fix automation failure based on SLAs. The added value of automation based on experiment is service agility and mass processing of tasks. Reputation of PaaS and its relative advantage is a critical adoption factor. If PaaS is associated with low quality, it diminishes the perceived relative advantage.

With respect to critic number two, the following was observed. PaaS automation requires deep understanding of how a platform is deployed and managed. PaaS automation developer needs to consider possible failure scenarios. These scenarios are simulated in lab.

Table 5. Critics, design consideration and observations

No.	Critic	Design consideration and observation
1	Automation of application platforms is not reliable. Automation quality is low and cannot be used for mission critical systems	Quality assurance should be integrated in the process of PaaS automation development
2	If automation is doing everything, labor will lose the technical skills and know how	With new technologies, a shift in labor skills is required. Automation requires high level of expertise by cloud service providers
3	The cost of building PaaS and the required automation is high	Financial Return on Investment analysis is required to calculate cost against expected return
4	Update of work procedures and policies is required in case of PaaS adoption	This is confirmed in the experiment. The update was mandatory to accommodate PaaS objectives at organization level
5	Automating the deployment of applications involves multiple functional group in Information Technology department	Segregation of duties based on technical functions is leveraged in the design to increase the level of automation quality and security
6	PaaS Orchestrator servers are empowered with privileged accounts and connected to applications and infrastructure components across the organization	The design provides control for the privileged accounts. The power of PaaS production Orchestrator was confined. The system securely manages the distribution of allowed operations through definitions. Unauthorized updates are detected by dual integrity control subsystem
7	Specific experts expressed their ability to achieve the same results using different automation approaches	Acceptable level of quality and security to implement PaaS is achieved in this experiment. Different approaches and designs should be experimented and compared objectively in future work
8	Application platforms are updated regularly with new features, security and bug fixes. There is an overhead of keeping track of changes and updating automation	A balance should be established between the value of update and automation development cost. Image based and plan based automation approaches were experimented. After the deployment of an older version, plans are executed to roll forward the platform to the required release

PaaS automation developer needs to be an expert in the platform being automated. After the deployment of PaaS automation, the developer is needed to troubleshoot and fix issues. Performance can be analyzed and improved. Upon the release of a new platform version or patch, developer needs to review and update automation. In the experiment, modularity and reusability approaches were adopted. Based on observation, labor technical skills about application platforms were enriched. There was a shift in the type of work being done by the labor. Instead of doing a deployment task manually and sequentially, the work is shifted toward platform deployment automation analysis, PaaS automation development and modeling, PaaS automation QA, and PaaS automation lifecycle management. Throughput of one technical labor is increased. IT expertise is a critical adoption factor of PaaS.

With respect to critic number 3, automation of database platform deployment was analyzed from human hours' perspectives. To deploy 100 database systems manually, a labor needs to work sequentially. Deployment of one database system manually requires around 4 h of work in average, based on experts' judgement. In total, 400 human hours are required to deploy 100 servers. On the other hand, development and QA of automating database system deployment requires an average of 80 h based on the study experiment. The created value is extended with the deployment of more servers while the initial investment cost from the cloud service provider is the same. Breakeven is achieved after the deployment of the 20th database system. Additional benefits beside human hours saving include service agility and parallel execution. Deployment of the server automatically was done in less than 30 min. On the other hand, cost of operating PaaS MS should be considered. In addition, customer support service is required in case of automation failure. Accordingly, financial feasibility study is required to measure return on PaaS automation investment. Table 6 summarizes the observed capital and operation cost elements associated with PaaS.

With respect to critic number 4, work instructions, policies and procedures were updated to achieve the experiment in the organization. An example for that is handling the use of root user which is a privileged account at LINUX OS system level. By focusing on the common goal of providing competitive and secure services to customers and with organization management support, legacy policies were updated to fit with the proposed PaaS MS. Organization stringent formalization may hinder the adoption of PaaS.

With respect to critic number 5, the experiment was conducted in organization where OSs, database systems and application servers are supported by different functional units. Each team has a set of privileged accounts to manage its services. In the experiment, it was found that deployment of database requires OS privileged account and database privileged account. The proposed design described above resolved SoD issues associated with the use of privileged accounts owned by different functional group. Organization size, structure and governance can be considered significant adoption factors.

With respect to critic number 6, the unlimited power of PaaS Orchestrator was controlled using the proposed MS. Only authorized artifacts are allowed to be executed by the Orchestrator. Authorization is achieved through the definitions in the HAs. The distribution of definitions from PI to HAs is achieved securely by the MS. Integrity of the definitions and the associated artifacts is monitored through Dual Integrity subsystem. Security is found critical adoption factor based on experts' opinion.

With respect to critic number seven, it is not believed that the proposed solution in this paper is the only possible management solution for PaaS. However, different solutions can be proposed and evaluated. This could be attributed to the lack of standardization which could hinder the adoption of PaaS CC.

With respect to the last critic, it was confirmed in the experiment that there is an overhead of maintaining application platforms delivered by PaaS. In the experiment,

Table 6. PaaS cost elements

Capital cost	
Element	Description
PaaS management system infrastructure	The management system requires cloud datacenter resources.
PaaS setup	Tools associated with PaaS requires installation, configuration and verification
Automation cost (off-the-shelf)	Automation could be supplied by a third party. License to use such automation is required if it is not an opensource
Automation cost (in house development)	Automation can be designed and built by PaaS cloud service provider. Development, quality assurance and deployment of automation require resources
PaaS tools licenses	PaaS system can be bundled in a container or designed as in this experiment using a set of technologies and tools. Each of these tools requires license if it is not an opensource
Initial labor training	Security team, IaaS administrator, PaaS administrator, automation developer training is required to prepare for PaaS configuration and setup
Operational cost	
Element	Description
Use case automation support cost	Automation may fail. Support is required to respond to customer incidents associated with automation. Based on SLA, the support could be required after working hours on a 24/7 basis
Use case automation lifecycle cost	This cost is required for in-house developed automation
PaaS management system monitoring & maintenance cost	PaaS system is achieved and controlled by a set of technologies. This system should be reliable and resilient. In addition, PaaS requires life cycle management
Labor cost	Associated cost with security team, Infrastructure as a Service team and PaaS administrator and developers
Vendor support cost	Required for off-the-shelf automation and tools
Datacenter operation cost	This cost is associated with the datacenter operation for PaaS infrastructure
Labor training (up-to-date) cost	Application market is dynamic. Demand for solutions varies over time. In addition, new applications are introduced. PaaS developer requires continuous training and skills development on these application platforms

flexibility, reusability, complexity and dependency automation properties [4] were incorporated in automation development to minimize the maintenance overhead. Modular and reusable components represent the logical units of PaaS automation plans. Parameter can be passed to these reusable units to control the use case. Also plan based automation and image-based approaches were utilized. By that, a base image of the platform is maintained. Then, new functions, updates and patches are added to the platform using plan artifacts to roll forward the platform to the desired version. Relative advantage of PaaS should be carefully assessed based on this critic and critic three. In addition, PaaS automation of distributed systems is associated with complexity as observed in the experiment.

5.2 Proposed PaaS TOE Model

Based on secondary data and the critical analysis discussed above, TOE model is proposed for PaaS perceived adoption factors (Fig. 4). Under Technology taxonomy, security, complexity [9, 30], relative advantage [31] and vendor lock-in [9, 32] constructs are included. Under Organization taxonomy, Information Technology expertise [33] and formalization [33] are included. Under Environment taxonomy, industry standard construct is considered for future empirical evaluation. Size can be measured in terms of employees' number or revenue amount. It is proposed to use size [30] as moderator in case the sample size is large.

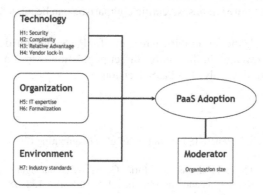

Fig. 4. PaaS derived TOE model

6 Conclusion

6.1 Research Contribution

Novel Delphi method was utilized in this research. Experiment captured different adoption stages of PaaS from potential adopter to adoption at a limited scope. PaaS adoption factors and requirements were analyzed and explored. TOE model is proposed based on the explored adoption factors.

6.2 Implication for Research and Practice

Practicality of PaaS for mission critical systems was demonstrated. The study revealed how critical systems can be managed by PaaS cloud service providers. Novel management system model was designed.

The proposed design is considered a management system for cloud service providers. It provides PaaS automation lifecycle management. Service interruption caused by PaaS automation failure may lead to reputation damage. The developed management systems design provides proactive and reactive security and quality control.

The study revealed the importance of directing adoption research efforts toward specific type of cloud computing. General cloud computing studies may overlook important factors associated with specific types of cloud computing.

6.3 Limitations and Future Work

Delphi expert panel was limited to 11 experts and from one organization. The study is exploratory research of adoption factors associated with PaaS. Similar IaaS adoption determinants exploratory study can be conducted in order to compare results.

The experiment can be repeated by different PaaS cloud service providers to test for external validity. It is suggested to experiment the design in public cloud and multicloud environments where IaaS layer is outsourced and offered by different cloud service providers. In future studies, forensic aspects of the design can be analyzed and tested. Cloud forensics is an emerging area of study.

Wide range of automation technologies in PaaS context is available and the model is not standardized. In future studies, scientific comparison can be made between different PaaS designs.

Future work should include empirical research for PaaS adoption determinants based on the TOE model revealed in this study. Target population is information technology experts in organizations involved in PaaS decisions.

References

1. Mell, P.M., Grance, T.: The NIST definition of cloud computing (2011). https://doi.org/10.6028/NIST.SP.800-145
2. Costache, S., Dib, D., Parlavantzas, N., Morin, C.: Resource management in cloud platform as a service systems: analysis and opportunities. J. Syst. Softw. **132**, 98–118 (2017). https://doi.org/10.1016/j.jss.2017.05.035
3. Deshmukh, S.N., Khandagale, H.P.: A system for application deployment automation on cloud environment. In: 2017 Innovations in Power and Advanced Computing Technologies (i-PACT) (2017). https://doi.org/10.1109/IPACT.2017.8245025
4. Wettinger, J., Andrikopoulos, V., Leymann, F., Strauch, S.: Middleware-oriented deployment automation for cloud applications. IEEE Trans. Cloud Comput. **6**, 1054–1066 (2018). https://doi.org/10.1109/TCC.2016.2535325
5. Lan, X., Liu, Y., Chen, X., Huang, Y., Lin, B., Guo, W.: A model-based autonomous engine for application runtime environment configuration and deployment in PaaS Cloud. In: 2014 IEEE 6th International Conference on Cloud Computing Technology and Science (2014). https://doi.org/10.1109/CloudCom.2014.80
6. Jinzhou, Y., Jin, H., Kai, Z., Zhijun, W.: Discussion on private cloud PaaS construction of large scale enterprise. In: 2016 IEEE International Conference on Cloud Computing and Big Data Analysis (ICCCBDA) (2016). https://doi.org/10.1109/ICCCBDA.2016.7529570
7. Boschetti, M., Baglio, V., Ruiu, P., Terzo, O.: A cloud automation platform for flexibility in applications and resources provisioning. In: 2015 Ninth International Conference on Complex, Intelligent, and Software Intensive Systems (2015). https://doi.org/10.1109/CISIS.2015.29
8. Tashkandi, A., Al-Jabri, I.: Cloud computing adoption by higher education institutions in Saudi Arabia: analysis based on TOE. In: 2015 International Conference on Cloud Computing (ICCC) (2015). https://doi.org/10.1109/cloudcomp.2015.7149634
9. Tashkandi, A.N., Al-Jabri, I.M.: Cloud computing adoption by higher education institutions in Saudi Arabia: an exploratory study. Cluster Comput.**18**(4), 1527–1537 (2015). https://doi.org/10.1007/s10586-015-0490-4
10. Ferrer, A.J., Pérez, D.G., González, R.S.: Multi-cloud platform-as-a-service model, functionalities and approaches. Procedia Comput. Sci. **97**, 63–72 (2016). https://doi.org/10.1016/j.procs.2016.08.281

11. Benson, J.O., Prevost, J.J., Rad, P.: Survey of automated software deployment for computational and engineering research. In: 2016 Annual IEEE Systems Conference (SysCon) (2016). https://doi.org/10.1109/SYSCON.2016.7490666

12. Wettinger, J., Breitenbücher, U., Kopp, O., Leymann, F.: Streamlining DevOps automation for cloud applications using TOSCA as standardized metamodel. Future Gener. Comput. Syst. **56**, 317–332 (2016). https://doi.org/10.1016/j.future.2015.07.017

13. Alex, M.E., Kishore, R.: Forensics framework for cloud computing. Comput. Electr. Eng. **60**, 193–205 (2017). https://doi.org/10.1016/j.compeleceng.2017.02.006

14. Wettinger, J., Andrikopoulos, V., Strauch, S., Leymann, F.: Characterizing and evaluating different deployment approaches for cloud applications. In: 2014 IEEE International Conference on Cloud Engineering (2014). https://doi.org/10.1109/IC2E.2014.32

15. Carvalho, J.O.D., Trinta, F., Vieira, D., Cortes, O.A.C.: Evolutionary solutions for resources management in multiple clouds: state-of-the-art and future directions. Future Gener. Comput. Syst. **88**, 284–296 (2018). https://doi.org/10.1016/j.future.2018.05.087

16. Mohamed, M., Engel, R., Warke, A., Berman, S., Ludwig, H.: Extensible persistence as a service for containers. Future Gener. Comput. Syst. **97**, 10–20 (2019). https://doi.org/10.1016/j.future.2018.12.015

17. Kozhirbayev, Z., Sinnott, R.O.: A performance comparison of container-based technologies for the Cloud. Future Gener. Comput. Syst. **68**, 175–182 (2017). https://doi.org/10.1016/j.future.2016.08.025

18. Kritikos, K., Kirkham, T., Kryza, B., Massonet, P.: Towards a security-enhanced PaaS platform for multi-cloud applications. Future Gener. Comput. Syst. **67**, 206–226 (2017). https://doi.org/10.1016/j.future.2016.10.008

19. Rodero-Merino, L., Vaquero, L.M., Caron, E., Muresan, A., Desprez, F.: Building safe PaaS clouds: a survey on security in multitenant software platforms. Comput. Secur. **31**, 96–108 (2012). https://doi.org/10.1016/j.cose.2011.10.006

20. Dukaric, R., Juric, M.B.: BPMN extensions for automating cloud environments using a two-layer orchestration approach. J. Vis. Lang. Comput. **47**, 31–43 (2018). https://doi.org/10.1016/j.jvlc.2018.06.002

21. Soldani, J., Binz, T., Breitenbücher, U., Leymann, F., Brogi, A.: ToscaMart: a method for adapting and reusing cloud applications. J. Syst. Softw. **113**, 395–406 (2016). https://doi.org/10.1016/j.jss.2015.12.025

22. Yasrab, R., Gu, N.: Multi-cloud PaaS architecture (MCPA): a solution to cloud lock-in. In: 2016 3rd International Conference on Information Science and Control Engineering (ICISCE) (2016). https://doi.org/10.1109/icisce.2016.108

23. Martins, J., Gonçalves, R., Oliveira, T., Cota, M., Branco, F.: Understanding the determinants of social network sites adoption at firm level: a mixed methodology approach. Electron. Commer. Res. Appl. **18**, 10–26 (2016). https://doi.org/10.1016/j.elerap.2016.05.002

24. Merfeld, K., Wilhelms, M.-P., Henkel, S., Kreutzer, K.: Carsharing with shared autonomous vehicles: uncovering drivers, barriers and future developments – a four-stage Delphi study. Technol. Forecast. Soc. Change **144**, 66–81 (2019). https://doi.org/10.1016/j.techfore.2019.03.012

25. Gupta, U.G., Clarke, R.E.: Theory and applications of the Delphi technique: a bibliography (1975–1994). Technol. Forecast. Soc. Change **53**, 185–211 (1996). https://doi.org/10.1016/s0040-1625(96)00094-7

26. El-Gazzar, R., Hustad, E., Olsen, D.H.: Understanding cloud computing adoption issues: a Delphi study approach. J. Syst. Softw. **118**, 64–84 (2016). https://doi.org/10.1016/j.jss.2016.04.061

27. Winkler, J., Moser, R.: Biases in future-oriented Delphi studies: a cognitive perspective. Technol. Forecast. Soc. Change **105**, 63–76 (2016). https://doi.org/10.1016/j.techfore.2016.01.021

28. Paré, G., Cameron, A.-F., Poba-Nzaou, P., Templier, M.: A systematic assessment of rigor in information systems ranking-type Delphi studies. Inf. Manage. **50**, 207–217 (2013). https://doi.org/10.1016/j.im.2013.03.003

29. Sîrbu, A., Pop, C., Şerbănescu, C., Pop, F.: Predicting provisioning and booting times in a Metal-as-a-service system. Future Gener. Comput. Syst. **72**, 180–192 (2017). https://doi.org/10.1016/j.future.2016.07.001

30. Klug, W.: The determinants of cloud computing adoption by colleges and universities. Dissertation, Northcentral University (2014)

31. Rogers, E.: Diffusion of Innovations. Free Press, New York (2003)

32. Taweel, A.: Examining the relationship between technological, organizational, and environmental factors and cloud computing adoption. Dissertation, Northcentral University (2012)

33. Hameed, M.A., Counsell, S., Swift, S.: A meta-analysis of relationships between organizational characteristics and IT innovation adoption in organizations. Inf. Manage. **49**, 218–232 (2012). https://doi.org/10.1016/j.im.2012.05.002

Author Index

Printed in the United States
By Bookmasters